Chuck Palahniuk

Chuck Palahniuk

Fight Club, Invisible Monsters, Choke

Edited by
Francisco Collado-Rodríguez

BLOOMSBURY

LONDON · NEW DELHI · NEW YORK · SYDNEY

Bloomsbury Academic

An imprint of Bloomsbury Publishing Plc

50 Bedford Square
London
WC1B 3DP
UK

175 Fifth Avenue
New York
NY 10010
USA

www.bloomsbury.com

First published 2013

British Library Cataloguing-in-Publication Data
A catalogue record for this book is available from the British Library.

ISBN: HB: 978-1-4411-4194-1
PB: 978-1-4411-7432-1
ePub: 978-1-4411-3845-3
PDF: 978-1-4411-5204-6

Library of Congress Cataloging-in-Publication Data
A catalog record for this book is available from the Library of Congress

Typeset by Newgen Imaging Systems Pvt Ltd, Chennai, India
Printed and bound in India

CONTENTS

SERIES EDITOR'S INTRODUCTION

Each study in this series presents ten original essays by recognized subject specialists on the recent fiction of a significant author working in the United States or Canada. The aim of the series is to consider important novels published since 1990 either by established writers or by emerging talents. By setting 1990 as its general boundary, the series indicates its commitment to engaging with genuinely contemporary work, with the result that the series is often able to present the first detailed critical assessment of certain texts. In respect of authors who have already been recognized as essential to the canon of North American fiction, the series provides experts in their work with the opportunity to consider their latest novels in the dual context of the contemporary era and as part of a long career. For authors who have emerged more recently, the series offers critics the chance to assess the work that has brought authors to prominence, exploring novels that have garnered acclaim both because of their individual merits and because they are exemplary in their creative engagement with a complex period.

Including both American and Canadian authors in the term "North American" is in no sense reductive: studies of Canadian writers in this series do not treat them as effectively American, and assessment of all the chosen authors in terms of their national and regional identity, as well as their race and ethnicity, gender and sexuality, religion and political affiliation is essential in developing an understanding of each author's particular contribution to the representation of contemporary North American society.

The studies in this series make outstanding new contributions to the analysis of current fiction by presenting critical essays chosen for their originality, insight and skill. Each volume begins with a substantial introduction to the author by the study's editor, which establishes the context for the chapters that will follow through a discussion of essential elements such as the writer's career, characteristic narrative strategies, themes and preoccupations, making clear the author's importance and the significance of the novels chosen for discussion. The studies are all comprised of three parts, each one presenting three original essays on three key recent works by the author, and every part is introduced by the volume's editor, explaining how the chapters to follow engage with the fiction and respond to existing interpretations. Each individual chapter takes a critical approach that may develop existing perceptions or challenge them, but always expands the ways in which the author's work may be read by offering a fresh approach.

It is a principle of the series that all the studies are written in a style that will be engaging and clear however complex the subject, with the aim of fostering further debate about the work of writers who all exemplify what is most exciting and valuable in contemporary North American fiction.

Sarah Graham

ACKNOWLEDGMENTS

I would like to thank very sincerely all the contributors to this volume on Palahniuk's exciting fiction. Most of us have never met in any "real" physical space but by virtue of cyberspace many of our ideas have been shared to make possible the pages that follow. Our combined thoughts have flown from three distant parts of the world before settling down here. I express my deepest gratitude to Sarah Graham, for her excellent work and for her sharp reading of the manuscript. My thanks also go to Laura Murray and her colleagues at Bloomsbury for their kind cooperation at the final stages of publication. Finally, I wish to thank my family, to whom this book is dedicated, for their love and their constant support.

I also wish to acknowledge that my work on this volume was funded by the Spanish Department of Research and Innovation and the European Regional Development Fund (FFI2012–32719), in collaboration with the Aragonese Department of Education (H-05).

Introduction: Chuck Palahniuk and the Posthuman Being

Francisco Collado-Rodríguez

This collection of essays on Chuck Palahniuk's fiction provides critical insights on three of his early works: his first and award-winning novel *Fight Club* (1996), *Invisible Monsters* (1999)—a book previously rejected by many publishers for its harsh content—and *Choke* (2001), a best-seller that, as happened to *Fight Club*, was adapted as a film. At the time of writing these lines Palahniuk has already authored 12 novels and 2 collections of alleged nonfiction essays that frequently address aspects of contemporary culture also dealt with in his fiction. The three books chosen for this volume belong to Palahniuk's early career as a creative writer because they played an essential part in establishing his status as a cult figure: his early fiction is not merely highly transgressive but also path-breaking, and the core of his literary vision becomes gradually explicit in the pages of these three early novels. These three novels are highly representative of the writer's particular style and insights; in the first two cases, they are also the works most frequently taught in colleges and universities, in a variety of curricular contexts. Also a best-selling book, *Choke* incorporates new nuances that will help readers to better appreciate Palahniuk's powerful perception of the ethos of contemporary Western life at the turn of the millennium. Additionally, other books such as *Survivor* (1999), *Lullaby* (2002),

Diary (2003), or *Haunted* (2005) soon garnered acclaim among readers and critics, helping to reinforce Palahniuk's position in the category of cult writer, a level that he attained following the release in DVD of David Fincher's film version of *Fight Club* in 1999.

By that time, different reactions among reviewers and readers had already marked Palahniuk's growing literary position as a transgressive writer. Due to its disturbing contents, *Invisible Monsters* had been rejected by 12 publishers (Costa 9–10) and would not be published till *Fight Club* became a critical and commercial success, but even this first published novel and its film adaptation were, and still are, the subject of intense critical debate on the boundaries literature should or should not cross.

Fight Club soon became a frequent subject of analysis for scholarly essays and literary reviews that debated many of the most striking topics presented by both the novel and its film adaptation. In one of the most influential essays on the film version, critic Henry A. Giroux understood *Fight Club* as a highly misogynous work, suggesting that the film was even dangerous for democracy. Giroux went as far as to argue:

> [I]t is crucial to understand how representations of male violence, scorn for everything that is feminine, and a proto-fascist politics in a film such as *Fight Club* resonate with a broader assemblage of historical and contemporary forces to reproduce rather than challenge some of the more oppressive forces in American society. (16)

But he was not alone in his criticism of *Fight Club*; the misogynous and fascist approach defended by Tyler's radical vision in both the novel and its film adaptation had already been denounced by other reviewers and critics. In some cases, they had simply confused Palahniuk's views with the ideology defended by the protagonists in his work, in a way that resembles the criticism suffered by Bret Easton Ellis only a few years earlier, following the publication of *American Psycho* (1991).

Like the work of Ellis, Palahniuk's fiction can also be associated with blank fiction. This trend, James Annesley contends, represents an exhausted life characterized by an "emphasis on the extreme, the marginal, and the violent," which goes hand in hand with a "sense of indifference and indolence" (1). Blank fiction novelists describe a mostly white and valueless society, characteristic of the conservative 1980s and 1990s, and obsessed with violence, indulgence, sexual excess, decadence, consumerism, and commerce. As a result, critics frequently associate this type of fiction with terms such as nihilism, late capitalism, or commodification, terms that fit Palahniuk's representations of contemporary life perfectly.

Palahniuk became interested in creating his peculiar kind of fiction—that he qualifies as "transgressional"—when, already in his thirties, he started to attend Tom Spanbauer's fiction-writing workshop in Portland. Spanbauer is the creator of the notion of "dangerous writing," a style based on expressing the writer's own fears of embarrassing sentiments and themes, which are filtered through a minimalist approach. Writing in connection with Amy Hempel's fiction in his piece "Not Chasing Amy," Palahniuk openly stresses the minimalist approach as a style based on "writing without passing judgment. Nothing is fed to the reader as 'fat' or 'happy.' You can only describe actions and appearances in a way that makes a judgment occur in the reader's mind" (*Stranger Than Fiction* 144). The author's praise for Spanbauer's ideas and minimalist approach openly points to his characteristically direct prose style and the presentation of disgusting, striking, and grotesque themes, situations, and characters.

Although some critics still insist on the old motto that readers should trust the tale and not the teller, a writer like Palahniuk, so willing to grant interviews and publicly disclose aspects of his private life, may be offering scholars a good excuse to see aspects of his real life reflected in his fiction. According to *The Cult*, the writer's official website, and also to information readers can trace in different interviews and in his two collections of nonfiction, Charles Michael "Chuck" Palahniuk was born February 21, 1962, and grew up living out of a mobile home in Burbank, Washington. His parents, Carol and Fred Palahniuk, separated and divorced when he was 14, leaving Chuck to spend his time on his maternal grandparents' cattle ranch. As the writer reports in *Fugitives and Refugees*, the date also marked the beginning of his work as a volunteer around hospitals as "you had to perform several hundred hours of volunteer work to be confirmed in the Catholic Church" (55). In August 2004, he also told Robert Chalmers in an interview with *The Independent* that his paternal grandfather shot and killed his grandmother after an argument over the cost of a sewing machine, killing himself after that. The event was witnessed by Chuck's father when he was only three. Many years later, in 1999, Fred Palahniuk was murdered by the jealous ex-husband of a woman he had met through a personal ad. Violence, divorce, trauma, and becoming a parentless teenager may help his readers to understand why Palahniuk's fiction does not qualify as mere entertainment and also why he has been associated with the particular literary trend known as blank fiction.

In 1986 he graduated with a BA in journalism from the University of Oregon and worked as a journalist for a local newspaper in Portland. Tired of his job, he engaged in different activities, including work as a diesel mechanic. He continued his job as an escort for terminally ill hospice patients and became a member of the Cacophony Society, said to be the inspiration for Project Mayhem in *Fight Club* and an obvious source for *Rant*. The year 1990 saw the publication of his first short story, "Negative Reinforcement." His first attempt at writing a novel, the 700-page manuscript *If You Lived Here, You'd be Home Already*, was rejected by a number of publishers (although some parts were recycled for *Fight Club*), as would be his second work, *Invisible Monsters*, so far his second biggest commercial success.

Palahniuk's perception of contemporary US society

The main reasons why *Invisible Monsters* was rejected initially by so many publishers probably lie in the harsh topics the book deals with and in the difficulties many readers may experience in perceiving the writer's irony and social messages. Palahniuk's novels can never be read at face value. If they could, his fiction would not have received the popular and critical attention it has since 1999. In his most acclaimed fiction, his characters' actions repeatedly reach a hyperparodic and grotesque level that works to emphasize the lack of moral purpose manifested in so many aspects of contemporary life. But, following one of the most important premises of the minimalist style, the writer shows his readers only the tip of the iceberg. It is for readers then to ponder on what they may see below the surface, although the author certainly provides us with some striking indications of the type of reality we might find down there.

The reality we can approach by looking under the minimalist surface is never a pleasant one. As the pages of this volume show, Palahniuk's eye is extremely sharp and critical. His perception has been filtered through and is a response to his knowledge of psychoanalysis, post-structuralist theories, and the rise of a new understanding of the self as posthuman, as well as to the increasing role the media has in turning the (post-) human being into a commodity. His work has been associated by some critics with theorists such as Jacques Lacan, Michel Foucault, and, more frequently, Jean Baudrillard (himself a post-Lacanian critic), as well as to fellow authors like blank fictionist Bret Easton Ellis, or Don DeLillo and Thomas Pynchon, masters of conspiracy theories that insistently demand that their readers consider new definitions of paranoia.

Palahniuk's prose shows some peculiar traits. He uses direct address ("you") very often, sometimes to bring the reader symbolically closer to the events his first-person narrators talk about; at other times, to intensify the dissolution of gender and body limits to which his protagonists are frequently exposed. But, as happens in all minimalist fiction, his style also intends to be conspicuously visual by offering readers sharp descriptions of events and portraits of personages that, far from representations of everyday reality, take us to the territory of neo-gothic landscapes, to environments sometimes not very different from the ones that can be found in portrayals of cyberpunk dystopic decadence or in horror fiction and film. Palahniuk's minimalist descriptions are close to William Gibson and John Shirley's views in "The Belonging Kind" (1981), a cyberpunk short story that anticipates the expansion of a thoughtless drug-addicted new human species, or to David Cronenberg's unsettling perception in *eXistenZ* (1999), a film that features characters with bio-ports that open and close their fleshy bodies, connecting them to an absorbing and gaming consumer's society that, saturated with new technologies, change us into posthuman creatures, devoid of the attributes that allegedly constituted the perfect humanist being: authenticity, independence, and free will. With artists such as Gibson or Cronenberg, Palahniuk shares Marshall McLuhan's illuminating perception of contemporary society. In his influential book *Understanding Media* (1964), McLuhan discusses how the media and the new technologies operate as "the extensions of man." These extensions have the capacity to extend the range of the human body and mind. However, the famous philosopher and social critic also warned his readers that for any extension to function, another thing has to happen: media and technological extensions require our "self-amputation," or the modification of human traditional capacities and bodies. For instance, the use of the telephone not only extends our physical capacity to communicate but it also amputates our older capacity to write. McLuhan pointed out that we tend to forget the consequences of such self-amputations and warned that any "invention or technology is an extension or self-amputation of our physical bodies and such an extension also demands new ratios or new equilibriums among the other organs and extensions of the body" (49).

Postmodernism, filtered by post-structuralist views, unremittingly convinced us of the notion that the world is a text from which we cannot escape. The real, in Lacanian terms, was always mediated by the symbolic and escaped any possible direct approach. For Baudrillard, in *Simulacra and Simulation*, our non-real symbolic world subsequently became the copy of the copy of a reality that had never existed, with the media in charge of controlling such mediated framing of our perceptions. In Baudrillard's version of life we are three times separated from the authentic. Periodically, since his first literary success Palahniuk's narrators and main characters (and at times the author himself) refer to an over-stretched copy of a copy of a copy, a pseudo-reality from which they insistently try to escape.

The beginnings: *Fight Club*, *Invisible Monsters*, and *Choke* as literary responses to the era of posthuman simulation

Violence, self-destruction, parental absence, pornography, the crossing of gender and body limits, are favorite themes in Palahniuk's fiction since his first published novel. Paradoxically, *Fight Club* was a literary product that, despite being fiction, encouraged the creation of a new factual reality. Following the success of the film adaptation, there was a proliferation of actual fight clubs, a first indication that the simulacrum may be manipulated and turned into real life. Palahniuk's story was adopted as rebellious banner by disaffected people, especially by a generation of new angry young men who imitated the behavior of Tyler's "space monkeys" and engaged in actual fights of physical self-punishment. More and more, as the author himself writes in *Stranger Than Fiction*, "what little was fiction [in *Fight Club*] is becoming reality" (228). Along the years, criticism on *Fight Club*—still Palahniuk's most successful novel—has debated the story's misogynist approach, its gothic ambience, the fascist tone of Tyler's terrorist project, the symbolic importance of soap, the connections of the story with Buddhism, or the traumatized condition of the protagonists, in this way proving that there is an extensive territory still to be discovered under the tip of the iceberg.

Possibly, the critical and commercial success of *Fight Club* lies in its significant capacity to question the 1990s status quo and to warn readers about the subtle ways the society of the simulacra has deployed to take over the human capacity to apprehend and understand reality, turning humans into mere commodities in the consumerist wheel of consumption and production. In the novel, the cycle is satirically exemplified in the production of expensive soap that the narrator's alter ego makes with the recycled fat of the liposuctioned bodies of the same rich people who will, in their turn, buy the soap. On the other side of the social spectrum, Tyler's awareness of the enslaved situation of many underprivileged males, who are only disposable peons in a society ruled by apparent democratic conditions and political correctness, helped readers to move if not into open action at least into questioning the role they played in this type of society.

Since the 1960s feminism made some significant political gains toward the recognition of equal rights for women. But those social gains also provoked fear in many men, who thought they had been deprived of some, if not most, of their patriarchal privileges. Some reviewers soon understood the protagonist's mental condition as motivated, at least in part, by the author's apparent belief in an excessive feminization of society, a condition almost explicitly presented in the novel in the symbolic figure of Bob, whose testicles have been removed but who, at the same time, is growing big female breasts between which he tries to console the faking—therefore inauthentic copy—nameless narrator of the story. For the sake of masculinity, symbolic Bob has to die, and then the narrator tries to put an end to his aggressive alter ego

(Jungian shadow or Freudian id) by shooting himself or, more exactly, by shooting the Tyler part of his unstable self. Meanwhile, Marla is the girl in the first of the love triangles that often recur in Palahniuk's fiction. What readers *see* of her figure is also opened to critical debate: she could be the perfect object of desire for the narrator were it not for the fact that she is also a faker who pretends to be seriously diseased to attend meetings of terminally ill people, meetings that ironically include a testicular cancer support group. In addition, the book is about a social revolution where the artificers, the "space monkeys," frequently work in menial jobs traditionally assigned to women, such as preparing and serving food, an issue that soon attracted the interest of gender critics. The soap is made and the revolution planned in an old shabby loft. This site of social resistance is located symbolically in Paper St, a first indication that *Fight Club* and, by extension, all fiction written by Palahniuk so far, is also about the power of writing as a viable alternative to the passive life lived by the servants of the simulated reality. Not surprisingly, Palahniuk has confessed in a number of interviews and in his nonfiction that writing for him has the power to offer a way out of our present commodified society.

However, he also defines his role as that of a romantic writer, as somebody interested in finding a way out of the isolation in which the contemporary self lives, even if it means exposing his readers to horrid scenes and impossible adventures with unexpected ends. "If you haven't already noticed," he writes at the beginning of *Stranger Than Fiction*, "all my books are about a lonely person looking for some way to connect with other people" (XV). Clearly, *Invisible Monsters*, the novel so often rejected by publishers, is about a way to connect with other people, but the results are esthetically striking indeed. The book condenses and amplifies some of the main topics present in *Fight Club*, but in a more radical way, both stylistically and thematically. This highly grotesque novel interrogates important issues such as the fragmentation and fluctuation of the self, the importance of the gaze in the social construction of reality, the role of mass media in the formation of identity or, ultimately, the physical and psychic limits (non) existing between gender and sex.

As in the previous book, *Invisible Monsters* opens with a scene that takes readers almost to the end of the story, which is then reported in retrospect. As Palahniuk also discloses in *Stranger Than Fiction*, always mediated by power relations and commodified simulacra, life in the United States "never works except in retrospect. And writing makes you look back. Because since you can't control life, at least you can control your version" (205). However, in *Invisible Monsters* the first-person narrator, who always narrates using the present tense, may be a traumatized being but she is not a psychotic individual. Shannon McFarland was a beautiful woman and former model turned into a monster after having shot off part of her own face (as the narrator in *Fight Club* does at the end of the story). In addition, as a result of her self-inflicted violence, she cannot talk properly anymore and writing becomes her central means of communication. In this way, parodying Ralph Ellison's classic protagonist, she becomes invisible to the superficial society of the end of the millennium, which had paid attention only to her former beautiful body and face. From her commodified former self, Shannon becomes the new monster in which nobody wishes to see herself reflected. If Freud seems to be an important source for *Fight Club*, in *Invisible Monsters* the influence of theorists Lacan and Baudrillard becomes prominent. The story is reported by the narrator sometimes as if it were a photographic session for a fashion magazine, sometimes as if it were a movie, in this way increasing both its experimental visual quality and its denunciatory aims—"Give me lust, baby. Flash. Give me malice. Flash. Give me detached existentialist ennui. Flash" (13).

For post-structuralist critic Jacques Lacan there is no authentic approach to ourselves because gaining access to our individuality is possible only by completing the mirror stage, which means that we are always condemned to misrecognize ourselves in the reflecting or mirroring Other. Palahniuk—via the novel's narrator—is sharply aware of an important social consequence existing in Lacanian theory: if you belong to a marginalized minority, be it in terms of race or physical difference, others will not look at you, therefore you will not see your reflection in them and you will not have any existence— you will not become a social being in the Lacanian symbolic. The simulated realm of the symbolic is based on the postmodernist notion of the world as text, and the text is the political property of a status quo where the media play a fundamental role. They enslave the individual in a game of pleasant images and superficial models that are to be imitated so that the cycle of consumerism goes on. By shooting her pretty face off, the narrator is carrying out a symbolic act of social revolution, affirming her wish to leave the cycle, and by publishing *Invisible Monsters* Palahniuk was consolidating his position as transgressional author.

Additionally, the book's transgression is effected by its insistence on (the necessity of) change, performance, and hybridity; traditional sex and gender boundaries are abundantly trespassed. They are denounced as conventional, worn out categories that are only used to trap the individual in the symbolic web of pre-established social roles. Accordingly, in the story nobody is how she or he appears, and the body is, like the self, always in a nonstable transition toward new definitions, new roles, and new names. On a textual level, the hyperparody of fashion magazines and road movies is contained within the more traditional structure of the modernist quest where the protagonist pursues the meaning of life, a pattern that finally gives way to an unexpected, even if perhaps ironic romantic ending where the love triangle is also resolved. But the powerful critique of the society of simulacra is always, page after page, carried out in a shocking, often harsh literary style, a feature that also marks Palahniuk's later fiction.

Brandy, the narrator's transsexual sister in *Invisible Monsters*, also belongs into the category of Palahniuk's teaching characters: a number of figures that the author has placed in many of his novels to directly *teach* the common reader, allegedly trapped by the forces of consumerism, about medical, scientific, and philosophical theories that frequently contradict the principles and ideas on which current Western societies are based. A cybernetic, posthuman interpretation of the individual applies in the narrator's didactic understanding that the same way "a compact disk isn't responsible for what's recorded on it, that's how you are. You're about as free to act as a programmed computer." Brandy's provocative perception is completed by her comment that "There isn't any real *you* in you . . . Even your physical body, all your cells will be replaced within eight years" (218). In effect, such understanding of the creature that we still call "human being" coincides with scientific views developed, among others, in the field of biochemistry and fits almost perfectly with the bleak description of humanity presented by Norbert Wiener, the so-called father of cybernetics, in his influential book *The Human Use of Human Beings* (1950). For Wiener, fluctuation, information, and change are our most important constituents:

Our tissues change as we live: the food we eat and the air we breathe become flesh of our flesh and bone of our bone, and the momentary elements of our flesh and bone pass out of our body everyday with our excreta. We are but whirlpools in a river of ever-flowing water. We are not stuff that abides, but patterns that perpetuate themselves. (96)

Wiener's theories about the posthuman being coincide, at least on a metaphorical level, with the postmodern understanding of life as a text and the Lacanian inescapable web of the symbolic. The newly understood being is constituted by patterns of information that can be gradually altered—and here we enter Pynchon's paranoid territory, also traceable in Palahniuk's fiction—by life events but also by reprogramming entities, that is the mass media, in charge of controlling and directing our informational patterns.

Similar views on the posthuman condition are systematically defended by another didactic, revolutionary character in *Choke*: the narrator's mother. Nevertheless, Ida Mancini's actions are presented as an important source of anxiety for the protagonist's traumatized, almost schizophrenic condition. Victor has a permanent need for love because his alleged mother—or kidnapper—forced him to grow up as a continuous transient, from foster home to foster home, amid her escapes from the police. A rebellious youth in the 1960s, Ida is now in a hospital, losing her memory, the only link with the past an individual has. By extrapolation, Palahniuk might be showing the reader the tip of American history as an iceberg quickly disappearing under the waters, to be replaced by the simulated history of Colonial Dunsboro in the 1730s, where the protagonist earns his living by playing a menial worker, an "Irish indentured servant" (22). The invented condition of this type of history reflects Victor's fantasy of becoming a new Christ, one more self-inflicted victim, as were the nameless narrator in *Fight Club* and the veiled protagonist in *Invisible Monsters*. Early traumas can be worked through by imposing a coherent narrative on the memories the victim may have (or invent) from the past, and that seems to be one of Victor's aims, even if he is still at the stage of acting out his trauma. His present condition is reflected in his compulsive needs, which make him addicted to sex, a theme that takes Palahniuk's narrative, once more, to the shocking grounds of transgressional fiction. But, again by extrapolation, the historical tip of this fictional iceberg may be hiding a critique of the American present as the land of addiction: to drugs, alcohol, sex, or any other category that may give some relief to a country disenchanted with a past that has brought about something very different from the promised land of the free; instead, it has been turned into a simulated reality where people are trapped and converted into commodities.

The function of individuals firmly and unavoidably depends on the society in which they live or from which they try to escape, and one of Palahniuk's aims in *Choke* is to offer his readers enough clues about the link existing between person and society so that we do not forget it. The very start of the narrative already warns readers that we are also trapped in the same net but, as happened to the men who wanted to become members of Project Mayhem, we are also tested at the beginning of the story. The narrator of *Choke* discourages his would-be readers several times with very direct advice: "After a couple of pages, you won't want to be here. So forget it. Go away. Get out while you're still in one piece." Thus, as happens in the case of many other addictions, readers decide to go on, even if what we read is intensively provocative and transgressive. For some people to go on reading the book may be even considered sinful, or the cause of secondary effects, as happens when taking drugs or smoking. For addicted Victor, writing his story represents a therapeutic attempt to get hold of his life as he stands between his nihilistic understanding of life and his impersonation of the new Christ, but it is also an invitation to everybody else to recall our memories and to visualize our personal addictions. Once again, Lacan comes to mind: if we need to *add* something to ourselves, it is because we lack something and need to fill the gap, a gap frequently associated in the pages of Palahniuk's fiction with the need for feelings and personal communion with other people. As developed in the third novel that this volume scrutinizes, the way out of the simulated life we live in is not an easy one. Victor Mancini sharply hints at the paradox:

> The only funny thing about Colonial Dunsboro is maybe it's too authentic, but for all the wrong reasons. This whole crowd of losers and nutcases who hide out here because they can't make it in the real world, in real jobs—isn't this why we left England in the first place? To establish our own alternate reality. (31)

Regrettably, alternate realities also end up being commodified and the slave remains a slave.

Some details on contemporary life: Palahniuk's other fiction

With so many novels written in a relatively short span of time, Palahniuk qualifies as a rather prolific writer. As might be expected, critics, reviewers, and fans have given different responses to his other novels and nonfiction books. Also published in 1999, a few months before *Invisible Monsters* was finally released, *Survivor* is a book highly praised for its innovative presentation of the story, allegedly narrated by the protagonist to a recording machine (or "black box") in a plane bound to crash, with the book's pagination progressing backward toward the zero page of final destruction. The fact that narrator Tender Branson is the only survivor of the suicidal cult of a fanatic sect and that he has hijacked an airplane bring about unnerving anticipations of contemporary events and highlights, as *Fight Club* did, the significance of violence and terrorism in the American contemporary ethos even two years before the events of 9/11. However, the author himself discloses on his official website that "*Survivor* is really about our education system because I feel, more often than not, kids are sort of taught or trained to be the best possible cogs in some big corporate machine ... They are sort of taught to be just good employees, to just fit in." Tender is a slave who finally learns to rebel against the system that used him as a robotic house-servant for a profit. *Survivor* is also a novel featuring an individual in need of love and sympathy although, despite the violence of its main topics and its explicit criticism of the system, it does not share the grotesque style so characteristic of *Invisible Monsters*.

In 2002 Palahniuk published *Lullaby*, a novel with neo-gothic elements which earned him the 2003 Pacific Northwest Booksellers Association Award, and a nomination for the Bram Stoker Award for Best Novel in 2002. Despite the presence of motifs and narrative devices already used in previous novels—such as the scene at the beginning from which the rest of the plot is presented in a long flashback, or the trespassing of bodily limits—*Lullaby* added to

Palahniuk's repertoire of social criticism its powerful warning on the capacity of words to modify reality. Words can be a powerful, even fatal, instrument, and Carl Streator's story serves as a deterrent not to use them in vain. The following year saw the publication of Palahniuk's sixth novel, *Diary*, a book also saturated with gothic elements where the power of representation was extended to plastic art; painting and writing condensed and mixed along its pages in the development of a story about their power of destruction but also about the possibility of redemption.

Published in 2005, *Haunted* continues the writer's interest in horror fiction, this time framed as a collection of stories disclosed along a main narrative that tells of the voluntary seclusion of 19 writers who decide to participate in a literary retreat, frequently compared in the text to Lord Byron's famous Villa Diodati. There, each one of them is expected to write the best novel ever, but what follows is a bleak presentation of the human appetite for power and social recognition. The book features the short-story "Guts," already published in *Playboy* in 2004 which, according to different sources is known to make audience members at Palahniuk's book readings faint, indirectly helping to consolidate his figure as a cult author and to bring about more controversial criticism of his works. In addition, Edgar Allan Poe and Stephen King became names associated with the writer's list of literary predecessors (see Coleman 166–79).

The next novel to appear was the best-selling *Rant: An Oral Biography of Buster Casey*, published in 2007, and one more technical experiment by the author. This time the narrative is composed of the brief and fragmented comments of a variety of characters about the protagonist, considered by some a murderer and villain, who propagated an epidemic of rabies across the whole country, while for his friends he is a generous person, a leader, and a savior. The book also recuperates the sense of the posthuman symbolic trap that characterizes Palahniuk's first novels by presenting a dystopic society where individuals have ports attached to their bodies and are divided by curfew into the apparently luckier Daytimers and the transgressive Nighttimers who engage in the eventually self-inflicting violence of *party crashing*. Palahniuk's following books, *Snuff* (2008) and *Pygmy* (2009), stand among the less successful novels written by the author so far. The first one focuses on pornography and some reviewers were quick to point out that the book was as boring, flat, and repetitious as pornography itself; the novel was not particularly criticized for the theme it treated but mostly for its sluggish narrative pace. *Pygmy* is the grotesque story of a young infiltrated agent from an unknown totalitarian regime who, as an exchange student, lives with an American family from an unnamed Midwestern location. The plot allows Palahniuk to criticize the political situation both in the narrator's totalitarian country but also in the United States. Unfortunately, as James Walkowiak states, there is "no way to explain why Pygmy, for all his state-sponsored education, writes in broken English" (F10), a characteristic that seems to have annoyed many readers.

Announced as homage to the Golden Age of Hollywood and released in 2010, *Tell-All* discloses the memoirs of Hazie Coogan, caretaker of the hyperfamous American actress Katherine Kenton, a woman of striking violet eyes, who loves jewelry and has married many times. Real and invented characters feature in a book that stresses again the power of writing to create and destroy reality, while questioning once more the valueless society of simulacra that systematically brings about violence and self-destruction. In 2011 Palahniuk published *Damned*, a novel that again divided reviewers about the qualities the later fiction of the novelist has. This time the narrator is a 13-year-old girl who allegedly has died of a drug over-dose and tries to make a new living in Hell while remembering her previous life. The report this new female Holden Caulfield shares with her readers oscillates between repulsive descriptions of life in Hell and some of the wittiest viewpoints that can be found in Palahniuk's fiction so far.

The leap of faith: Palahniuk's nonfiction and his Ars Poetica

In his two collections of alleged nonfiction, the author further confuses the traditional borders between invented and factual life. *Fugitives and Refugees* (2003) is an unconventional tourist guide to Portland, Oregon, where the reader is introduced not only to the parks and museums of the city but also to its haunted houses, underground tunneling, and to places where it is possible to "knock off a piece." The 11 "postcards" of the book, representing some of

Palahniuk's personal memories, help to blur the limits between the common and the extraordinary by presenting cases and events that no doubt helped to build the writer's peculiar perception of life.

Not surprisingly, his second nonfiction work is called *Stranger Than Fiction* (2004). The book is a compilation of "true stories" in which the writer rearranges essays and articles previously published, where the reader's traditional ability to differentiate fact from fiction is continuously put to the test. The collection features some of the most striking experiences Palahniuk has had so far in his life together with some of his opinions on reality and writing. In its pages, the writer discloses that one of the main devices he uses to gather information before writing a novel is to join different groups of people. In their meetings, he can experience what can be understood as a face-to-face emotional encounter with the other. The experience, he affirms, contradicts the American Dream, where you want to get so rich that "you can rise above the rabble" (XV). The world is made of people, he says, who want to tell you their stories, and his role as a writer is, therefore, to be a listener before re-telling those stories in his own fiction.

In one of the pieces in the book, "Monkey Think, Monkey Do," the novelist explicitly addresses his fiction and gives a turn of the screw to preceding blank fiction works. He refers to the liminal space existing between fiction and factuality: waiters who really litter their customers' food, projectionists who collect single frames from porno movies and cut them into G-rated films . . . Those things happen to be in *Fight Club* because Palahniuk knew people who did them in real life and he attributes the success of both book and film to their reflection of the violent ethos of a transgressive generation that demanded the writing of transgressive fiction such as *American Psycho*, *Trainspotting* or his own novel (213). Palahniuk offers some examples of people who fight against everything they think keeps them down, but the writer ends his essay in a combative mood, inviting his readers to take a more active part in life:

[Y]ou can make what Kierkegaard called your Leap of Faith, where you stop living as a reaction to circumstances and start living as a force for what you say *should be*.

What's coming is a million new reasons to go ahead.

What's going out is the *cathartic* transgressive novel. (215; my emphasis)

His use of the term *cathartic* can be linked to the committed character of the literature he proposes. Palahniuk is fully conscious of the power of his "transgressional" fiction to modify our experiences of reality; the disappointment and resentment of the social losers that he describes in his fiction have brought them together in life, in imitation of what happened in *Fight Club*. Literature, in his own understanding of art, exists also to accomplish an effective emotional communication between the writer and the other. In this sense, his work advances from the dubious moral territory of blank fiction into the open affirmation of an ethical purpose, as his first novel already shows.

PART I

Fight Club

Introduction

As stated at the beginning of this volume, David Fincher's film adaptation of *Fight Club* in 1999 represented the start of Chuck Palahniuk's life as a cult writer. The success brought about by the release of the film meant the re-evaluation of a novel went on to leave a powerful imprint in the current lives of many young American males and win for its creator fame and critical appraisal, but also some controversial comments and reviews that defined Palahniuk's book as the product of a misogynistic and proto-fascist author. The actual emergence of many fight clubs following the success of film and novel and of young men even asking the writer if they could hit him real hard—as he told Erik Hedegaard in the 2005 interview for *Rolling Stone*—place *Fight Club* among the selected number of books which have created a new reality from their fictional pages.

Nevertheless, in the case of *Fight Club* controversies mainly arise when readers and critics alike take the story at face value. Cammie Sublette is in part right when she affirms that "Palahniuk's readers are not really prepared for historical ambiguity and controversy, for few of them read widely and even fewer have been exposed to the kind of genuine historical scholarship that historians deem significant" (35). The issue, of course, could be applied to many other authors, whose books are read by a variety of readers who provide them with different and often contradictory interpretations. But Sublette seems to be referring here to the increasing number of young males who saw themselves reflected in the role of the "space monkeys" who, in the pages of the novel, chose to follow Tyler Durden in his anarchist endeavors. Dressing in black, participating in actual fight clubs, and developing an understanding of their own condition as caught in the traps of consumerist society became actual signs of the young males' desire for social change that elevated Palahniuk's first published novel to the status of a "revolutionary" book. On the other hand, critics like Henry A. Giroux understood *Fight Club* as an extremely misogynous and fascist work that, in view of what was already happening in the United States in the period, could even endanger the foundations of democracy.

In a sense, many of the followers and detractors of the book rooted their divergent positions in the same frequent misunderstanding of the book's different ontological levels: they substituted the actual writer for the fictional narrator and his alter ego, Tyler Durden. The three chapters in this first part of the volume do not fall into the old trick of narrative "credibility": two of the contributors, James R. Giles and Laurie Vickroy approach the fictional minds of narrator and alter ego from different but complementary perspectives that draw on their expertise in psychoanalysis, the role of violence in our current society, and trauma studies. Eduardo Mendieta, on the other hand, approaches *Fight Club* from a cultural and sociological perspective, identifying the implications of the whole text within the sociopolitical context in which it was written.

Giles's "Violence, Spaces, and a Fragmenting Consciousness in Chuck Palahniuk's *Fight Club*" also coincides with Mendieta's reading of the novel in pointing out that the book is strongly committed to criticism of consumerist excesses in present US society and to denunciation of the menial social roles left for a whole generation of young American males. However, Giles approaches his analysis mainly from a detailed Freudian reading of motifs in the story that are frequently understood as symptoms flowing from the narrator's psyche, the problematized constructor of the narrative. From the nameless narrator's mind everything flows, including an ever-increasing violent reaction to his living conditions, violence that constitutes one of the main sources for the popularity of book and film. Giles also employs René Girard's and Georges Bataille's theories to explain both the narrator's attempt to gain control of his anger and the combination of homoeroticism and self-destruction that pervade his report. Additionally, this contributor also makes use of Lefebvre's theories on space to explain the connections between this category and the representation of violence in the novel. Giles finally pays detailed attention to the book's opening and concluding scenes, two important parts in the narrative that frequently play with the readers' expectations in many other novels written by Palahniuk.

This first chapter on *Fight Club* further complements the interpretation provided by Mendieta because Giles is also interested in analyzing the narrator's social motivations while the second chapter provides some insights into the cultural implications of the whole text. The two chapters together provide readers with additional perspectives on the importance that the different narrative levels of a novel have, especially on those occasions in which the story is told by an unreliable narrator, as the case is in *Fight Club*.

Drawing on examples from some contemporary popular films, which bring echoes of the main issues discussed in *Fight Club*, Eduardo Mendieta's "The Avatars of Masculinity: How Not to be a Man" offers a philosophical and sociological approach to masculinity in the novel, pointing at its failure in a post-industrial society that has men trapped in a vicious enslaving cycle of production–consumption amid a collective imaginary that still expects them to behave as heroes. Norms, socialization, and ethics are key terms in his analysis. Mendieta clears the path for readers to recognize Palahniuk's early understanding of the sociological and political implications that in time, as we know now, would result in contemporary movements such as Anonymous or Occupy Wall Street, and other similar popular reactions against the current status quo. Palahniuk's first published novel is for Mendieta also a "parody of male bonding" and he sees the lack of understanding of its satiric tone as being responsible for the (mis)readings that linked Durden's with Palahniuk's own sociopolitical views.

In the last chapter dedicated to *Fight Club*, "Body Contact: Acting Out is the Best Defense in *Fight Club*," Laurie Vickroy brings us back to the level of the narrative and the workings of the narrator's mind. But her contribution also offers an interpretive link that goes from the protagonist's behavior to the social reaction the book provoked. More specifically, Vickroy tries to demonstrate "how Palahniuk uses traumatic symptoms to articulate the crisis of ungrounded identity in contemporary society." In her view, trauma has become a structural condition in present American life; aware of that, Palahniuk invites his readers to extrapolate from the case presented by his protagonist and to draw a moral from it.

The writer's characterization of his protagonists allows him to deal with functional and shifting identities, but it also depicts "traumatic psychic splitting and fragmentation." To develop her analysis, Vickroy lists some of the symptoms Palahniuk uses to portray his troubled protagonist and evaluates the popularity of fight club and self-mutilation with regard to the psychological notion of acting out. Men, in her view, are more likely to act out their trauma issues than seek therapy, which would explain not only the narrator's reactions but also the popularity the book has among young men. Vickroy goes on to debate Marla's importance in bringing the protagonist back to consciousness and the realization that he is also Tyler. Violence and wanting revenge mean, in this third analysis of the novel, to be stuck in trauma, an alternative that the narrator finally rejects by shooting himself/Tyler, in a climactic scene where the (manipulative) author seeks to invest his work with a final moral that not all readers of the book understood.

1

Violence, Spaces, and a Fragmenting Consciousness in *Fight Club*

James R. Giles

The diversity of critical responses that Chuck Palahniuk's *Fight Club* has inspired is the result of the novel's complex narrative structure and point of view. The unnamed narrator's fragile identity disintegrates throughout the novel, making it difficult for him and the reader to distinguish between fantasy and reality. This chapter contends that the narrator's identity is undermined by a profound self-hatred and masculine insecurity originating in his Oedipal relationship with his father, his hatred of his work, and an intensifying fear of death. Out of the disintegration of his ego emerges the character of Tyler Durden, the narrator's projection of a super-masculine rebel against the capitalist system. The narrator hopes that association with Tyler will enable him to construct a strong and stable masculine identity. Instead, his creation of Tyler, who equates masculinity with pain, violence, and irrationality, embodies the climactic moment in the destruction of the narrator's identity. While irrational rebellion appeals to the narrator because of the stifling conventionality of his life, irrationality in itself can hardly form the basis of a stable identity. Thus, reality and fantasy merge in the novel; and it becomes increasingly difficult for the reader, as well as the protagonist, to distinguish between actual and imaged people and spaces. In addition, the character of Marla

Singer functions as a guide to the boundary between the actual and the fantasized in *Fight Club,* especially in its concluding section.

A fragmenting consciousness

A cult favorite first as a novel and then as a film, Chuck Palahniuk's *Fight Club* has been interpreted, among other things, as a satire of excessive American consumerism, an exploration of fascist ideology, and as either a straight or a satiric depiction of an extreme cult of masculinity. The cult status of novel and film derives in part from the fact that all of these approaches are valid. Moreover, especially in the case of the novel, they are all rooted in an examination of a disintegrating personality. That the narrator is nameless is significant; his identity is fragmenting throughout the text as his grasp on reality falls to pieces.

Several interrelated factors are responsible for the critical condition of the narrator's identity. First, an essentially Freudian conflict with a simultaneously absent and threatening father lies at the core of the long-repressed anger that increasingly engulfs the narrator's psyche as the novel progresses. The narrator's job with an exploitive insurance company creates an intense self-hatred in him, and his absent father and cynical boss merge in his consciousness as representatives of a repressive male authority. Father and boss also come to embody a patriarchal American capitalism that advocates unchecked consumption. While his job identifies the narrator as a servant of the capitalist system, he hates the exploitation and waste associated with it. Finally, though he is apparently quite young, he becomes obsessed with death and his intensifying desperation at the inevitability of his own demise leads to his entrapment in reminders of physical decay, with what Sartre called "facticity." Not surprisingly, the narrator is also haunted by feelings of sexual inadequacy that are manifested in castration anxieties. His obsession with death leads to his attending support groups for people with life-threatening illnesses; the most significant for the novel's thematic development is a support group for testicular cancer victims. The group is called "Remaining Men Together" and it is led by Robert Paulson, known as Big Bob, whose testicles were removed six months earlier and who, because of hormone therapy, has developed breasts. Big Bob functions as an ironic embodiment of the narrator's own fear of emasculation.

Inspired by Tyler Durden, an alter-ego that emerges out of his subconscious during his sleeping hours, the narrator comes to believe that the destruction of his present self will enable him to find a renewed vitality and thus transcend both death and what he describes as his "tiny" life. At one point, Tyler tells the narrator that "'if you lose your nerve before you hit the bottom . . . you'll never really succeed.' Only after disaster can we be resurrected" (70). That the narrator feels he is being devoured by the quotidian necessities of his life and his job is a key factor in his fears of emasculation and death.

While Tyler Durden is not the first nor the last of the identities that emerge out of the narrator's subconscious, he is the most important. It is Tyler who introduces the narrator to the concept of fight club, an organization initially devoted to promoting brutal physical combat between strangers in isolated buildings throughout the city. Besides its sheer brutality, the most important aspects of fight club are its secrecy and elaborate set of rules; the first and second rules of fight club are "you don't talk about fight club" (48). Since fight club exists only in the narrator's fragmenting consciousness, the rule of secrecy makes complete sense.

The motif of the absent father, which is extended to include contemporary American male society as a whole, significantly receives its first extensive development in the context of the origins and rules of fight club. Tyler is in the process of enumerating the rules when the narrator's thoughts abruptly turn to his father and his traumatic childhood:

> Me, I knew my dad for about six years, but I don't remember anything. My dad, he starts a new family in a new town about every six years. This isn't so much like a family as it's like he sets up a franchise.
>
> What you see at fight club is a generation of men raised by women. (50)

Fight club, with its code of rules and its constantly accelerating membership, constitutes the narrator's projection of an exclusively male family to substitute for the family that he never had as a child because of his father's irresponsibility—even if ultimately fight club also becomes a "franchise." The reference to "a generation of men raised by women" in the quotation above derives its clearest meaning from the narrator's castration anxieties. The legacy of an unfeeling, absent father has left the narrator deeply insecure about his own masculinity. Also significant is the virtual invisibility of the mother in this passage. The reader does not know whether the narrator simply considers her unworthy of notice or has been so psychologically harmed by her that he does not want to acknowledge her existence. In discussing *Fight Club,* one must certainly consider the issue of misogyny. Undoubtedly, a rejection, even a hatred, of women is present in the text; but whether it endorses a misogynistic vision or merely depicts it as a central aspect of the narrator's damaged psyche is less clear.

The narrator's subconscious projects fight club with its ritualized system of male aggression and violence as a means of transcending the emasculation of his generation of American males. Kevin Alexander Boon, like other critics, reads *Fight Club* as a study of a conflicted contemporary white male consciousness: the novel "addresses the identity crisis of white, heterosexual, American men in the late 20th and early 21st centuries who grew up in paradoxical cultural environments that makes heroes of aggressive men while debasing aggressive impulses" (269). A formula of sorts starts to emerge in the novel: masculinity is equated to the experience of pain and ultimately this equation will extend to the valorization of mutilation.

Later in the book, an unnamed mechanic raises the motif of the absent father to still another level: "if you're male and you're Christian and living in America, your father is your model for God. And if you never know your father, if your father bails out or dies or is never at home, what do you believe about God?" (141). That the mechanic, like Tyler Durden and the other anonymous members of fight club, exists only in the mind of the narrator is worth noting as illustrative of Palahniuk's narrative device of extension and intensification. First, the absent father motif is treated exclusively in the context of the narrator's childhood; then it is extended to include all contemporary American males in an exclusively secular context; and finally, in the mechanic's comment, it takes on a spiritual dimension. Paul Kennett perceptively describes the novel's Freudian overtone in this way: "the Narrator continually reaches out to the narrative of patriarchy, rooted in the Oedipal complex, to provide him with a meaningful identity sanctioned in the eyes of an authoritative Other, a transcendent Father" (48). However, the mechanic's comment also illustrates the existentialist nature of Palahniuk's novel. God is absent in the novel, and his characters, in the face of a preoccupation with death, must struggle to find some sustaining spiritual meaning on their own. Fight club represents the narrator's need for such meaning. Emerging out of the narrator's subconscious and taking over more and more of waking consciousness, Tyler, the unnamed mechanic, and the anonymous members of fight club take on the personas of a new faith that is rooted in aggression and violence and is thus doomed to fail. The device of extension and intensification is most clear in the steadily increasing number of figures that emerge from the narrator's profoundly damaged psyche. Initially Tyler Durden stands alone but then fragments into all the members of fight club and then into all the members of the narrator's generation.

The narrator's self-hatred is rooted almost as much in his job as in his memories of an absent father and an invisible mother. Comparable to Palahniuk's introduction of the father conflict by way of an account of the origins and rules of fight club, the text transitions into the initial discussion of the narrator's job from a description of Tyler Durden's petty assaults on the social order. Employed by an automobile company, the narrator determines the economic feasibility of recalls. He applies a formula prescribed by the company to determine whether recalls should be ordered, a formula that is loaded to make it almost impossible to initiate a recall: "Everywhere I go, there's the burned-up wadded-up shell of a car waiting for me. I know where the skeletons are. Consider this my job security" (31).

Although angered by the company philosophy that carelessly disregards public safety and even more by his own role in applying that philosophy, the narrator does not have the courage or confidence to quit his job. Rather, he initially finds release from his complicity in the capitalist system in imagining Tyler's ineffectual rebellion against it. Krister Friday discusses his rebellion in the context of "a narrative of 'white male decline'" (5). The narrator imagines Tyler as working several menial jobs, including that of a movie projectionist. In this role, he finds gratification in splicing pornographic images into family-oriented films, one of which is of an erect penis: "towering four stories tall over the popcorn auditorium, slippery red and terrible, and no one sees it" (30). The audience members are subliminally aware of the image even if they do not actually see it; and some, especially children, are reduced to tears by it. The image of the erect penis seems to be Tyler's, and by extension, the narrator's, way of "giving the finger" to mainstream consumerist society and, as an act of rebellion, is just about that effective and meaningful. In keeping with Palahniuk's narrative motif of extension and intensification, Tyler's acts of rebellion accelerate throughout the novel until they culminate in massive violence.

This imagined rebellion constitutes the key to the cult popularity that the character of Tyler Durden has achieved. For many young males trapped in dead-end jobs, he embodies the open attack on the system they in their helplessness would like to undertake. In fact, any individual acts of rebellion they might imagine, except of course for violent ones, would be ineffectual and as subterranean as Tyler's image of a four-story tall erect penis.

The complicity of Palahniuk's narrator in a corrupt system takes on murderous overtones later in the novel. The insurance company for which he works does not issue a recall for automobiles containing a kind of leather that contains an illegal substance "so strong that it could cause birth defects in the fetus of any pregnant woman who comes across it" (96). A recall would cost the company more than its initial profits. The narrator knows that "if anybody ever discovers our mistake, we can still pay off a lot of grieving families before we come close to the cost of retrofitting sixty-five hundred leather interiors" (ibid.). While the narrator is tormented by such corporate cynicism and irresponsibility, he has no intention of becoming a whistle-blower. Another instance of his metaphoric emasculation, his complicity intensifies the profound self-hatred that fragments his identity.

The constant air travel involved in the narrator's job further contributes to his feelings of insignificance and emasculation:

The charm of traveling is everywhere I go, tiny life. I go to the hotel, tiny soap, tiny shampoos, single-serving butter, tiny mouthwash and a single-use toothbrush. Fold into the standard airplane seat. You're a giant. The problem is your shoulders are too big. Your Alice in Wonderland legs are all of a sudden miles so long they touch the feet of the person in front. Dinner arrives, a miniature do-it-yourself Chicken Cordon Bleu hobby kit, sort of a put-it-together project to keep you busy. (28)

The pervasive irony of this passage originates in the narrator's sense of being the opposite of a giant, a temporary traveler in a sphere of essential unreality. On planes and in airports, he feels that his existence has been miniaturized and destabilized, that everything surrounding him is designed to be discarded, to be thrown away. Such a throw-away life is the fate of those working in contemporary corporate America.

Late in the novel, the narrator acknowledges Tyler's fantasized existence to Marla Singer:

> I hated my life. I was tired and bored with my job and my furniture, and I couldn't see any way to change things.
>
> . . .
>
> I felt trapped.
>
> I was too complete.
>
> I was too perfect.
>
> I wanted a way out of my tiny life. Single-serving butter and cramped airline seat role in the world.
>
> . . .
>
> I took a vacation. I fell asleep on the beach, and when I woke up there was Tyler Durden, naked and sweating, gritty with sand, his hair wet and stringy, hanging in his face. (172–3)

In this acknowledgment that Tyler exists only as a fantasy, elements of self-deception remain. The narrator implies that the creation of Tyler was a conscious, willed act. In fact, as is indicated in his admission of being asleep just before his alter-ego appears, Tyler emerges only during the narrator's sleeping hours. Eventually, Durden clarifies this to the narrator: "we're not two separate men. Long story short, when you're awake, you have the control, and you can call yourself anything you want, but the second you fall asleep, I take over and you become Tyler Durden" (167). Sleep is, of course, a state in which will and control are absent and the narrator quickly loses control of his fantasy. Moreover, haunted by the memory of his absent father and the fear of death and hating his job, he exists in an ongoing state of futility and desperation.

Intensely aware of the "tiny" nature of his life, the narrator recalls the power once possessed by the British Empire to name the world and perceives that power as being replicated by international corporations:

The IBM Stellar Sphere.

The Philip Morris Galaxy.

Planet Denny's.

Every planet will take on the corporate identity of whoever names it first.

Budweiser World. (171)

His internal torment is two-edged. He realizes the disastrous consequences of such limitless corporate power as well as his own helplessness in the face of it. To name is to possess; to rename is to destroy the past and thus to destroy traditional anchors of reality.

Along with his Oedipus complex and his hatred of his job, the third main overriding factor behind the fragmentation of the narrator's identity is his fear of death. His evocation of Tyler Durden is, in part, a desperate attempt to make death attractive. Throughout the novel, Palahniuk reverses clichés celebrating life. The narrator's attendance at meetings for people suffering from terminal illnesses is one such instance. He imagines Marla Singer, whom he encounters at such meetings, as saying that "she wanted to have Tyler's abortion" (51). In fact, the narrator's relationship with Marla originates in and is sustained by his fear of, and fascination with, death. Along a similar line of criticism, Andrew Hock Soon Ng places Marla in the context of Sartrean existentialism to contend that: "from an existentialist framework, Marla is the 'fleshiness' that finally confronts the Narrator with the facticity of his being" (121). Later, reversing another cliché, the narrator reflects on the "amazing miracle of death, when one second you're walking and talking, and the next second, you're an object" (146). In addition, the unnamed mechanic who lectures the narrator on the significance of his absent father assumes the role of a perverse savior when he says to the narrator: "believe in me and you shall die, forever" (145).

The narrator's mental castration, his hatred of both his job and his way of life, and his fear of death result in the outbreak of violence, a complex emotional reaction that Palahniuk brings to a mystical level to keep his readers trapped in the pages of his novel.

The appeal of violence

One manifestation of the narrator's self-hatred is a growing attraction to violence, especially to a male cult of violent behavior and ideology. Increasingly unable to deny the appeal of violence, the narrator tries to control it through the highly regimented fight club concept. His method of attempting control can be understood in the context of ideas of René Girard and Georges Bataille. In developing his theory of "sacred violence" (1972), Girard focuses initially on classical Greek drama and folklore and then on the concepts of Freud and Claude Lévi-Strauss, among others. For him, violence is linked to the practice of ritual sacrifice:

> Violence is frequently called irrational. It has its reasons, however, and can marshal some rather convincing ones when the need arises. Yet these reasons cannot be taken seriously, no matter how valid they appear. Violence itself will discard them if the initial object remains persistently out of reach and continues to provoke hostility. When unappeased, violence seeks and always finds a human victim. The creature that excited its fury is abruptly replaced by another, chosen only because it is vulnerable and close at hand. (2)

I contend that Tyler Durden's idea of fight club is rooted in the irrational. A result of the issues described in the previous part of this chapter, the narrator's fantasized violence is directed inward at himself because the initial objects that motivated it (father, mother, capitalism, death) remain "persistently out of reach." Moreover, it exists exclusively in the realm of fantasy until the end of the novel. The protagonist's hostility is profoundly irrational, a sense of persecution that pervades every level of his being; it cannot be unappeased and seeks the closest human victim available: the narrator himself.

Girard further argues that human beings have historically feared outbreaks of reciprocal violence that threaten the very foundation of the social order. In order to control the threat of reciprocal violence, societies have arbitrarily chosen sacrificial victims on whom to practice violence—Jethro Rothe-Kushel has discussed the film version of *Fight Club* in the context of Girard, identifying Tyler Durden as a sacrificial victim (2004). But a key aspect of *Fight Club*'s appeal, especially to males, is that in contemporary American society, it is difficult to find sacrificial victims that can be attacked without bringing about retaliation. One cannot readily attack an international corporation or pervasive social corruption, and any attempt to isolate a surrogate for such abstractions is virtually impossible. Of course, Americans still attempt to do so; thus the popularity of conspiracy theories, the legalized persecution of illegal immigrants, and the racism that lingers in American society. But the roots of the narrator's persecution complex are too deeply personal for him to identify surrogates among African Americans or Hispanics. Moreover, he seems too intelligent to focus on such common scapegoats.

Fear of death has historically been a motivation in what Girard describes as the need to isolate surrogates on whom to inflict nonreciprocal violence; and certainly the narrator shares that fear. But again in contemporary American society, such surrogates are difficult to find. Women and gay men remain targets for heterosexual male insecurity and rage and, as mentioned, *Fight Club* contains undeniable misogynistic overtones. Homophobia is a largely elided motif in the novel, but it is nevertheless present.

The anger, fear, and self-hatred that pervade the narrator's being demands concrete manifestation and out of the narrator's subconscious emerges first Tyler Durden. The novel's account of the narrator's first meeting Tyler at a nude beach initially seems a curious, even discordant, element in the book. There is no other mention of the narrator being a devotee of public nudity. Nude beaches are often identified as gay spaces, but again *Fight Club* never defines the narrator as being gay. There are nevertheless homoerotic overtones in Palahniuk's description of the narrator's meeting with Tyler: "Tyler was naked and sweating, gritty with sand, his hair was wet and stringy, hanging in his face. . . . I asked if [he] was an artist" (32–3). The homoeroticism of the beach scene seems to be one aspect of Tyler's appeal to the narrator as a projection of social rebellion, as someone who has escaped the capitalistic trap in which the narrator is enmeshed. An imagined bohemian existence with its freedom from social conventions would have strong attractions for him: thus "I asked if [he] was an artist."

In the contexts of Palahniuk's belated coming out of the closet and a recurrent note of romance in his novels, Jesse Kavadlo calls the author of *Fight Club* a "closet moralist" (5). The novel's subsequent scenes of semi-nude young men engaged in ritualized acts of physical violence can be read in this same context. That the fight club combatants are brutally assaulting each other in secret, isolated spaces echoes the necessary secrecy of pre-Stonewall gay meeting places and the self-hatred produced in some gay men by the persecution of the dominant heterosexual society, a self-hatred sometimes manifested in sadomasochistic activities.

Complicating a gay interpretation of fight club is the fact that it exists only in the narrator's mind. The abandoned buildings where the fights occur have no counterpart in reality; thus any attempt to read them as designated gay meeting places is undercut. The rebellion of which they are manifestations is a private, internal one, doomed to failure. Tyler and fight club constitute a desperate attempt by the narrator's subconscious to control the disintegration of his identity. The attempt is doomed from the start by its evocation of violence as a mode of control. Violence is, of course, irrational, a condition that resides at the core of the narrator's fears and insecurities. Thus, in addition to its gay overtones, the nude beach scene can be read as the narrator's first confrontation with his anger and fear. Initially, his subconscious transforms these negative emotions into an attractive image, one that will increasingly consume the narrator's identity. The novel's progression from the narrator's initial encounter with a nude Tyler Durden to increasingly violent descriptions of fight club combat illustrate the intensifying disintegration of the narrator's identity, a disintegration that will culminate in an act of self-mutilation.

The elaborate rules of fight club, which are recited like a mantra throughout the text, represent an attempt to impose order on what is profoundly irrational; and ultimately it cannot be ordered. Moreover, the fundamental irrationality of fight club is obvious from the beginning. The narrator describes its origin as being an instant outside a bar when both he and Tyler Durden are drunk, and Tyler abruptly asks the narrator to hit him. The narrator comments that neither he nor Tyler had ever been in a fight previously: "if you've never been in a fight, you wonder. About getting hurt, about what you're capable of doing against another man" (52). Here, the narrator is equating masculinity with pain and the ability to inflict pain. Behind this is the concrete reality of physical pain in contrast to the abstract pain inflicted by the company for which the narrator works.

Initially, he resists Tyler's request, but the latter explains the necessity of such violent aggression: "Tyler explained it all, about not wanting to die without any scars, about being tired of watching only professionals fight, and wanting to know more about himself. About self-destruction" (ibid.). Because of the anger, guilt, and self-hatred that define him, the narrator longs for self-destruction. This first spontaneous fight soon escalates into the ritualized violence of fight club and the narrator imagining that he sees physically scarred and bruised young men wherever he goes. These battered figures are an early indication that, despite its rules, the narrator's projection of fight club as a means of controlling the irrationality of the violence that calls out to him is unraveling from the start.

In *Erotism: Death and Sensuality* (1957), Georges Bataille develops a theory that human existence is binary in nature that can be meaningfully applied to the alienation of the narrator of *Fight Club* and his embrace of an imagined and self-destructive violence:

> [O]ne cannot fail to observe mankind's double nature throughout his career. There are two extremes. At one end, existence is basically orderly and decent. Work, concern for the children, kindness and honesty rule men's dealings with their fellows. At the other, violence rages pitilessly. In certain circumstances the same men practice pillage and arson, murder, violence and torture. Excess contrasts with reason. (186)

For the narrator of *Fight Club*, the affirmative half of this "double nature" is meaningless. Since he is unmarried, childless, and alienated from his parents, family can never be a meaningful anchor for him. He is profoundly aware of this lack, and first Tyler Durden and then the half-naked young men of fight club emerge out of his subconscious as surrogate brothers, as well as images of the male sexuality that is compromised in his own identity. This imagined family is compromised by its homoeroticism. There are overtones of incest in his evocation of a surrogate family—Tyler and the young men are imagined as lovers as well as brothers.

In addition, the narrator's experiences with his parents and at work have taught him that human beings are anything but kind and honest, that they are in fact embodiments of selfishness and greed. The company for which he works, and which one feels that Palahniuk intends as representative of corporate America, operates in a decidedly indecent fashion. Its decisions concerning recalls are based on a kind of order, but it is an inhumane and destructive order. Bataille further argues that work, since it is rooted in reason, has historically served human beings as a barrier against unchecked excess that inevitably leads to violence. From the moment that Tyler asks the narrator to hit him, violence becomes the central ingredient in the story; fight club is born. The descriptions of fighting in the novel become increasingly brutal until they culminate in this: "one more punch and my teeth click on my tongue. Half of my tongue falls on the floor and gets kicked away" (201). Violent excess rather than controlling reason is the defining ingredient of the narrator's fantasized fight club. Such devotion to excess negates any possibility that the narrator will control the fantasy; in fact, as the novel progresses, it increasingly controls him. Three distinct stages of fight club emerge gradually, each stage more defined by excessive violence than the previous one.

The stages of *Fight Club*

The first stage represents the creation and growing expansion of fight club. One of the novel's more surrealistic elements is the narrator's descriptions of seeing more and more battered and even mutilated young men wherever he goes, especially in connection with his job:

> Now I go to meetings or conferences and see faces at conference tables, accountants and junior executives or attorneys with broken noses spreading out like an eggplant under the edges of bandages or they have a couple stitches under an eye or a jaw wired shut. . . .

According to my boss, there are fewer and fewer gentlemen in business and more thugs. (54)

These images of badly mutilated young men at business conferences constitute an early clue of the fundamental unreality of fight club. Obviously, no corporation would retain such employees, much less send them to high-level conferences. There is meaningful irony, however, in the boss's comment about the decreasing number of gentlemen in business. The boss, of course, is one of the individuals who decide not to issue recalls, even when the lives of consumers are endangered. He, like those above him on the corporate ladder, is himself a dangerous thug, no matter the decency of his public appearance.

Soon, on a second stage, fight club extends beyond the promotion of simple fighting and assumes a broader mission, "Project Mayhem," the promotion of random acts of sabotage, primarily against corporations. "Project Mayhem" operates according to a set of rules, promulgated of course by Tyler Durden, that mimic those of fight club itself: "the first rule about Project Mayhem is that you don't ask questions about Project Mayhem" (119). Moreover, like the corporate world, it functions through committees:

Arson meets on Monday.

Assault on Tuesday.

Mischief meets on Wednesday.

And Misinformation meets on Thursday.

Organized Chaos. The Bureaucracy of Anarchy. (ibid.)

That Project Mayhem is modeled on the corporate world demonstrates that the narrator has been co-opted by that world and that, ironically, he does not resist it in his fantasy of rebellion.

The initial description of Project Mayhem contains an important clue about the structure of Palahniuk's novel. After listing Project Mayhem's committees, the narrator refers to them as "support groups. Sort of" (ibid.). Support group meetings, for instance, "Remaining Men Together," constitute one of the novel's four narrative spaces that clearly exist on a level of external reality; the narrator's office and the airplane seats in which he travels are two of the others. His attendance at Remaining Men Together, pointing to his necessity to establish human links, and his encounter with Marla Singer, pointing to his sexual insecurity, trigger his subsequent retreat to the nude beach where the apparition of Tyler Durden takes place.

At first, Project Mayhem is devoted to relatively innocuous, even childish, acts of vandalism:

> [Y]ou have to go to the import beer festival this weekend and push over a guy in a chemical toilet. You'll get extra favor if you get beat up for doing this. Or you have to attend the fashion show at the shopping center atrium and throw strawberry gelatin from the mezzanine. (120)

But as excess and violence replace reason and control in the narrator's fantasy, Project Mayhem engages in extreme acts of vandalism. The increasingly dangerous actions of Project Mayhem represent the third stage of fight club. What begins in fights between anonymous young men is transformed into underground warfare against the corporate world.

One form of this warfare involves the kidnapping and threatened or actual castration of the victim. This "cut-and-run" practice has its origins in the loss of his testicles by Big Bob of Remaining Men Together. Inevitably, the narrator imagines himself as a near cut-and-run victim. Big Bob, in fact, intrudes into the narrator's fantasized fight club space and, in it, is killed by the police while undertaking a Project Mayhem assignment. Subsequently, Big Bob, now known only as Robert Paulson, assumes the status of a martyred hero of Project Mayhem. In addition, the narrator's imagined cut-and-run experience foreshadows his ultimate disfigurement. The complexity of Palahniuk's narrative is epitomized in the manner in which this disfigurement is recounted. It actually occurs in the novel's opening pages, which introduce the novel's fantasized spaces, but is not clearly revealed until its concluding scene, which unfolds in the novel's fourth reality space.

The spaces of *Fight Club*

A brief summary of Henri Lefebvre's analysis of space in *The Production of Space* (1974) sheds light on *Fight Club*'s juxtaposition of fantasized and real spaces. Writing from a Marxist perspective, Lefebvre begins by positing three essential kinds of space: "the *physical*—nature, the Cosmos . . . the *mental*, including logical and formal abstractions; and . . . the *social*" (11). In discussing the ways in which spaces interact during the processes of production and commodification, he introduces a second triad: "*spatial practice*," "*representations of space*," and "*representational spaces*, embodying complex symbolisms, sometimes coded, sometimes not, linked to the clandestine or underground side of social life, as also to art . . ." (33).

Both of Lefebvre's triads contribute to an understanding of the structure of *Fight Club*. After its opening pages, which transpire in a complex mixture of physical and mental or more specifically fantasized spaces, the novel essentially unfolds in physical and social spaces until it abruptly shifts to mental space(s) after the scene in which the narrator meets Tyler Durden on the nude beach. It returns to the initial mixture of the physical and the mental in its concluding scene. In addition, Lefebvre's concept of representational spaces is especially relevant to Palahniuk's novel. The key stages of fight club are certainly coded and linked to the "clandestine or underground side of social life." Since *Fight Club* is a novel, they are also linked to "art." Moreover, a complex mixture of the concrete and the symbolic characterizes all the novel's spaces. Collectively, the narrative takes place in physical space, mental space, social space, and symbolic space, sometimes in only one of these levels, but more often in a complex mixture of them. Thus, the underground world of fight club exists only as a projection of the narrator's consciousness, but it originates in his Oedipus complex, his hatred of his job with its "tiny life" and the guilt that results from his continuing in it, and in his fear of death.

The narrator's apartment and Tyler Durden's house on Paper Street illustrate the complexity of space in *Fight Club*. After he returns from a business trip to find that his apartment has blown up, the narrator lists the furniture and material possessions that were destroyed in the explosion and expresses relief at their destruction:

> You buy furniture. . . . Then the right set of dishes. Then the perfect bed. The drapes. The rug.
>
> Then you're trapped in your lovely nest, and the things you used to own, now they own you.
>
> Until I got home from the airport. (44)

It is unclear what caused the explosion, one implication being that Tyler Durden, or the narrator as Tyler Durden, intentionally blew up the apartment as a means of escape from a capitalist system defined by excessive commodification. One can, nevertheless, assume that the apartment did exist in the realm of reality. Even more complex is Paper Street and Durden's house on it. Tyler's origin in the narrator's subconscious and the series of surreal events that unfold in his house would seem to indicate that the Paper Street setting exists strictly on the level of fantasy.

Especially bizarre is the novel's account of the Paper Street Soap Company that is run out of Tyler's Paper Street house. Tyler introduces the narrator to raiding trash containers outside medical centers in order to steal collagen suctioned out of the bodies of overweight women. The collagen becomes the secret ingredient in Paper Street soap. Moreover, Marla Singer has inherited from her mother a "collagen trust fund":

> [W]henever her mother grew any extra fat, she had it sucked out and packaged. Marla says the process is called *gleaning*. If Marla's mom doesn't need the collagen herself, she sends the packets to Marla. (91)

After Marla puts some of her inherited packages of collagen in the freezer, it is transformed into soap. The soap is produced by Project Mayhem volunteers utilizing an assembly line method of production supervised, of course, by Tyler Durden. The extended episode of the Paper Street Soap Company and the fate of Marla's mother's collagen has misogynistic overtones—why do they not use collagen suctioned also out of men's bodies?— and further echoes the Nazis' practice of making soap out of concentration camp victims. It is also the prime example of *Fight Club*'s surreal black humor.

That Project Mayhem is presented from a black humor perspective is further evidence of the essential unreality of Tyler's house and of Paper Street itself, as is a key scene in which the narrator allows Tyler to burn his hand with lye. The burn scene perfectly illustrates the spatial complexity of Palahniuk's novel. In the course of administering the burn, Tyler gives an extensive lecture on the history of human sacrifice, while the narrator thinks about a time in Ireland where he "first wanted anarchy . . . and learned about little acts of rebellion" (76). Since Durden is a fantasy of the narrator, one can assume that the lecture about human sacrifice emerges out of the narrator's own consciousness as does his memory of an earlier time in Ireland. His recalling the time when he was initially drawn to anarchy and to little acts of violence constitutes the roots of Project Mayhem. The burn scene also highlights the narrator's intensifying self-hatred and obsession with pain and self-destruction, especially as he reports that it represents "the greatest moment of our life" (75). The "our" here is fascinating, an indication of the narrator's fragmenting consciousness.

The opening and conclusion of *Fight Club*

Any distinction between reality and fantasy spaces virtually disappears in an extended scene that constitutes *Fight Club*'s opening and conclusion and describes events occurring in the same time frame. The novel leads into this climactic moment through an account of the final, extreme stage of Project Mayhem, a program of destruction of large, corporate buildings that function as representatives of the capitalist, consumerist culture. The building that houses the narrator's office is one of these structures, and its explosion kills his boss. The narrator identifies first Tyler, and then himself, as being responsible for the explosion: "The problem is, I sort of liked my boss. . . . Except Tyler didn't like my boss. . . . I wanted out of my job. I was giving Tyler permission. Be my guest. Kill my boss" (186–7). As elsewhere in the novel, the narrator can only imagine his alter ego rebelling against the cynical capitalist structure that employs him.

The imagined bombing of his office building and killing of his boss shocks the narrator into a partial awareness that Tyler exists only as a projection of his own subconscious. Just prior to the novel's climactic scene, he tells Marla Singer that Tyler is "the other side of my split personality" (196). Nevertheless, he believes that he must act to stop Tyler from carrying out the last act of Project Mayhem, the bombing of the 191-story Parker-Morris building.

In the novel's penultimate chapter, Tyler is holding the narrator prisoner on top of the Parker-Morris building with a gun stuck in his mouth. He tells his hostage that "the last thing we have to do is your martyrdom thing. Your big death thing" (203). When the narrator refuses to cooperate, Tyler vows to go after and kill Marla. Abruptly Marla appears, running across the roof and followed by all the members of the illness support groups she and the narrator have attended. She orders the narrator to put down the gun but, in the last line of the chapter, he pulls the trigger. This chapter functions as a lead-in for the novel's opening. Palahniuk's departure from linear time here works to intensify the novel's suspense and as an illustration of the narrator's fragmented consciousness. The novel begins on top of the Parker-Morris building with Tyler holding the gun in the narrator's mouth and telling him that "this isn't really death. . . . 'We'll be legend. We won't grow old.'" In part, this extended scene constitutes the narrator's fantasized escape from the death he has always feared. In this context, the novel's last chapter will encapsulate the irony that pervades *Fight Club*. The narrator imagines Tyler shooting him in the face. Thus, the savior, whom the narrator has constructed out of his imagination as a means of reaffirming his own identity, attempts to murder him. The irony is intensified by the probability that what really occurs is a suicide attempt by the narrator. If so, the suicide represents an irrational attempt to escape death by embracing it, an attempt that leaves him still alive, but disfigured and trapped in a mental institution.

The narrator imagines a photo sequence of the demolition of the building in which "the last shot" will be of "the tower, all one-hundred and ninety-one floors" collapsing on "the national museum which is Tyler's real target" (14). The imagined defacing, if not actual devastation, of art and culture is reported throughout the novel; and the destruction of a national museum constitutes the culmination of this motif as well as a repudiation of the nation's cultural past. At one point, the narrator says that he "wanted to destroy everything beautiful I'd never have" (123). This comment exemplifies the narrator's perverse reaction to his entrapment in a society and civilization dominated by gross "facticity" and corporate cynicism.

While Tyler holds the narrator hostage on top of the building, the "space monkeys" of Project Mayhem are carrying out a program of demolition against the interior of the building. The novel's stress on this program of annihilation forces the reader to consider the possibility that the assault on the Parker-Morris building is occurring in reality as well as in the narrator's imagination, that it simultaneously exists in reality and fantasy space(s). But, even though there is no concrete indication in this opening chapter that Marla Singer is present on the Parker-Morris roof, the narrator abruptly asserts that "I know all of this: the gun, the anarchy, the explosion is really about Marla Singer. . . . We have sort of a triangle going on here. I want Tyler. Tyler wants Marla. Marla wants me" (14). The narrator's assertion that he wants Tyler gives credence to a homoerotic reading of the novel, but also to an interpretation that Tyler exists as a projection of all the things the narrator wishes he had, but knows that he does not, including sexual vitality and the courage to rebel against an exploitive capitalism.

Marla Singer provides another key to the novel's complex spatial structure. The reader can assume that, as an habituée of support groups, she exists in reality. The narrator meets her at these groups and immediately dislikes her, labeling her a "fake" because she does not, in fact, have a terminal illness. Neither, of course, does the narrator, and his labeling Marla a "fake" is, in part, an indictment of himself. In the fantasy space of Paper Street the narrator imagines her betraying him by sleeping with Tyler Durden. The narrator, in fact, becomes as obsessed with her as with Tyler, in the process of which he transforms her from the flesh-and-blood habituée of support groups to an object of simultaneous sexual attraction and revulsion both in the real and fantasy spaces.

In the concluding chapter of the novel, the narrator imagines himself in heaven, where he is interrogated by God "across his walnut desk with his diplomas hanging on the wall behind him" (207). In fact, the narrator appears to be incarcerated in some kind of institution, probably a home for the mentally ill. That the God here is most likely a psychiatrist is another example of the novel's black humor. For a moment, the narrator seems to have attained some degree of wellness, repudiating not only the existence of Tyler Durden, but his alter-ego's philosophy as well: "we are not special. We are not crap or trash, either. We just are" (ibid.). Nevertheless, he bears Tyler's mark: "the bullet out of Tyler's gun, it tore out my . . . cheek to give me a jagged smile from ear to ear" (ibid.). Rather than death, the narrator has experienced disfigurement. That he persists in saying the "bullet out of Tyler's gun" indicates that he has not reached a state of wellness. His physical disfigurement is a metonymic representation of his still-fragmented consciousness. A likely reading of the novel's extended conclusion is that the narrator, belatedly realizing that he cannot control the irrationality that pervades his consciousness, has attempted suicide.

A further indication of the partial nature of his healing is his comment that "Marla's still on Earth, and she writes to me. Someday, she says, they'll bring me back" (ibid.). Despite his mixed feelings about her, Marla remains his anchor to reality and, fake devotee of terminal illness support groups though she is, his hope for ultimate psychological and sexual healing. In this concluding chapter, Marla seems to have returned from fantasy to reality space. Both in the narrator's consciousness and in actuality, she is "on Earth."

2

The Avatars of Masculinity: How Not to be a Man

Eduardo Mendieta

Introduction

If Simone de Beauvoir's incisive dictum in *The Second Sex* (1949) "One is not born, but rather becomes, a woman" is true for woman, it must also be true for man. The biological facts of sex are the raw material which historical forces, ideologies, ideals, and social practices shape into distinct gender identities. Sex is the tabula rasa on which gendering practices inscribe normative expectations about what we are supposed to do with our organs of reproduction, our whole bodies, and eventually all our acts. It is for this reason that the history of societies, nations, and civilizations are also the history of gendering practices. That we have been slow, even too late to recognize that gendering practices and their corresponding gendering norms have a history should not be registered as an objection to the very recognition of that history, but rather that neglecting, failing to recognize, even denying it is itself part of the history of gendering practices. Gender is most at play precisely when it is hoisted upon an allegedly ahistorical sex. It is one of the greatest virtues of literature, and the novel specifically, that it has contributed to our becoming conscious of the historicity of gender (see De Lauretis 9–82). All great novels in the literary canon (and not simply the Euro-North American one) are in one way or another meditations on what it means to be male or female in a given society. Don Quixote, the hopeless romantic; Casanova, the gigolo of the Renaissance; Madame Bovary, the heroine of a proto-feminist insurrection against the banality of stultifying domesticity; even Roa Bastos's "I, the Supreme," the metonym for all Latin American caudillos; from its beginnings in literary history the novel has been always about the avatars of gender. The history of literature is the history of self-reflection on the different regimes of gendering. It is from this perspective that Chuck Palahniuk should be read within this long history of the novel as a medium for the reflection on distinct "American" gendering practices. His work certainly should be read in conjunction with that of Philip Roth, James Baldwin, Saul Bellow, John Updike, and Don DeLillo, as well as Bret Easton Ellis and Jonathan Franzen, because all these male writers have meditated deeply, provocatively, courageously, irreverently on what it means to be a male in America during these past 50 years. While most, if not all, of Palahniuk's fiction is suffused with references, reflections, and dogged insistency on the constructedness of masculinity, *Fight Club* is the novel where he is most deliberate about deconstructing fin de siècle American masculinity. Indeed, it would be both interesting and useful to attempt a typology of the male protagonists, or antagonists, in Palahniuk's novels. Such a typology or compendium would reveal how not only consumerism, hypersexuality, violence, but also popular culture and religion condition the ways in which masculinity is inscribed and circumscribed. In 2005 I offered a reading of Palahniuk's work as a diagnosis of the crises of "American Culture." In the following pages, however, I will limit myself to offering a reading of *Fight Club* that shows not only how this novel is about the avatars of masculinity, but also how it offers a quasi-Nietzschean reading of the practices of "American" civility that render people docile subjects of servility. The critique of American masculinity is also a critique of an ethos of docility and trust. Tyler Durden, I argue, turns out to be the "Übermensch," the new Nietzschean superman who, in *Thus Spoke Zarathustra* (1891) is the bridge between the man produced by empty eroticism, rampant consumerism, post-heroic militarism, and what men may become beyond post-imperial, post-hyper finance capitalism, post-American economic might; that is, what men must become in a nation that must co-exist with other nations in a world of dwindling resources and intensifying global precariousness. The Nietzschean "overman" is a most appropriate figure to help us decipher the critical dimension of Tyler Durden, not simply because Nietzsche was inspired by the quintessential American writers, Ralph Waldo Emerson (see Ratner-Rosenhagen 1–27), but also because the overman is a figure of moral transformation and critique of the status quo. When Nietzsche's Zarathustra announces that he has come to teach the overman, he adds: "Human being is something that must be overcome. What have you done to overcome him?" (5). The overman is also a figure that in Nietzsche's corpus could be read as part of his rejection of the Plato's philosopher-king. The overman escapes Plato's cave by escaping the notion that we are merely prisoners of false knowledge. Tyler Durden, as an American Zarathustra, also traces an escape route.

The overman is a call to transform ourselves into the moral exemplars we ought to become, but this demands that we reject everything that has rendered us docile, servile, and resentful creatures.

Disciples of servility

We are not anything at birth, but whatever we become is part of a process of congealing some social glue. We become ourselves by being socialized into our individuality. Self-hood is an accomplishment that is enabled by the society against which and through which we claim: "I am myself." Individuality reflects the society that enabled it. Conversely, we can only be ourselves as we assume a particular attitude to the norms and mores of the society to which we belong. To be an individual is partly the result of subscribing to the practices and expectations that bind our society together. There is no individuality without a relationship to one's society, that is, to the necessity of having to subscribe to a certain code of civility. There is no society without the individuals who continuously replenish the lubricant of social co-existence. The key ingredient in the lubricant of sociality is surely trust, as sociologists since Emil Durkheim have argued. To be socialized as individuals is to be socialized into trust, that is, to trust others and to be trusted. Most of the time we are able to operate on autopilot, so to say, because we ceaselessly and unconsciously rely on others. The everyday life of communal existence is predicated on countless and uninterrupted acts of reliance. Civility is precisely the routinization of such faith in others. You stand on line to buy something, and you believe that someone else is not going to simply jump ahead of you without having waited. We wait our turn, because others do as well. We merge on the highway without trepidation, confident that either the car on the lane you are merging onto will shift to the left or that they will decelerate. Our quotidian existence is sustained by countless such acts of faith. Without our submission to its etiquette, we would be living in a Hobbessian world of mutual mistrust, cynicism, and simmering violence. In his *Leviathan* for Hobbes, in the state of nature, before the compact that gives birth to civil order and thus industry and culture, we are wolves to each other. We are caught in the zero sum calculus that we are all potentially murderers and victims, and no one is safe from another's will to survive by taking one's life and property. Hobbes's solution, however, is to transfer the fear of mutually assured destruction to the sovereign, who terrorizes us all into submission. Now we are all at the mercy of the terrifying beast that is the state—after all it is called a Leviathan, a biblical creature of punishment and judgment. Trust, it could be argued, is the only way in which we thwart the Leviathan and its bloody sword, and look at each other without cowering fear.

Fight Club stages the drama of a social etiquette of trust that has turned into a social etiquette of servility. When faith in the others is ceaselessly manipulated to turn persons into docile subjects, trust does not operate to coordinate social cooperation, but to impose submission and compliance. When reading *Fight Club* it is easy to be distracted from this key theme by the foregrounding of violence in the "fight club." Yet, we miss an important link Palahniuk is surely establishing between how a social order is maintained and what it means to be a particular type of male in that society. To be socialized into masculinity is partly to be socialized into submitting to certain codes of male behavior. There is no social order if we refuse the roles we are assigned, but part of submitting to those roles is to reaffirm the interconnections of our social order. It is for this reason that what happens in the dark basements of bars, that is fight clubs, is mirrored by what the members of fight club do during the day in their underpaid service jobs. One of the challenges members of "Project Mayhem" have to face is to get into a fight with someone on the street, without responding back. In a wonderful Nietzschean exercise, they push the boundaries of civility until people snap and fight back, but without the instigator responding. The point? It is time to be "outraged!" But why are we not outraged? Note that this is different from "road rage"—which is rage occasioned by different reasons. Interestingly, in the *Nicomachean Ethics*, book 2, Aristotle gives a distinct place to "outrage"—or "righteous indignation"—in his catalog of virtues. The passage merits quoting:

> Righteous indignation is a mean between envy and spite, and these states are concerned with the pain and pleasure that are felt at the fortunes of our neighbours; the man who is characterized by righteous indignation is pained at undeserved good fortune, the envious man, going beyond him, is pained at all good fortune, and the spiteful man falls so far short of being pained that he even rejoices. (1108b)

In all virtue ethics, in fact, to be able to be outraged is indispensable for moral action, because to be moved by the harm done to someone urges us to demand redress for the injury that has been done. Without outrage, we would hardly be moved to repair the ethical fabric of our social existence when moral harm and injustice have been committed. In this sense, Project Mayhem aims to make us aware of the ways in which social order is predicated on the code of civility, which can also turn into a code of servility.

In *Fight Club*, "a generation of men raised by women" (50) fight each other, first, so as to break through all the conventions that determine masculinity and, second, so as to enter a space of willful, deliberate trust. A fight might be conceived here as the staging of trust as its most extreme. If a theater performance signifies the very act of acting—that is, what we see is the very act of acting—a fight is the staging of the act of trusting. The blood drawn by the naked punches of an anonymous other, in which each one has rendered himself vulnerable to the other, becomes a baptism into a deliberate community of trust. While this deliberate faith is fashioned underground, during the day members of Project Mayhem go about dismantling the confidence that has turned humans into morose and enslaved sites of respectability. "Where is your outrage?" is the unasked question implied by their theatrics of disrupting social trust. "Time to be outraged!" is the silent motto of these men who in daylight deliberately abuse the trust of their unsuspecting customers in order to show both their having become aware of that trust and their own willingness to start a new project of social trust.

The men in Project Mayhem are the everyday men, the anyone and everyone of daily life. They are the silent men "who serve with pride." As Tyler says to the commissioner who is trying to shut down Project Mayhem:

> We're the people who do your laundry and cook your food and serve your dinner. We make your bed. We guard you while you're asleep. We drive the ambulances. We direct your calls. We are cooks and taxi drivers and we know everything about you. We process your insurance claims and credit card charges. We control every part of your life. (166)

These men control the lives of everyone else, and yet they had not usurped that power precisely because they submitted to the etiquette of a trust turned into servility. However, Project Mayhem is about awakening men to precisely their quiet, inertial power. It is time for "outrage" specifically because a lot of these men, the men who go to fight club to punch themselves into a live masculinity, have become the disposable and silent servants of an underpaid, insecure, and meaningless service economy. The men of fight club are the children of a post-industrial economy. They are the men of a generation whose standard of living will be worse than that of their parents. They have been raised on exorbitant expectations that because they can never be cashed out in social reality turns them into failures. Fight club males are men who have introjected failure, but who now seek to vomit this psychological poison by challenging the social system that condemns them to abysmal expectations. Speaking like the prophet of our post-industrial, post-Keynesian, post-Fordist cities, Tyler proclaims: "We are the middle children of history, raised by television to believe that someday we'll be millionaires and movie stars and rock stars, but we won't. And we're just learning this fact" (ibid.)

What happens when a society is no longer able to deliver on the expectations it rises for its members? What happens when those expectations are imbricated with what it means to be a specific type of male, and becoming that type of male is no longer possible on the basis of those expectations? The fabric of that society begins to unravel. The fight clubs in *Fight Club* should be read as allegories of a new type of social resistance in which class or economic struggle becomes at the same time a fight against social meaninglessness and numbing social submission that prostrates men before the unreachable heights of defunct role models. Men cannot but feel betrayed, and they in turn betray that society. They opt out of the social contract of trust that sustains that society. In *Fight Club*, the issue of trust is linked to the question of the norms of gender. Some years later, in *Choke* (2001), Palahniuk offers another staging of the relation between trust and servility. The protagonist of this novel, in fact, makes a point of exploiting people's basic faith in the others, or what we could call in its most extreme form, "gullibility," as readers of this volume will find in part 3. To the silent assent to an etiquette of servility based on exploited trust, the response of the men of fight club is the loud yell of outrage. Sometimes outrage is what urges men to violence, but sometimes outrage is what urges men to social change, the change that would allow them to be men differently.

The fetishes of consumerist masculinity

David Dobkin's 2011 film *The Change-Up*, dreadful as it is, can help illustrate a key theme in *Fight Club*. In the movie, Dave and Mitch, two friends who grew up together but have drifted apart, are reunited. They realize that prima facie each other's life is more appealing. They would rather lead the other's life. The younger one leads a life devoid of responsibilities. He is the perpetual teenager. He is a ladies man, and as viewers find out, even works in the soft porn industry. The other is a successful lawyer, father of three, who is married to a beautiful blond wife, and is about to become a partner in a large corporate law firm. As things go, they fulfill their mutual wish, and each wakes up in the other's body. The movie then falls into the typical clichés, following the already well-known stages of bland Hollywood Bildungsroman: at first utter disbelief, followed by attempts to convince spouses that Mitch is the real Dave, and Dave is Mitch. After this fails, they settle into each other's life. In fact, they begin to enjoy each other's life. The father of three gets to play, sleep late, even have a date with his gorgeous secretary (for after all, is it not a fantasy all men have, to sleep with their young, hot secretary?). Meanwhile Mitch, now living as Dave, gets to play the family man. Being a gigolo, viewers learn, is full of hazards, inconveniences, and disgust. While, in contrast, being a responsible father, husband, and soon to be partner of a big law firm, is not only full of hard work, but also of gratifying accomplishment. However, underneath all the Hollywood schlock and sentimental drivel is one interesting idea: that what men crave are a good challenge, meaningful responsibility, and earned success. The stereotypes, as predictable as they are, are also telling: in one case, a driven, workaholic husband, who has grown distant from his wife, the other a carefree sex machine who feels failed and underappreciated. They are embodiments of work without meaning and sex without respect.

On the other hand, *Fight Club* does not tread on such hackneyed stereotypes of masculinity. It is too subtle and sophisticated to give us such cartoonish archetypes. Tyler Durden, who might be deemed the main protagonist of the book, is the alter-ego of everyman. But who is this "everyman"? Everyman is everyone, but also no one. All males are him. And in the novel, they are all unsatisfied losers trapped by an ever-demanding consumerist society. The male characters in the book, eventual members of fight club, are overworked, doing meaningless tasks which they know entail fraud and an economy of failure. Everyman, embodied in the nameless narrator of the book, descends into the rut of work and returns to his catalog-furnished apartment. His success is measured by the beautiful, but also useless things he accumulates. In his fiction, Palahniuk frequently warns readers that people buy things to stand in for success, but then they become prisoners of those fetishes. Perhaps one day they come to realize that now ". . . you're trapped in your lovely nest, and the things you used to own, now they own you" (44). Here, the writer is giving his readers the latest version of the classic story told by Plato in book 8 of *The Republic*, of the moral and political degeneration of society by the corrosive effect of possessive individualism and the bewitching power of its fetishes. From timocracy through oligarchy and democracy to tyranny, the story is one in which the things people produce to make their lives more civilized, less violent, less filled with privation, turn them into their servants and protectors. At stake, however, is the satisfaction of some corporeal desire. The gratification of consumption has something fundamentally erotic about it, which is why they are closely and ironically aligned in *Fight Club*: "The people I know who used to sit in the bathroom with pornography, now they sit in the bathroom with the IKEA furniture catalogue" (43). Both pornography and consumerism draw not only on the same urge for immediate gratification, but also on the scopophilia that is instigated by a society that is so relentlessly driven by visual stimulation. While *Fight Club* alludes continuously to what I understand to be empty eroticism and the pervasiveness of pornography in American culture, Palahniuk has written more explicitly and extensively about these themes in novels such as *Survivor* (1999) and *Snuff* (2008), clearly showing his concern about the issue. The latter book in fact explicitly focuses on the pornography industry and culture, suggesting that they are nothing but the ultimate stage in the process of commodification of human beings ... In Palahniuk's first published novel Tyler Durden is the alter-ego of this everyman who, bursting from the narrator's unconscious, will fulfill his desire to be freed from his material things, and his compulsive masturbatory sexuality, which chain him to the cyclical task of working in order to have more of the picture perfect things in catalogs, from IKEA, Maxim, Playboy, and GQ. In his role, Durden will sabotage the culture of advertising that tethers men to the culture of consumption. Accordingly, part of the story in *Fight Club* is what Tyler and his "space monkeys" do to bring down both advertising and consumption.

Likely, one of the main reasons for the success of *Fight Club* is the overriding concern of its story with the effects of a consumerist culture that is ceaselessly renewed and energized by an advertising industry. As a mechanic, "pure Tyler Durden," tells the narrator: "Advertising has these people chasing cars and clothes they don't need. Generations have been working in jobs they hate, just so they can buy what they don't really need" (149). Thus, Palahniuk's novel warns readers again that they live in a society in which even teenagers and young adults are overworked and overscheduled with odd jobs so that they can meet the credit card bills that pay for their fancy smart phones, expensive designed cloths, and sporty cars. Regrettably, the society denounced in the pages of *Fight Club* is still trapped in the conditions that Fredric Jameson described to explain the rise of the postmodern period more than 50 years ago:

I believe that we should understand the emergence of postmodernism [in the 1960s] in terms of the emergence of consumer or multinational capitalism. In many ways, its formal features express the deeper logic of this social system. We need only think of the way our sense of history has disappeared, of how our entire contemporary social system has little by little begun to lose its capacity to retain its own past. We live in a perpetual present. We might say that the media help us forget the past. (204–5)

Within this perpetual present, the level of consumerism has created a great "spiritual" emptiness, and a cultural malaise. The men of fight club are the children of a civilizational discontent brought about by rampant consumerism and empty eroticism. Tyler Durden is the American *Übermensch*, born from social outrage, who will try hard to bring down the consumerism machine, with its glossy advertising images and aromas, so as to liberate men from the soulless prison of modern American culture. Project Mayhem is a spear aimed at the heart of this sick culture.

Men of war

Thus far I have been profiling two of the three cardinal points of reference for the inspection of masculinity in fin de siècle America: consumerism and eroticism. The third is militarism. The men in *Fight Club* are the children and grand children of the two generations of men who forged America into a world empire by fighting the "good wars." But, since Vietnam, men in the United States have not fought a "great war." If anything, they have fought disgraceful, meaningless, even Machiavellian wars, wars not for the nation, but for some intractable economic interest. The mechanic, repeating Tyler's ideas, makes it very clear: "We don't have a great war in our generation, or a great depression, but we do, we have a great war of the spirit. We have a great revolution against the culture. The great depression is our lives. We have a spiritual depression" (149). So much of American identity is tied up with war, the great wars of the last century. American young males in the novel grow up and live in the shadow of the heroes of the great patriotic wars. However, they cannot fight in any such great war anymore; contemporary society denies them the possibility of heroism. Even if the nation had to fight such a war now, it would be fought mostly by professional soldiers with the help of sophisticated technological weapons.

Fight Club was written before the 9/11 attacks and before the subsequent wars in Iraq and Afghanistan, yet it can be argued that this novel speaks to the present generation of men warning them about the demands of mystified militarism. For some of them, the life of the soldier remains a powerful ideal, but one which is increasingly distant and even incomprehensible to most men in contemporary America. Recent demographic analysis of the professional army reveals that most soldiers come from military families, and that most come from a handful of states: Texas, California, Virginia, New Mexico, Colorado, essentially across the southeast and southwest, forming what is popularly referred to as the "gunbelt" (Thompson 2011). This military concentration in only a few states seems to indicate that soldiers are growing more distant from the everyday life of most citizens. There seems to be a rift between the ideal and the actuality of military life in contemporary American culture, a fracture that separates the old notion of masculine valor traditionally associated to ethical behavior from the present understanding of the military as mere servants of economic powers. It is this rift that is aptly captured in James Cameron's *Avatar* (2009). A paraplegic marine (and one should reflect on this synecdoche beyond the exigencies of the plot) takes up the place of his dead brother in an important mission on a distant planet evocatively called Pandora. Departing from the cultural tradition of the heroic soldier that fights for his motherland, Cameron's film features a marine, left maimed by war, who is going to redeem himself, as a soldier, and as a man, by fighting an anti-colonial war fought against the economic status quo. In this movie, the military are at the service of corporate greed, which is portrayed as having absolutely no regard for the natives. But in order to redeem himself, the hero has to cease to be an US soldier, and even an American. He must renounce being an US soldier so that his transformation becomes complete. He in fact takes up the fighting ethos and weapons of the natives. Yet, despite all the movie effects and computer-generated imagery (CGI), Cameron's story is classic Americana, going back to eighteenth-century narratives of captivity and heroic awakening to the injustice of one's nation's war. Far from being socially subversive, Cameron's critique of the corporatization of the US military, and the rapacity of corporate interests is not, however, a critique of militarism. In the end, the hero of *Avatar* is saved by war. The film reconciles present militarism with the old mythology of the American West—which traditionally tried to justify American Expansionism in ethical terms—a trope so rigorously analyzed by Richard Slotkin in his famous trilogy (1973, 1985, and 1992). Unlike what happens in Cameron's film, which tries to reinstate the ethical validity of American violence as a way to bring about a blissful social order, this key American trope becomes one of the main concepts that Palahniuk's *Fight Club* aims to deconstruct.

Tyler Durden behaves as the perfect soldier, the alter-ego of all those American men who are children and grand children of the generations who fought in the two world wars. The narrator's alter-ego will fight the good fight. He can make explosives in the kitchen. Tyler knows all there is to know about weapons. He also knows how to organize men in search of meaning, community, solidarity, and loyalty, into an army of devoted soldiers. Tyler Durden is the perfect soldier. Accordingly, Project Mayhem is the perfect war. It is the war that is going to redeem these men. "We wanted to blast the world free of history" (124), confesses "everyman" who has doubled into Tyler Durden. The world weighs heavy with unrealizable expectations upon the shoulders of a generation without a "great war." So, if they do not have such a war, they will create one:

> It's Project Mayhem that is going to save the world. A cultural ice age. A prematurely induced dark age. Project Mayhem will force humanity to go dormant or into remission long enough for the Earth to recover. . . . This was the goal of Project Mayhem, Tyler said, the complete and right-away destruction of civilization. (125)

Fight Club does show us the building of the anarchist army that will save the planet from humanity, and humanity from its cancerous civilization, which has rendered them zombies of consumerist life. It should be noted that the theme of apocalypticism is recurring in Palahniuk's fiction. It is central in *Survivor* (1999) and *Lullaby* (2002), where an impending final destruction is to be accelerated or averted.

Tyler Durden will give this generation of men who crave for meaning a war that will grant them honor and meaning, a war to end all wars.

Yet, Tyler Durden is the alter ego of an impossible masculinity. He is the American male on steroids, precisely what American males must be cured of. *Fight Club* has been read in a myriad of ways, but some of these interpretations reveal incomprehension while some others present facile readings. Of the latter type are those who read the novel as an endorsement of Tyler Durden's gratuitous violence and anarchistic militarism. These read Tyler Durden as the extreme fighter, the total warrior. But, in fact, *Fight Club* satirizes as much this aspect of Durden as it does the dependence on communities of soldiers to create meaning. If anything, the protagonist's alter ego is an anti-hero, what men aspire to become, but cannot and should not. Project Mayhem is a parody of male bonding. The narrator remarks that what "you see at fight club is a generation of men raised by women" (50). They are presented as men yearning for guidance, mentorship, role models, discipline, but in the absence of their fathers, they create their ersatz families. Militarism is as much a malady as is consumerism and empty eroticism. The "space monkeys," as are designated the nameless men who join Project Mayhem, are caricatures of men who trade one meaningless task for another hoping to find community and loyalty. So the former army of consumers turns into the armies of a war against commercialism: war and consumption fuse into each other. The men of fight club wage war against consumerism because consumerism has driven them to war. Awareness of their own enslaved condition, among the fetishes of the affluent society for which they work, has brought about the collapse of their social trust.

An American Zarathustra

That we are always escaping caves, breaking the chains of dogma, liberating ourselves from the illusory images of consumption and satiated sensuality seems to be the message of Tyler Durden. There are indeed caves of illusion and geographies of escape in *Fight Club*. The book transverses between three symbolic spaces: the underground spaces of fight club, the brightly lit spaces of daily servility, in which fight club loyalists perform their pedestrian and little acts of anarchy, and the crumbling, abandoned, and then occupied house where Tyler Durden sets up shop to build his army of "space monkeys." Three topoi, three liminal spaces, three pilgrimage destinations, so to say. Each projects an allegory for what must be overcome, and is itself not the way it is overcome. Tyler Durden is born, grows and discovers himself by transversing these spaces. As pointed above, he is the new parodic American Zarathustra, come to announce an American overman but this creature of the future is itself not yet born, and it will not be born so long as the horizon is marked by voracious consumerism, loveless sensuality, and anachronistic militarism. In his parodic representation of Nietzsche's Zarathustra, Tyler Durden ascends from the basements of fight club to announce the coming of a different type of man. However, although many readers and some critics took the parody seriously, what Durden preaches cannot be taken for the remedy. Nor does his alter-ego offer a better solution: "Maybe self-improvement isn't the answer. . . . May be self-destruction is the answer" (49), the narrator guesses early in his story, anticipating his own attempted suicide. Certainly, the novel offers no easy way out. Neither the annihilation of culture nor self-destruction can be acceptable answers but *Fight Club* warns its readers that we cannot hide from the malaise that poisons contemporary culture. There has to be an alternative to either improving what is sick or destroying what is dying. . . .

How can you be a male in post-imperial America? Evidently, the answer is not in this novel, not in ten novels, not in all novels. Yet, Palahniuk has written one of the most eloquent works of fiction about the challenge of being a male in a culture that invests so much of its cultural capital projecting images and puffing up role models that are no longer tenable. What makes Palahniuk distinct and different from other male writers of the last few decades, whom David Foster Wallace so aptly named "The Great Male Narcissists," (Wallace 1997) is the way in which he, most specifically in *Fight Club*, has inquired into the condition of male identity in a post-racial, post-authenticity, post-identity politics and culture. Tyler Durden is certainly white, but his struggle is not distinctly white. The everyman of which Tyler Duren is the alter ego is the post-industrial, post-capitalist American male.

The Nietzsche references are not unwarranted. Palahniuk's entire work is intensely preoccupied with the daily habits of docility and servility; note, for instance, that this is a key to *Choke* (2001),

Lullaby (2002), and even *Snuff* (2008). Many people are so polite, to the extreme of not being outraged by blatant exploitation. Cultures survive because they are reproduced through socializing new generations of members into certain practices of trust, social etiquettes of mutual respect. But when the fabric of mutuality is manipulated to render subjects servile, rebellion, resistance, cynicism, and pessimism ensue. *Fight Club* is in part about the need to reclaim something of the basic goodness of American culture from its distortion by consumerism, pornography, and militarism. Doubtless, the book is a brilliant meditation on how culture is predicated on the production of gendering roles, or norming sex into certain roles. *Fight Club* is not only about how present American culture makes it impossible to be a man, but also about how not to become a certain type of man while resisting the avatars of American masculinity.

3

Body Contact: Acting Out is the Best Defense in *Fight Club*

Laurie Vickroy

Trauma and its contexts

The unnamed, unidentified protagonist/narrator of Chuck Palahniuk's novel *Fight Club* embodies the depersonalizing effects of a world practically devoid of human caring and meaning, which the author elevates to trauma. Similar to many contemporary trauma narratives Palahniuk's novel depicts socially induced traumas originating in powerful ideologies, in this case, a capitalistic society that fuels inequalities and alienates people from themselves and each other. The protagonist, who seems to suffer from issues of childhood neglect and shame, seeks comfort from his pain-filled isolation in cancer support groups, but when his pain threatens to become conscious, it precipitates a dissociative psychic split. Out of this split emerges Tyler Durden, an alter ego or split-off aspect of himself that incarnates the narrator's psychic defenses and allows him illusions of control, but leads him away from potentially healing connections. Palahniuk complicates healing from trauma, particularly for men, because clinically speaking this necessitates acknowledging helplessness that contradicts masculine identity formed in bodies acting out. The protagonist's attraction to trauma culture and his own repetitive behavior convey a sense of profound struggle to understand a typically empty existence in a social context that ignores psychological and existential pain. By examining the protagonist's gendered-inflected shame, and the narrative unraveling of his "unknowing knowing" of his psychic split, I intend to demonstrate how Palahniuk uses traumatic symptoms to articulate the crisis of ungrounded identity in contemporary society.

Trauma is a psychological wound resulting typically from events that are so overwhelmingly intense that they impair normal emotional or cognitive functioning. Such events are often violent, involving war, rape, or physical brutalities, and the bodily humiliations or violations that result from such events can have devastating effects on individuals' self-regard and ability to achieve intimacy (Herman 108–10). While trauma often involves horrific events, individuals can be traumatized by daily life situations or patterns of emotional or physical abuse, notes Kai Erikson (457). Trauma victims, who may suffer from a tainted or diminished sense of self, may unconsciously deploy defense mechanisms that help protect them from re-experiencing pain, including suppressing memory or dissociating, that is, distancing themselves physically or emotionally from the sources of their fears (Herman 51–6). But while these defenses may protect against further trauma, they can also jeopardize human relations, making victim–survivors skeptical or distrustful of others (Herman 42–7). At its worst, trauma can create feelings of helplessness and guilt, and destroy in victim–survivors the belief that they can act independently or meaningfully in the world (Janoff-Bulman 19–22). If it is normal for people to try to overcome their fears and acquire a sense of relief by psychically both approaching and avoiding what causes anxiety, those who have been traumatized experience an extreme version of this: they are at once driven toward, and fearful of, remembering (Laub and Auerhahn 288). *Fight Club*'s narrator seems severely repressed, with little access to his memory or his own feelings, which emerge in acting out in the guise of a split-off part of his psyche.

Fight Club also resembles other trauma narratives in how it raises questions about victims' identities and the possibilities for successful human connection (Vickroy 11–13). The novel presents how a dissociated world, blind to the consequences of its destructive actions, creates a deeply isolated protagonist who longs for attachments but has few means to achieve them. The narrator's postmodernist tone of irreverence reflects his discomfort with feeling but also recreates an environment that limits individuals' ability to act and create a cohesive identity. Palahniuk's approach to characterization may be conceptualized in a postmodern sense, of functional and shifting identities, but it can also be interpreted as depicting traumatic psychic splitting and fragmentation. The narrator's seemingly traumatic breakup with his father cuts him off from the past: "I knew my dad for about six years, but I don't remember anything" (50). He also compares his father's negligence to his own capitalistic environment in the way his father had set up his new families like "franchises" (Kavadlo 13). Like many men in the novel, he indulges himself in rage-filled acting out that seems over-determined (i.e. having repressed and multiple causes), and yet an understandable response to a belittling world. The fights, which are eventually revealed to be the protagonist's self-mutilation, are symptoms of trauma that relieve him of his emotional numbness, and make him feel alive and in control. The protagonist's history of his father's abandonment and the suggestion that his mother raised a "thirty-year-old boy," is acted out rather than remembered, as he tries to reconstruct his nurturance by replacing his father with Tyler.

The narrator also exhibits symptoms of failure and shame. He feels ashamed of being de-masculinized, of not living up to, or knowing, male models of adulthood. This process begins with losing his father and continues with his mothers' implied overprotection, and his feminization by consumer culture (e.g. his obsession with his IKEA-furnished home). These are examples of Sandra Lee Bartky's contention that society regularly shames individuals: "shame is manifest in a pervasive sense of personal inadequacy that, like the shame of embodiment, is profoundly disempowering" (85). The narrator feels almost disembodied, effaced on many levels, and this is why recapturing his body's power with violent physical contact is so vital to him. Scheff and Retizinger establish that "shame leads to violence . . . [when]. . . . It is hidden to the point that it is not acknowledged or resolved" (3). This certainly is true of the repressed narrator who tries to redeem himself by enacting violence that initially seems to have no purpose other than an outlet for anger provoked by Tyler. Marla also shames him, making him so self-conscious about attending support groups that they no longer can function as part of his defenses, and as such he must revert to other defenses and create Tyler. These defenses continue to mask his shame and rage and fend off self-consciousness.

In recent years American men's place in the social and economic hierarchy has declined, and some critics interpret the novel as part of a backlash against the partial gains of women. However, other critics have noted how the novel addresses men's sense of diminishment primarily in the new service economy. In *Fight Club* the narrator begins to recognize that money-making activities and the "scripted interactions of the service economy" de-individualize their employees (Lizardo 236). He first worries about fulfilling his role as the good consumer but this does not satisfy his need for male companionship particularly. Worn down with relentless travel, and work as a corporate recall campaign coordinator, the narrator is exposed to potentially traumatic information such as his description of seeing photos of people's legs cut off by exploding turbo chargers that the negligent company will not replace (99). He does not discuss his feelings about this, but a normal ethical reaction to this knowledge that he is a part of a negligent company should be shame-inducing. When he becomes empowered as a man by fight club he can see this as something that he can hold over the company and perhaps use to undo it.

Trauma and characterization

The characterizations and storytelling in *Fight Club* utilize many trauma symptoms: splitting, dissociation, diminished sense of self, shame, helplessness, defensive and self-defeating behavior, and violent acting out that is more common to male victims. The narrator's self-portrait resembles Bessel Van der Kolk's description of trauma's effects on character development, including: impaired trust, inability to attribute responsibility appropriately (he is unaware of his own actions), and identifying with the aggressor (his father, then Tyler) rather than his own vulnerability (and Marla's). Further, victims perceive themselves as "unlovable, despicable and weak" (Van der Kolk 197–8). The narrator tries to escape helplessness through violent action, and fearfully avoids (possibly because of self-loathing) emotional intimacy with Marla, to whom he is attracted, through most of the novel. His emotional distance is apparent as he observes that Big Bob's shirt has a "wet mask" of how he looked crying as they embraced (22), but he does not report feeling any emotion except relief; he can only approach his own pain vicariously through others'.

The narrator/protagonist's first noticeable symptom of trauma is his relentless insomnia which he describes as an "out of body experience" (19), adding that with the "insomnia distance of everything, you can't touch anything and nothing can touch you" (21), in this way indicating a dissociated state (Gold 16; Van der Kolk 189). This is the first of many living-death metaphors in the novel, including his death-like existence of monotonous travel and regulated environments (work, hotels). He is initially cured of his insomnia, "resurrected" through participation in a cancer support group, where the threat of death to other members (though it is not actual for the protagonist) makes him feel more alive (22). He can respond to individuals, particularly males who try to comfort him, like Bob, but he does not respond as well to women, however. He cannot sexually comfort the dying Chloe as she wishes. Though he would like to help, she is terrifyingly too near to death. His response to her may indicate his shame around not feeling manly, which makes him shy away from women generally. However, the support groups' focus on bodily suffering does allow the narrator to consider the idea of death as a relief from his own emotional pain— "Every evening, I died, and every evening, I was born" (ibid.).

When Marla appears at the support groups, she recognizes a fellow "faker" and makes him feel self-conscious and ashamed of his fraudulent participation. If his repressed emotions have been released in the safe context of these groups, when Marla in effect shuts down this outlet, his psyche will have to seek relief elsewhere. Because she is an object of potential intimacy, Marla also makes him feel more vulnerable and defensive. She has enormous influence on him, though he denies it through most of the novel, to the point of openly rejecting her several times—"The last thing I want is Marla moving in, one piece of crap at a time" (90).

After she appears so does his alter-ego Tyler (who perhaps has emerged earlier), a decisive father substitute and a bolder provisional self who is unafraid to aggressively resist forces that oppress average men: humiliating and morally compromising jobs; the false promises of the American Dream; and their fathers' failures to provide them with a clear path to male identity. Tyler also persuades the narrator to join him in challenging his superiors at work through blackmail and violence. Though their jobs certainly add to their misery, these confrontations do not address the protagonist's deepest unresolved fears of living with the knowledge of mortality, and his failure to form intimate connections to others. Tyler is a product of the narrator's trauma, resulting in his fragmented personality (George 71), and fulfills his need for a more cohesive identity. Despite the provisional sense of control he gains through Tyler, he merely repeats earlier dysfunctional family relations by acting out his anger and hostility toward his parents, replaying how they ignored one another in his treatment of Marla. He then engages in self-mutilation, another kind of acting out, which is reactive, symptomatic behavior, bringing temporary relief but no healing or connection. These are all typical defensive strategies of the traumatized. Tyler helps the protagonist escape from an identity shaped by consumerism and family (George 73), but in fact becomes the vehicle for the defensive maneuvers listed above. He becomes over-reliant on Tyler, feeling inferior to him until he realizes that his alter ego's violent proclivities (really his own suppressed rage) must be stopped.

The beatings administered in the fight club he creates provide (as with the cancer support groups) displaced confrontations with the men's traumatic fears of the real world. They can create new, untarnished identities, and find temporary relief as self-inflicted bodily pain trumps psychological pain in the short term. The popularity of fight clubs and reenactments in the book, film, and by audience members demonstrate that many others share the narrator's own fears: "Most guys are at fight club because of something they're too scared to fight," he says (54). As a symptom of trauma, his self-mutilation acts as a means of self-soothing, or a release from mental anguish; it is often a means for victims to break away from experiencing a "sense of complete disconnection from others and disintegration of the self" (Herman 108). Self-harm can also "be a way of expressing the anger that has been carried for so long [and] ... that has to be repressed over the years as a means of survival" (Bray Haddock 22). It also feels less dangerous than expressing anger to others directly (Favazza 273). The narrator's wounds are not only emblematic of life and action, but also self-punishment for his previous passivity and his doubts about his manhood.

The protagonist/Tyler split embodies the workings of dissociative identity disorder (DID) (formerly called multiple personality disorder), a rare and extreme manifestation of trauma. A person with DID is typically split between a "primary passive identity and alternate identities with contrasting names and characteristics. In at least a third of cases, self-mutilation may be inflicted as a punishment by one alternate personality or another" (Favazza 247). This seems the case with the self-wounding narrator's symptoms as he succumbs to Tyler's stronger personality; Tyler beats and burns him with lye and rationalizes this punishment as providing the protagonist/narrator with essential knowledge of pain and death. He is essentially punishing himself for what he sees as his cowardice, helplessness, and his failures to act, and develops a hero worship of Tyler, who is the wish fulfillment he needs to replace the father who has abandoned him and for whom he harbors buried hostilities. Forgetting important personal history is also a typical symptom of DID (Bray Haddock 9) and relevant to the protagonist's forgotten but crucially reenacted relationship with his father.

Palahniuk's narrative strategy involves the protagonist hiding that he already knows about Tyler until the end of the novel so that he can build suspense and reconstruct the disorientations and conflicts of trauma. If traumatic symptoms are accurately portrayed, of necessity victims will engage in self-defeating, defensive and repetitive behaviors that may tempt readers to pass moral judgments on the characters. Palahniuk wants readers to note how his characters "sabotage any chance of bonding with another person" (Kavanagh Interview 184). The characters' ethical failures can also be attributed to trauma, if it deprives sufferers of agency and perspective. In effect, their limited circumstances and mindsets can place them outside of normal ethical frameworks. Many narrator/protagonists in trauma fiction try to create an illusory sense of agency and order against feeling fragmented but it is merely self-protective (Tal 3; Vickroy 24). Narrators that mimic forms and symptoms of trauma are "characterized by repetition and indirection" (Tal 3). They can seem unreliable, not because they are depicted as deliberately dishonest, but because they are unaware and defensive.

If readers are led to see the emotional and cognitive limitations of survival mode, they may be able to consider to what degree the traumatized are capable (or not) of being able to bear responsibility for others and themselves, or to treat others fairly and compassionately. If a narrative can effectively bring readers into experience that lies outside their normal behavioral contexts, they may be persuaded toward a more complex if sometimes irresolvable view of human ethical response under duress. For this to be possible, texts have to signal for readers the effects of traumatic circumstances since readers' cognitive responses to texts involve the ability to attribute mental states to characters. These circumstances must adequately counter the effects of Attribution Theory, or readers' tendency to see characters' behavior as influenced more by character traits than their specific circumstances (see discussions in Palmer 245, Gerrig, Zunshine). Further, Geoffrey Hartmann has said that these literary works of trauma depict behaviors that are "externalizations of an internal state" (541) and fittingly, *Fight Club*'s narrator focuses on externals and physical acting out because he is disconnected from his internal life.

Palahniuk demonstrates the traumatic effects on his protagonist's personality, with his callousness toward others also extending to himself in his self-punishment. His mind works in an indirect and defensive mode where he describes traces of emotional events that indicate experience but never feelings themselves, as with the mask of his tears that he sees on Bob's shirt, or the mask-like remnants of blood on the floor after a beating at fight club. Marla is an indicator through much of the novel of his coldness, or emotional distance, but also she helps him recognize and act on his situation. Readers are taken through his gradual process of becoming aware of his split self, and how he takes responsibility, and tries to atone for his own cruelty and violence seemingly perpetrated by Tyler.

The narrator's dissociative state is his primary traumatic symptom, seen in both his behavior and storytelling strategies. The narrator's isolation, which may have originated in his family, is reinforced in a culture of detachment. He tries to break from the dissociations that defensively help him cope with an impersonal, alienating post-industrial world that Steven Gold argues creates emotional numbing and denies individual's agency (16). The protagonist's dissociation is the result of disturbed attachments in his family, work, and social life, accumulating, I would add, to the point of trauma. He is unable to fully express his anger until he finds a voice through Tyler, but, ironically, he is silenced by Tyler as well, often demonstrating the "absences or intermittences in speech, [the] residual muteness" characteristic of trauma (Hartmann 552). Tyler articulates what the protagonist cannot: his unconscious, unfiltered, and unsocialized rage, with violent consequences that the narrator cannot own.

His narrative "internalizes the rhythms, processes and uncertainties of traumatic experience, including the obstacles to self-awareness and communication: silence, denial, ambivalence of memory, dissociation and repression" (Vickroy 3). His reports of Marla's and Tyler's behavior demonstrate the narrator's defensive disconnection and avoidance of the truth. For example, his silent hostility toward her and her frustration demonstrate that he is unaware of any sexual intimacy with her except as Tyler. His over-determined admiration for Tyler reflects his own need for such a figure and prevents him from recognizing Tyler's (i.e. his own) sadomasochism and slows the discovery of his own deeds as Tyler. The narrator presents himself as having few memories of the past, wanting to jettison his upbringing along with other controlling forces that Tyler demands as part of his philosophy. The protagonist occasionally expresses anxiety, for instance acknowledging his father's rejection of him, and fear that Marla will take Tyler from him, but humorously (i.e. defensively) glosses over it, feigning ironic detachment with *Reader's Digest* body metaphors: "I am Joe's clenching bowels" (62). He demonstrates disconnection from his feelings by displacing his anger through Tyler. "These are Tyler's words coming out of my mouth. I am Tyler's mouth" (155). He draws the reader's attention primarily to immediate events, and remains more focused on Tyler than Marla, demonstrating further his dissociation and faulty judgment in looking to Tyler who is the angry destructive part of himself, and pushing off Marla, a fellow isolated victim who tries to connect with her own and others' suffering, and with whom he might have a relationship.

Bodies acting out

Until he can confront Tyler's existence he is consigned to repetitively seek reinforcement in bodily action. His identification with Tyler and fight club appear to be antidotes to the narrator's sense of shame and failure for not living up to masculine and adult conceptions of self that he tries to recover through bodily strength, sexual prowess, and aggressive action. These temporarily allow him to reject the limitations the world places on him. The fight club members have experienced communal trauma, and have lived with the disasters their lives have become. Tyler articulates the men's rage at the culture offering up fantasies of rock stardom, etc., and helps the others engage in collective resistance to their own devaluation. However, Tyler as a fantasy figure embodies the perfect body type, and the dangerous, callous masculinity featured in advertising that offers men an illusion of control and women glamorized threats of violence. The rough sex that he seems to have with Marla as Tyler underscores this dissociated, mediated intimacy that seems to transcend inhibition and shame. However, it does not accomplish the real emotional intimacy and friendship that the narrator needs but fears. He seeks refuge in media-driven images of masculinity that shun vulnerability and full humanity and mask why he has difficulty accepting Marla's love: she is like him, and he hates himself.

The narrator's focus on his own body becomes the concrete manifestation of his identity, an externalization of his psychological issues, and a platform for agency and control for his defensive personality. It becomes emblematic of living life fully: "I just don't want to die without a few scars" (48). It may also demonstrate the narcissism (but not vanity) of the provisional self in being so male identified, following from the protagonist's notion that becoming a man is his sole salvation. The focus on the male body in the novel illustrates its concerns with masculinity, the likelihood that men are expected to prove themselves in violent situations, and their propensity to externalize their responses to traumatic (often violent) events with action (hence the overwhelming male presence in prisons vs the female presence in mental health facilities, as women are socialized to internalize their reactions to pain). The vulnerability of women's bodies and the ill are contrasted with the toughness of the fight clubbers' bodies.

Many writers of trauma narratives depict bodily humiliations to represent aspects of traumatic experience, making it more visceral for the reader. Prominent examples are Larry Heinemann's graphic Vietnam veteran novel *Paco's Story* (1986) and Toni Morrison's

Beloved (1987), about the effects of slavery, and though bodily injury is more part of the circumstances of trauma in those novels, Palahniuk, similarly, shows that wounding and scars can also become associated with the possibility of healing through the body, and making connections with sympathetic others. *Fight Club*'s protagonist proudly alludes to the results of his fights, the unhealed hole in his cheek, his bleeding mouth, black eyes, etc., and how these horrify some but link him to hundreds of men seeking to challenge their lowly life status. He delights in terrifying his boss by beating himself and bleeding on him, describing himself from the perspective of the culture he wants to destroy: "the monster drags itself . . . hooks its bloody claw" (116). Palahniuk is creating analogies to war trauma and how men are more likely to act out their trauma issues than seek therapy (Gold 18, citing Kessler).

Embodiment provides a more revealing forum for trauma and anxiety with Marla. Her fears of illness and mortality are centered in her body's signals of illness and aging. Like the narrator, she punishes herself and tries to recover from traumatic fears of death and stasis through the body. However, she also invites his concern and friendship around her body as she asks him to feel her breasts for lumps. She offers connection and healing with her body by fulfilling the narrator sexually, though he can only acknowledge this in a displaced fashion. When she attempts to seduce him as himself and not Tyler, he refuses her.

The protagonist's relationship with Marla is the most important actual one, stirring his feelings and defenses. Through much of the book his psychological defenses lead him to cut himself off from her (though as Tyler he encourages her presence), perhaps associating her with his devalued mother: "I'm a thirty-year-old boy, and I'm wondering if another woman is really the answer I need" (51). However, Marla persists and confides in him and he eventually wants to protect her from Tyler's violence. Marla's first appearance disconcerts him because she sees through his pretense of being a true cancer victim and makes him self-conscious so he can no longer displace his own fears in the support groups; she knows what he is doing because she is looking to do the same. Self-loathing and self-mutilating like him, she nevertheless has a relatively more integrated personality than him and more directly engages her fear of death, at times amusingly, by saving her mother's lipo-suctioned fat for collagen anti-aging treatments. She and the protagonist take the existentialist path of recognizing death as a way to appreciate life, though at times they wish for it as an escape or punishment. Marla persists with the narrator despite his constant resistance to her. He seems to love and then ignore her, making her feel she says, like a "discarded Christmas tree." She becomes his reality base and conscience, calling him on his inauthentic victimization, his hypocritical capitalism (selling expensive human fat soap), and eventually helps bring him to greater self-awareness. He is loathe to recognize this, and critics have pointed out that because of the male focus of the novel, readers (especially the fight club imitators) often do not recognize her as the life impulse that sustains the protagonist because they take Tyler and his charming and dangerous ways at face value (Kavadlo 9–10). The narrator has to get past the "allure of Tyler" to discover Marla, who saves him (8).

For traumatic memory to be integrated with normal memory, a patient has to undergo a therapeutic "controlled reliving experience" of traumatic events (Herman 182). The protagonist does not undergo this type of remembering, but he does gradually become aware that Tyler is a destructive, dissociated part of himself. In *Fight Club* others must indicate to him that he himself is Tyler. The narrator unveils his gradually evolving awareness through the ways he reports Marla's words and reactions to him. For instance, he dreams of sex with Marla (which he has actually had), but convinces himself that Tyler is doing it because he cannot yet succumb to this kind of intimacy: "Marla looks at me as if I'm the one humping her" (68). She helps illustrate his struggle with memory and his own split self, calling him on Tyler's actions and the black eye "Tyler" gave her. His traumatized state leaves him unable at first to comprehend that for Marla he and Tyler seem to be the same person and that he is responsible for Tyler's actions.

He defends himself against this knowledge through most of the novel, keeping himself and Tyler separate through the secrecy rules of fight club. Thus he can avoid others' opinions of Tyler, his destructiveness, or the illusion of connection he provides. Tyler's existence depends upon the protagonist's unawareness; Marla represents consciousness, though, and Tyler disappears when she appears to help save the suicidal protagonist toward the end of the novel, a reversal of their appearances at the beginning of the story. The narrator's treatment of her demonstrates his emotional split, the impulse toward her versus his tainted sense of self, his inability to envision a woman as part of his healing or future. If we read his symptoms, we get clues as to the real and destructive effects of Tyler on him, though he cannot recognize this until very late in the novel. For instance, his insomnia returns once he joins Tyler and stops going to support groups. He recognizes the paramilitaristic regimentation of Tyler's anti-corporate Project Mayhem, referring to his recruits as "space monkeys." However, he still buys into some of their activities until his friend Bob is killed. At this point in the narrative Tyler is unavailable to him, circumventing his conscience and doubts. Noting evidence of murder in the back yard, he tries to protect Marla. Other critics have pointed out that Tyler and the men engage in conformist repetitions of "institutionalized violence and disregard for human life," (Gold 26) which the protagonist eventually recognizes he must stop.

The protagonist's psychological resistance persists as Tyler eludes and seemingly abandons him once the latter doubts Tyler, but he nevertheless repeatedly reassures himself with Tyler's mantras, feeling he needs Tyler as this (in Tyler's words) "model for god" for whom he keeps searching: "I am nothing in the world compared to Tyler. I am helpless" (146). This dependency persists despite the fact that the satisfaction he experienced from fighting is diminished (123), and his participation in Tyler's project to destroy a tainted world by sabotaging corporations and the rich and powerful does not provide resolution of his trauma. Though the protagonist has the impulse to return to the origins of the trauma in hoping to repeat the father–son relation with Tyler, Tyler, enacting the protagonist's defenses, wants to liberate the men from social identity—"You're not your family . . . you're not your problems . . . you're not your age . . ." (143). Though all these have their limitations, they are also things the narrator needs to confront, not continue evading. Personal history matters, and must be worked through, not merely denied.

He is slow on the uptake, but Marla and the recruits (who recognize *him* as Tyler) force him to become aware that he has done the things he has attributed to Tyler. He eventually has to fight for his own identity against Tyler, who wants to take over: "There isn't a me and a you anymore" (164). Tyler confronts him when he resists Tyler's destructive anarchy, but Tyler admits to all he has done that the narrator has remained unaware of, and refuses to leave: "I wouldn't be here in the first place if you didn't want me" (168). Comically personifying the narrator's pathological split, his desires to know and not know, Tyler asserts his dominance despite the protagonist's identification of him as his own "dream . . . projection . . . He's a dissociative personality disorder. A psychogenic fugue state" (ibid.). However, the narrator's ability to diagnose his condition does not preclude the need to continue to enact and not resolve his pathology.

Once Marla has witnessed him murdering someone as Tyler, and he has given her a black eye, the protagonist knows he has to confront this part of himself and protect her, and he enlists her to help him suppress Tyler and prevent more violence. The narrator will eventually have to take responsibility for all of Project Mayhem and the deaths it has caused. He is once again shamed and feels he must pay: he offers himself up to be destroyed by fighters, and then wants Tyler to kill him. In the climactic scene, he holds a gun to his own head to get rid of Tyler even if it costs his life. Tyler disappears when Marla and support group members approach to help him, and now that he is assured Marla loves him, not Tyler, he makes sure Tyler "dies" by shooting himself.

He survives and the final chapter situates him in a mental hospital, a respite where he can rely on others to take care of him, but some of the orderlies remind him they still admire his actions as Tyler Durden. At least some of his traumatic patterns remain. He sees his therapist as God, again searching for an all-knowing figure to lead him. In the end he is given time to reflect and he is still ambivalent regarding his life dilemmas: is the solution manly action or his growing connection to Marla? The brief but profound satisfactions of answering masculine shame with violent physical conflict and the provisional identity he creates via Tyler do not heal the narrator, in fact, they almost destroy him, but still seem as appealing to him as the potentially healing compassion and forgiveness he gets from Marla and the support group.

Clearly violence and wanting revenge represents being stuck in trauma. Steven Gold attributes this emotional stasis to being unable to change the soul-destroying social context in which "the characters are so hopelessly mired that even their attempts to transcend it are ultimately doomed to replicate or even compound its flaws" (26). Palahniuk does not try to sentimentalize his wounded characters. He visits the consequences of people's rage taken to the extreme, but his focus on the temporary relief fight club brings to the characters is what many in the viewing audience of the film adaptation focused on, creating their own fight clubs. In his Afterword to *Fight Club* Palahniuk points out that for centuries men (and women) have been able to cope with their oppression and frustrations through fighting, knowing they cannot affect the larger forces (218). The urge to action is compelling even if it does not alter the sources of trauma in the long run. From the standpoint of healing psychological trauma it is perhaps a step forward in confronting fears, but is less complete than engaging in the emotionally painful work of braving the deeper fears of one's existence that cannot be confronted alone because we seem to be wired to bury them if left to our own devices. The author's use of trauma is overstated in a realistic sense in that there is no evidence for the severity of the trauma that the narrator's symptoms would indicate. Palahniuk uses this for dramatic effect: to highlight the multiple and fragmented nature of postmodern identity; to illustrate the severe effects of commodification and dehumanization of contemporary corporate-run life; and to suggest existence itself can be a trauma to which we have little access.

PART II

Invisible Monsters

Introduction

Invisible Monsters had been rejected by 12 publishers before the success of *Fight Club* opened the market to almost anything the author wanted to publish (Costa 9–10). Undoubtedly, the vast number of early rejections can be explained by the book's highly transgressive topics and scenes, despite which some critics have seen in it a significant example of the novelist's ethical demands. Intensively provocative and critical of the conflicting social and cultural ideologies existing at the turn of the millennium, *Invisible Monsters* opens fire against traditional family relations but also against the postmodernist celebration of gender and sex crossing, fragmentation, performance, and the exaltation of beauty and external appearances as the marks that define the individual's entrapment as a social commodity. Elsewhere I have defined this novel as a hyper-parody of different ideological notions that are still pervasive in present life. Namely, the (Lacanian) emphasis given to the recognition of the self in the mirroring Other, the importance of beauty and fashion, the consideration of the (post)human being as trapped in the media culture of simulations, or the poststructuralist understanding of life as a story of which we end up having only fragmented memories (Collado-Rodríguez 197–8). All these motifs, among others, become the target of Palahniuk's ironic fiction by means of a number of literary strategies but also with the help of other critical notions that the contributors of this part perceptively analyze in the three following chapters.

Clearly a favorite work of his author, *Invisible Monsters* has recently become an unstable text: following the release of a new

version of the story as a graphic novel—with KGZ as graphic
artist—2012 was also the year of publication of *Invisible Monsters
Remix*. Once again suggesting a trespassing of, this time, genre
limits, Palahniuk announced to his followers that in both written
and filmic narratives something could always be added to. He had
now his own "Director's Cut" of a book whose violence, sexual
perversions, and unbelievable transgressions have inevitably
offended many traditional readers and reviewers.

Andrew Slade's "*Invisible Monsters* and Palahniuk's Perverse
Sublime" offers a sustained and illuminating analysis that clarifies
some of the most controversial issues the novel deals with. The
contributor starts by contending that *Invisible Monsters* is a novel
about a search for identities that is never at ease with the search
itself. In other words, Slade identifies a deep conflict between
the protagonists' need to respond to a demand that has become
one of the most relevant cultural issues at least since Modernism
(*know thyself*) and the fact that "they are ill equipped to do so."
The chapter first evaluates the role anxiety plays in the characters'
behavior, reinterpreting the story in view of Freud's theories in
"Family Romances" and Lacan's notions of the Mirror Stage. The
imaginary, the visible, the invisible, and the reflective other are
notions that Slade connects to authenticity and identity formation
along a convincing argument. He points to the writer's use of the
stable family structure as a mechanism to deal with the instability
of identity that the book so abundantly displays. The chapter
then turns to some of the textual strategies used by the novelist to
evaluate the postmodern insistence on the idea that reality is only a
construction, with authenticity always escaping from any possible
ontological anchor. The concept of (lack of) authenticity allows
Slade to break a new path through the text and convincingly argue
that fetishism is elevated in the novel to the grandeur of the sublime,
even if it is a perverse sublime. Being one of the most controversial
issues in the novel, perversions are offered here as a key notion to
assess the characters' behavior and the role the sublime plays for
the resolution of their own family relations.

Richard Viskovic and Eluned Summers-Bremner's chapter "The
opposite of a miracle: Trauma in *Invisible Monsters*" offers a
number of perceptive hints toward the interpretation of the end of
the novel in ethical terms. The contributors use trauma studies as a
sustained framework to disclose some of the hidden mechanisms of

the book. The story, they contend, seems to overflow with traumatic situations. However, the novel also discovers a postmodern indifference toward violence and, therefore, toward the actual pains of trauma: simulation has absorbed reality; accordingly, trauma has been displaced by the *appearances* of trauma. Furthermore, in this chapter the authors convincingly argue that the explicit traumas of the protagonists are actually there to conceal the true nuclei of trauma in the novel. Opposing to a certain degree Andrew Slade's claims, Viskovic and Summers-Bremner understand the fragmented presentation of the story as a symptom that "the exact cause of the characters' suffering cannot be definitely known," at least till the end of the book. Trauma studies—especially the pathbreaking theories defended by Cathy Caruth and Shoshana Felman—allow the contributors to search and find the foundational moments that help explain why the protagonists stopped being real people and turned into performative roles. Understanding surgery as a metaphor for testimony makes Viskovic and Summers-Bremner to reinterpret the role that identity and gender play in the novel, complementing Slade's angle by stressing the importance that performance plays in *Invisible Monsters*. Finally, the mechanism of disconnections, so explicitly present in the plot, offers the authors a way to deal with the surprising and ethical turn at the end of the novel.

Sonia Baelo-Allué's contribution, "From Solid to Liquid: *Invisible Monsters* and the Blank Fiction Road Story" offers a contextualized reading of Palahniuk's novel that starts by claiming that the book is structured as "a blank fiction road story that lacks a point of departure and a point of arrival." The analysis of *Invisible Monsters* as blank fiction, together with the role played in the book by its road story structure and the fluid nature of its characters' identities take Baelo-Allué on a scholarly quest for the ethical impulse to be found at the end of the novel. The alternative interpretation, as chosen by some reviewers, would be the lack of both real feelings—especially love—and enough resilience to fight back the protagonists' traumatic symptoms. By drawing on James Annesley's seminal work on blank fiction, the chapter first proposes that Palahniuk's novel can be better understood in the context of this mode, as blank fiction helps to explain the ambiguous and contradictory readings the novel produces. Violence, fashion, and consumerism combine with the narrator's interpretation of the story as if it were a number of photos for a fashion magazine and with the road story genre to contribute to the detached quality of the narration, providing it with the atmosphere of shallowness so characteristic of blank fiction. Baelo-Allué's detailed analysis of the road story structure in Palahniuk's book also helps to explain the protagonists' need to search for a real life beyond the consumerist expectations imposed by the society of simulations. The apparent aimless journey, in the contributor's interpretation, ends in an act of liberation: the road, as a space of mythic trials, finally brings about the alleged resolution of previous conflicts and the rebirth of the protagonists. However, by means of the fight between what Baelo-Allué perceptively discusses as the characters' solid versus liquid identities, *Invisible Monsters* ends up being a narrative with an indecisive end, as befits the blank fiction mode.

Freud, fetishism, the sublime, trauma studies, consumerism, simulacrum, the road story genre, or blank fiction offer different, often complementary, angles for interpreting one of the most transgressive novels ever written by Palahniuk, which still offers at the last moment an invitation to existential despair or a leap of faith into the waters of ethical behavior.

4

Invisible Monsters and Palahniuk's Perverse Sublime

Andrew Slade

The Sublime is an idea belonging to self-preservation.

—EDMUND BURKE

Introduction: Searching for identity

Invisible Monsters is a novel about the search for identities—sexual, family, gender, social—that is never at ease with the search. The characters in the novel wish to put an end to the need to search for an identity and to draw to a close the need and urge to represent themselves to others. These are characters who wish to be what and who they are without apology or argument but are ill-equipped to do so. They cannot find the means by and through which to put the seeking to an end. It may be tempting to diagnose them as if they were people who could sit on the couch—if they wanted to—as living in fear and denial as addicts chasing a sense of belonging that addiction pretends to offer but fails to make good on. It might be tempting to figure out what is wrong with them as if therapy is what they need and what the novel intends. It might be tempting to do as Brandy Alexander pleads and to seek to live a life beyond labels and definition, beyond the claims of identity and family, of the law and the troubles of living a life of desire in a world that demands that we conform and renounce our most intimate desires. These characters cannot, for whatever reasons, be as they are without anxiety.

Palahniuk's novel is no morality play in which the answers to human problems are presumed. Instead, the novel can show the drama and great effort involved in the struggle to accept the identities we forge for ourselves—identities that are distinct from those childhood influences that we idealize, idolize, abhor, or destroy with an energy and ambivalence that can be frightening to recall. The central characters in the novel seek identities to live out in the moment. At the same time, they seek constantly to be someone other than they are. None of the characters in *Invisible Monsters* wants to be who they are. All of them struggle with the relationships that suggest to them a fixed and stable identity. The novel's narrator, Shannon McFarland, is a daughter and a sister by virtue of her position in a family. While such a basic observation might seem too simple to mention, Palahniuk uses these basic relations as rigid designators against which his narrator and character can fight for a sense of authentic existence apart from those fixed points that she believes define her. The same can be said about her parents—who are minor figures in the novel—and her brother, Shane, who appears as Brandy Alexander.

Freud, Lacan, identity formation, and the family

In his essay, "Family Romances" (1909), Freud describes the process of coming into our identities as a romance. No romance is without drama or pain where moments of sentimentality brush up against the resistances of lived experience and the desires of others. The romance is a family affair: the struggles between fathers and sons, mothers and daughters, and the murderous wishes of the children against everyone even while the same children, sweet and tender and angelic, caress their mothers, fathers, and brothers and sisters. Extra-familial relations also fuel the drama of the romance. Children will seek models other than their parents to test their own possibilities and to try out different ways of being in relation to themselves and others. The romance implies a level of experimentation and imaginative work that leads us to achieve an identity. For Freud, this achievement is an accomplishment. How can it be otherwise with so many other desires seeking to control and shape us as we manage to break away for ourselves? *Invisible Monsters* can be understood as a reinterpretation of the family romance in as much as it is a novel about the struggle to articulate an authentic identity.

In his most famous essay, "The Mirror Stage as Formative of the *I* Function as Revealed in Psychoanalytic Experience" (1936, 1949), Jacques Lacan characterizes the process of acquiring a specular, imaginary ego distinct from the other as the effect of a drama. Lacan writes that:

> The mirror stage is a drama whose internal pressure pushes precipitously from insufficiency to anticipation—and, for the subject caught up in the lure of spatial identification, turns out fantasies that proceed from the fragmented image of the body to what I will call an "orthopaedic" form of its totality—and to the finally donned armor of an alienating identity that will mark his entire mental development with its rigid structure. (78)

The acquisition of the imaginary ego is a struggle from a position of insufficiency to one of anticipation, that is, from dependence on the other to the threshold of a distinct identity to an identity as "armor" that the subject puts on. The distinct specular identity that Lacan describes—and which has been widely cited and commented upon—implies an ambivalence of defense and aggression. The distinct specular ego has a protective function. It protects us from attacks from without and it keeps the fantasies of our interior life from getting too far away from us. The specular identity that Lacan describes is like a shell. Palahniuk's characters are on the lookout for a substance of identity that is not an alienated identity. They are looking for what belongs essentially to the interior of the shell.

Neither Freud nor Lacan suggest that there is an essential character in the drama of the family romance or as the effect of the mirror stage. No authentic being is inside that armor that could resolve the conflicts of an alienated ego. The drama of the assumption of identity is a struggle fraught with conflict and ambivalence. How can we hate, as we all do at particular moments, those we most cherish and most love? How can those who protect us, hold us so dear that we never want to be without them become objects that we blame, deride, detest, despise, and wish to be without? What parent has not wished, however secretly, to be childless? If, at one moment or another, you do not want to kill your mother, you have got a problem. If your father does not disgust you, get to therapy. If you are unlucky enough to have a brother or a sister, there are ways around that injustice too. Every time my students say that their brother or sister is their best friend, their closest ally, they forget the most banal cliché about friends and enemies and who you should keep close to you. If you are that close, I ask, what is the reason for it? What is it about your friends that you need to keep them so close? Freud and Lacan knew about the fantasies that form the core of our desires for love and belonging and they knew that even the most warm, sentimental, nostalgic feelings have a deep and violent side to them as well. They knew that our most tender love could become, sometimes without warning to ourselves or others, the most violent and aggressive desire. Children love their mothers and fathers and also, sometimes often and often with great guilt, wish to kill them. The younger child may idealize the older ones and secretly—sometimes not so secretly—want them dead. The older child wishes the younger one to disappear, to go away, or to die. Juliet Mitchell has recently emphasized the importance of the brother or sister in psychoanalytical accounts of the family and identity. While much psychoanalytical theory focuses on the vertically oriented, intergenerational conflict, in her book *Siblings: Sex and Violence* (2003) Mitchell reflects on how the relations between brothers and sisters may fuel conflict in the formation of identities. Fantasies about parents and siblings share the quality of ambivalence.

The ambivalence of the fantasies that constitute family relations form the structure on which we assume our identities as the armor we wear to protect us. The characters in *Invisible Monsters* suffer from the ambivalent desire that emerges from the formation of identities in the standard course of family life. The family in Palahniuk's book is in many ways a stereotype of what passes as the conventional, American family—two parents and two children, a boy and a girl, Shane and Shannon McFarland. Shannon is beautiful and becomes a model—Shane commits the ultimate crime against the family and against the father by transitioning his identity and body from male to female. The stereotypical family serves as a stable structure against which Shannon and Shane—Brandy Alexander—revolt. Palahniuk uses the stable family structure as a mechanism to work through the fluidity of identity that the novel displays and which his work as a whole tends to demonstrate. Flux and fluidity are only visible upon a stable ground. The family functions as that stable ground that allows him to illustrate the experimentation with identity that Shannon comes to admire in her brother and Brandy Alexander.

Shane becomes Brandy and seeks an identity beyond the limits of the one given to him by his location in the constellation of Mom, Dad, and Shannon. Shane is not transgender or transsexual as an authentic expression of identity. He does not feel that conflict between his most intimate sensibility and his body that characterizes the experience of many trans people. Shane becomes trans as a way to deny the reality of his family life and the identity assigned to him in that structure as son and older brother. Sex reassignment surgery does not give him an authentic bodily experience that his birth denied him, rather it gives him a chance to become free from all of those expectations that the family, commanded by the father and enforced by the mother, forces on to all of us. In this novel, an experience of authenticity is central to freedom and the function of father and the family seem to be the chief obstacles to the access to that authentic existence. "Brandy says, 'Don't you see? Because we're so trained to do life the right way. *To not make mistakes.*' Brandy says, 'I figure, the bigger the mistake looks, the better chance I'll have to break out and live a real life'" (258). The real life that he seeks has less to do with gender or sex identity than it does with a refusal of the father's function in the transmission of identity and of the place the he is forced to occupy as his father's son.

The novel as magazine: From authenticity and fetishism to the sublime

Invisible Monsters unfolds like a glossy magazine article—that is how Shannon tells us to read it—as if it were, "a *Vogue* or a *Glamour* magazine chaos with page numbers on every second or fifth or third page" (20). Jump around, she says, read it to find the products that we like to see since we are all products anyway (12). The novel insists that the reality that we share is a construction and that the authentic life is absent or that it is to be found in the unreality of the constructions themselves. Everyone knows that the glossy magazines are full of fakes. The models are airbrushed, digitized, and photoshopped to look however the editors want them to look. The referent to the real of photography has been erased in the service of selling products to the products we have all become. The erasure of the referent implied an erasure of the difference between consumer and product. If everything is a product then there is no difference between the product and its consumer: both are produced. Everything is reducible to glossy construction. If authentic life has yielded to the constructions of the glossy magazines then either authentic existence is an object of nostalgia or yearning or we can, "just go with the prompts" (21) that the glossy magazines give us and live life authentically in constructions. The highly wrought, malleable, contingent, inauthentic life of the glossy is authentic life.

Palahniuk's novels are obsessed with authenticity, as Eduardo Mendieta has claimed in his essay, "Surviving American Culture: On Chuck Palahniuk" (2005). The obsession with authenticity, with finding and being the real thing, whatever that might be, is at the center of *Invisible Monsters* as the sublime figure of a fetish. A fetish can be a perfectly benign object in the economy of desire yet, in Palahniuk's text, the fetish becomes the object of a perverse fascination. *Invisible Monsters* is a novel that elevates the fetish to the grandeur of the sublime. The main character in the novel, the "queen supreme" Brandy Alexander, the narrator's transsexual brother, becomes the object of the narrator's quest to know herself by knowing her brother, by situating herself in the economy of a family where identity is malleable and constructed. Brandy Alexander serves as the narrator's sublime fetish that gives an authentic meaning to her life. Shannon seeks to cover the flash and jumps of her glossy magazine narrative of a life with the grandeur of the queen supreme whose overvalued presence puts the narrator in proximity with her brother's real life, all the while turning her real life into an unliveable, monstrous fantasy. Palahniuk's perverse sublime turns the fetish into the core of identity. The hero of this novel, the queen supreme Brandy Alexander, dies as such seeking a way out of the tyranny of labels and the glossy magazine products that she covets.

The psychoanalyst Paul Moyaert describes three essential values of the fetish. In one sense, a fetish is a relic or a token of a loved one.

Among certain widows, for example, it is a common practice to keep the ring of the lost husband on a chain to be worn around the neck. The ring is a token of the lost husband that signifies a presence of the absent husband. A fetish can also support or scaffold desire. It is a structure that bears desire on its way. When the beloved wears the fetish, desire for the beloved becomes inflamed. This fetish can be clothing, a gesture, a scent. Any of these can support the advent of desire all the way to its end or waning. These two senses of the fetish operate well within the range of the common life of desire. The third sense of the fetish is perverse. A fetish is perverse when the fetish takes on a life of its own outside of the economy of desire (55). In perverse fetishism, the fetish is isolated from the common course of desire and absolutized as the source of pleasure and meaning. This fetish does not signify beyond its own lustrous appearance, it is unequivocally itself, beyond any doubt. According to Moyaert, the perverse fetish attains a value beyond measure for the pleasure of the subject. Without the fetish, the subject's desire comes abruptly to a halt. Desire is given over to the fetish that alone determines the course, the aim, and the pleasure of desire. The fascination with the lustrous fetish eclipses everything that is not the fetish.

Invisible Monsters operates according to the logic of a fetishism that is perverse at its core. The fetish object, the Queen Supreme Brandy Alexander, is elevated beyond the ordinary circuit of desire. She is elevated and absolutized as the defining signifier that anchors all meaning and significance. The characters in *Invisible Monsters* circulate around her and acquire their significance in relation to her luminous presence. All of these characters exist at the margins of social life, people who in another time would be openly and regularly attacked as perverts. In the American political and cultural imaginary, the pervert is a freak of social life. Perversions are imagined as moral deficiencies and perverts are imagined to be degenerates who live on the periphery of social life where their presence is doubtful and shocking to those who do not live on the margins. They can be tolerated as long as they are closeted, as long as they "don't go around shoving it in everybody's face," as colloquial usage in the United States sometimes puts it. The name pervert, in this frame, is a sign of hatred. The appeal to the pervert attempts to justify hatred as a socially accepted and acceptable, even desired, set of beliefs. Those people are sick, as the saying goes. While I am not using the term in this sense, Palahniuk's text banks on this sentiment being attached to these characters. Without these marginal characters, the central and stable hetero-normative family structures cannot be put into question.

According to Freud, perversion is a descriptive category. Perversion is the use of an organ for a purpose other than its anatomically determined one or it arises when we stop the regular aim of genital sexuality at a preliminary object. Perversion is not a different kind of desire, but a possibility of all desire. All desire has the potential to become perverse. In *Three Essays on the Theory of Sexuality* (1905), Freud writes, "Perversions are sexual activities which either (a) extend, in an anatomical sense, beyond the regions of the body that are designed for sexual union, or (b) linger over the intermediate relations to the sexual object which should normally be traversed rapidly on the path toward the final sexual aim" (150). The pervert seems to want it all—who does not?—and tries to get it all. The pervert is hyper-attached to his pleasure. The fetishist is a pervert whose identity and desire are bound to the presence of the fetish.

Bruce Fink is right to point out that the pervert only seems to get what he wants and that Freud emphasizes the subject's "refusal to give up satisfaction" (179) as the chief characteristic of the pervert's desire. The pervert cannot yield to the basic reality that we cannot always get what we want. Perverse desire is not perverse because of its object, as the tradition of cataloguing perversions in the manner of Kraft-Ebbing suggests. The pervert's object does not satisfy his desire and he refuses to yield to the reality that the object is incapable of providing the satisfaction that he wants. The pervert chooses an object that will not satisfy though he cannot bear to admit that the object will not satisfy him. The pervert holds "two incompatible positions at the same time," as Laplanche and Pontalis describe the fetishist (119). The name for this defence against anxiety is disavowal. Like other subjects, the pervert does not have what he most wants—he is castrated, in psychoanalytic terms. Disavowal is his defence against castration anxiety.

Disavowal is a structure that characterizes perversion in the same way that repression characterizes neurosis (Fink 170). *Invisible Monsters* is not a ghost story about the return of the repressed or a gothic novel where the representations circulate around objects that are highly invested with repressed material. The disclosure of the secrets of this novel's representation will not serve as the key that will allow us to resolve the conflicts that it stages. Finding the hidden, repressed thoughts in *Invisible Monsters* will not disclose the truth of the novel. Instead, *Invisible Monsters* is about disavowal of the family. Bruce Fink describes disavowal as a "making believe about the paternal function" (170). According to him, disavowal involves something like the following thought:

> I know full well that my father hasn't forced me to give up my mother and the jouissance I take in her presence (real and or imagined in fantasy), hasn't exacted the "pound of flesh," but I'm going to stage such an exaction or forcing with someone who stands in for him; I'll make that person pronounce the law. (170; inverted commas in the original)

We can follow Fink's description of disavowal in Brandy Alexander's discourse on identity. Brandy constructs the father as giving a command that he never gave in order to institute a new law over and against which the uncompromising father will persist as if actually present and powerful. By choosing to become trans, Shane becomes Brandy as a way out of the demand the father never issued to get a pleasure she was never denied. Brandy Alexander is the name of Shane's disavowal—she becomes the castrated body to escape the pressures of castration anxiety. The position that Brandy occupies has to be strongly distinguished from people who experience Gender Identity Disorder and who seek sex reassignment surgery. Such people transition from one sex and gender to the other as part of an effort to live authentically and they can succeed at it. Shane becomes Brandy to uphold two contradictory positions that he attributes to an other and at whose hands he continues to suffer as Brandy Alexander.

In Shannon's narrative of disavowal, Brandy becomes the Fetish object. Brandy's body is a body that is wrought, constructed, and idealized. She is doubly marked by the ostentatious names of lipsticks and rouge—"Burning Blueberry," "Rusty Rose," "Aubergine Dreams," "Plumbago." Scattered throughout Shannon's narrative of Brandy Alexander these names signal the malleability of identity. Shannon banks on the name of the color giving Brandy some depth where all that she has is surface. The emphasis on the surface is in the service of the disavowal of the depth and dynamism that identity linked to the family implies.

Shannon is a failed daughter and Shane is a failed son to parents who have failed to parent even if they—belatedly—try to rectify their choices. The dramas of their identities descend through the mother and father who are represented as clueless of their children's worlds or concerns. For Thanksgiving dinner before Shannon is disfigured and after Shane has disappeared—died of AIDS, he construes for his parents—Shannon sits at the table with a new tablecloth that her parents made from fabric that they had intended to sew into a panel for the AIDS memorial quilt. They believed their son to be gay and so part of a culture that operates with specific codes that they do not understand, "We just ran into some problems with what to sew on it," (90) her mother tells her. The problem that they encountered is one of signification and shame. Whatever colors they use on the panel, they fear that they will signify something about Shane that they do not want others to think is true. Even in death, the parents prefer their son to be closeted. One set of colors signifies "leather sex" (91); a pink triangle is a Nazi symbol for homosexuals (91). Red signifies fisting, yellow watersports. The conversation strains over the table with Shannon wishing for new parents—"Give me new parents" (90)—and the parents doing their best to perform as parents who could have produced children who could have lived in the world—though they have been unable to do so. That the children have failed means that the parents have failed. The parents are not villains or despots—they might have been good enough for their children to live quality lives. Precisely this characteristic of the parents allows Palahniuk to show Shane's mania for authenticity against the wish of all children to come from a good enough family that can propel them to a fecund and joyous life, an authentic life.

The parents are not authentic enough for Shane to develop his authentic identity—Shane fails to assume the place in his family that he believes that he is required to assume. He believes that he is required to assume it precisely so that he can refuse it. In time, Shannon needs the parents to prefer her to her brother—"Shane's dead," she laments, "but he's more the center of attention than he ever was" (92). The conflict and drama of the family in *Invisible Monsters* has a vertical structure and a horizontal one. The vertical structure produces intergenerational conflict. This is the conflict that Freud describes in "Family Romances." The horizontal conflict is the ambivalent love between Shannon and Shane and the idealization that proceeds from Shannon to Brandy

Alexander. These conflicts take place in the conversation at the Thanksgiving table as the enumeration of the ways that certain sexual practices are signified. The miscommunication occurs at the end of that dinner when Shannon thinks her parents ask her to tell them what "felching" is. It turns out that her mother had asked her about "fletching" a turkey (93–4). The process of disavowal is an effort to force the father to demand of the son and the daughter that which he never demanded. Shane becomes Brandy Alexander to materialize his response to that very demand. In this passage, Shannon supports Shane's disavowal by giving the father what he never demanded—an account of felching. Brandy Alexander is thus the fetish at the center of *Invisible Monsters*. Felching is the signifier of the brother who is present as his disavowal.

The disavowals that characterize *Invisible Monsters* take the form of the most extravagant and lustrous characters of the novel as the sublime figures around which the discourse of the novel unfolds. Edmund Burke writes that the sublime has its source in anything that is "terrible, or is conversant about terrible objects, or operates in a manner analogous to terror" (36). Feelings of terror put us in touch with "the strongest emotions of which the mind is capable of feeling" (36). For Burke, our strongest feelings are linked with pain and death rather than with the positive pleasures of those that "the most learned voluptuary could suggest or than the liveliest imagination, and the most exquisitely sensible body could enjoy" (36). The sublime is a pleasure that is attached to elements of experience that threaten us. Though the experience may in the end prove exhilarating or enlivening, in the first instance we come into contact with pain and displeasure. The experience of the proximity of pain and death, "the king of terrors" (36), from a certain distance can produce the most intense of pleasures. Those most intense pleasures of the sublime Burke names delight.

Delight is not a positive pleasure, but a negative one that we feel when terror, pain, or death press in upon us and yet we are relieved from having to experience terror, or pain, or death. We brush up against them and feel their power over us and, even so, are relieved that they do not destroy us entirely. In the modern history of aesthetics, the sublime is also associated with all of those things that are lofty, noble, or command respect, reverence, and awe. The sublime object humbles us without humiliating. At the moment before we would cross over into the pain and terror of death with an impossibly massive or powerful object that would, in the very next instant, destroy us, a distance appears and we are relieved from terror and given over to the exaltations of delight. Kant describes the experiences as a momentary checking of the vital forces followed by an outpouring of them that is all the stronger (246). The classical sublime is an experience of exaltation that proceeds from proximity to destruction. For Kant, the sublime puts us in touch with our suprasensible vocation (ibid.)—a sense of who we ought most essentially to be. Without the encounter with pain, however, there is no exaltation—without pain, no delight.

The fetishist's object brings him to the brink where his enjoyment expends and depletes itself to make way for his enjoyment again. The feeling rather than the object drives the fetishist toward his pleasure leading him to mistake his enjoyment for his object. The fetishist moves from a benign enjoyment to a perverse one. The shift is not a matter of quantity or power, but of structure. In nonperverse fetishism, as Moyaert describes it, the fetish stands in the place of a lost object—as a token—or as a screen for the object of desire that activates and sustains desire for the object. The fetish is a station on the way of desire and not the destination. The fetishist turns the fetish into the destination of his desire to make good on the promise of delight that will annihilate, he hopes, the separation between himself and the object that the fetish cloaks. In seeking to overcome that separation he passes over the object in favor of the effects of the fetish.

In the *Critique of Judgement* (1790), Kant is clear that the sublime is an emotion attached to a structure of the mind as the faculty of imagination seeks to present the unpresentable to the faculty of judgment. The sublime sentiment, an experience of pleasure in the pain of that failure, is the destabilizing feeling that accompanies the presentation of the unpresentable. The perverse fetishist invests the fetish with a power and magnitude that surpasses the power and magnitude of the object that bears his fetish. The fetish itself is a sublime object. The object becomes the support for the fetish and the subject tries to combine the affect with the object. To make the object bear the sentiment, the subject will have to come up short. *Invisible Monsters* demonstrates the subject coming up short from start to finish. Virtually no character gets what he or she wants. The fundamental experience of these characters is to not have what they want—in psychoanalytical language, they suffer their castration.

That is, they lack the object that could satisfy their desire. If an object appears that seems to satisfy their desire, it is an object that will have been isolated and removed from its common location in communal and social life. Shannon describes her breakfasts with Manus and his understanding of an object that can satisfy his desire by which he means every man's desire:

> At home in my apartment I'd have Manus with his magazines. His guy-on-guy porno magazines he had to buy for his job, he'd say. Over breakfast every morning, he'd show me glossy pictures of guys self-sucking. Curled up with their elbows hooked behind their knees craning their necks to choke on themselves, each guy would be lost in his own little closed circuit. You can bet almost every guy in the world's tried this. Then Manus would tell me, "This is what guys want."
> Give me Romance.
> Flash.
> Give me denial. (69)

Shannon and Manus come to a point of conflict surrounding the object of desire and the source of pleasure. Manus and Shannon are an impossible erotic couple; she seeks romance, even if the romance that she invokes is laced with irony, as the path along which desire travels. Manus is tied to the impossible image of a male body circled around itself in its autoerotic, oral and genital pleasure. Shannon continues the narrative,

> Each little closed loop of one guy flexible enough or with a dick so big he doesn't need anyone else in the world, Manus would point his toast at these pictures and tell me, "These guys don't need to put up with jobs or relationships." Manus would just chew, staring at each magazine. Forking up his scrambled egg whites, he'd say, "You could live and die this way." (69–70)

To live and die this way is an articulation of a vocation, a way of life. The fetishist believes that the fetish—whatever it might be—is the total object of all satisfaction—you can live and die by it. Of course, that is an error. The pervert's sublime object derails his or her desire. The characters in this novel chase their objects as if getting them to close the circuit of desire like Manus's self-sucking men, and liberate the subject into a vocation beyond life and death where they can be authentically themselves.

The sublime object as perverse sublime is fascinating and frightening like all sublime images. Attachment to that object will situate the subject in a place where he or she will always come up short. Every guy has tried to do this, Manus says. Every guy wants to, wishes he could; every woman envies it even if she may deny that envy. The perverse wish—as articulated by Palahniuk in this novel—is to be a completely closed circuit. This is the narrative that Shannon wishes to deny or disavow. Brandy Alexander is the most sublime of these closed circuits because she represents the masculine and feminine configuration of the body. She is the perfect example of the closed circuit around which the rest of the universe gravitates. Brandy Alexander is the most sublime of perverts!

Conclusion: The real as copy and the perverse sublime

Invisible Monsters invests the delight of sublime sentiment in the figure of Brandy Alexander and the universe that circulates around her: "On the planet Brandy Alexander, the universe is run by a fairly elaborate system of gods and she-gods. Some evil. Some are ultimate goodness. Marilyn Monroe, for example. Then there's Nancy Reagan and Wallis Warfield Simpson" (76). Palahniuk's narrator, Shannon McFarland, seeks the truth about her brother, Shane, who has become Brandy Alexander. In this maniacal search, Brandy becomes the focus of all agency and action. She is the planet at the center of a universe that is organized and run by fakes. Palahniuk's vision of social life is one in which feelings override objects and where the objects themselves have been so extricated from the authentic site of their social value that the question of authentic meaning becomes irrelevant. The truth of an object is the truth of its copy. There is no original though his characters long for their origins. Shannon introduces Brandy Alexander and Evie Cottrell in a burning manor house in the opening sequence of the novel. At that early stage in her narrative, truth lacks an original model—the world is composed of copies of copies: "What's burning down is a re-creation of a period revival house patterned after a copy of a copy of a copy of a mock-Tudor big manor house. It's a hundred generations removed from anything original, but the truth is aren't we all?" (14). Just as a house can be copied from an original model, human identities get forged through copying other models. Much of the drama of *Invisible Monsters* centers around the conflicts between characters who are—literally—models, and the discourse of the rhetoric of the novel—the glossy fashion magazine—is a showcase of models. All of these models are copies of some other copy. Brandy Alexander is not satisfied with the copy or being a copy—she is in search of the original.

If the world is made up of copies of copies without an original model, if our identities function in the same way, there is no reason for us to fret about who or what we are. Yet, the narrative of *Invisible Monsters* is obsessed with the original and authentic model of identity. If Shannon's view of the relationship between the model and the copy is the right way to view the world, what reason can there be to seek an authentic model? Shannon's narration does not accept the absent model as absent. Instead, the absent model of the copies of copies becomes first an object to be found again, and once it is named, it becomes the most sublime fetish from which all reality derives its meaning.

Had Palahniuk's narrative sought to find the lost object, it would remain a neurotic's narrative with a neurotic's sublime at the center of the narrative. The neurotic's sublime is a fetish, to be sure, but only in the sense that it is a token or a screen for the neurotic's lost object. The neurotic's sublime masks repressed material and points toward it. Palahniuk's narrative is a pervert's narrative with a perverse sublime. The pervert is overrun by the affect of the fetish that he mistakes as the enjoyment of the object. A perverse fetishism seeks the presence of the fetish to gain the sentiment of the sublime. The sublime sentiment, as Kant describes it, involves an encounter with a limit to the vital forces followed upon by an outpouring of them that is all the stronger. The fetishist convinces himself that he is alive by seeking the outpouring of vital forces through the fetish—the most sublime object. The fetishist believes that he is most alive when he is alone with the object that alone seems to satisfy his desires. But, the satisfaction is merely a seeming satisfaction that masks the anxiety and suffering that motivate the choice for the fetish or other perversion. Palahniuk's characters follow this path in their search for an authentic existence.

In *Invisible Monsters*, Palahniuk presents a perverse sublime. I have argued elsewhere that mutilation is the textual figure that announces Palahniuk's sublime. All of his characters, in one way or another, are mutilated or undergo an experience of mutilation. The mutilated body becomes the occasion of a sublime sentiment and the source of access to an authentic life. As much as his characters undermine the stability of identity and an authentic existence, and approach identity and authenticity with an ironic pose, nearly every one of Palahniuk's characters yearn for both as if being known for wanting what they want is as painful as not getting it. They plead for an authentic existence. The authentic existence that the characters of *Invisible Monsters* seek is an existence undetermined by the power and force of the father. They seek a world where the father's demands never have to be met but in which they construct a more outrageous set of demands for themselves. The sublime of *Invisible Monsters* is a perverse one that gives its characters a life that is bound to pain in the search for an authentic existence and freedom. Yet, the freedom that they find is a freedom to suffer, it is pleasure in pain in the name of an authenticity that is impossible to materialize.

5

The Opposite of a Miracle: Trauma in *Invisible Monsters*

Richard Viskovic and *Eluned Summers-Bremner*

Invisible Monsters opens on a scene of apparent carnage. Brandy Alexander lies shot and is bleeding on the floor. The shooter, Evie Cottrell, stands halfway down a staircase, naked inside the burnt shell of a wedding dress and still holding the shotgun she used to shoot the bleeding woman. A third person—narrator Shannon McFarland—stands above the shot woman as witness to the carnage. Shannon sums up the situation: "Nobody's all-the-way dead yet, but let's just say the clock is ticking" (11).

These first pages seem to overflow with trauma. Arson, mutilation, and murder are only the most immediate and visible. But Shannon lets us know the macabre scene she sets before the reader is not what it appears to be. The blood pooling on the floor is "less like blood than it's some sociopolitical tool" (12), the fire is only "a sustained chemical reaction" (15) set by the narrator for "set dressing" (14) and the prospect of murder is as meaningless as "killing a car" (12). Is this a traumatic moment? It could have been. Instead the narrator has hidden the trauma, reducing the traumatic events to scene setting and the people to archetypal characters, "the murderer, the victim and the witness," (16) each fighting for the limelight. According to the narrator, this is not a traumatic moment at all because these are not real people and this is not real trauma. Is the narrator right? If not, could the real locus of trauma be elsewhere?

Looking into the characters' personal histories reveals earlier events that could be characterized as traumatic. Brandy was mutilated by an exploding hairspray can. Shannon was disfigured by a gunshot wound. These appear to be traumatizing events, but both are deliberate, self-inflicted, and done in response to something else. These two people were wounded long before what appear to be the major traumas of their lives.

Palahniuk foregrounds the narrator's indifference to the violence around her. The scene provides a snapshot of the postmodern condition, where simulation and reality have become separated and simulation has expanded and effaced the reality for which it formerly stood, as Jean Baudrillard describes in *Simulacra and Simulation* (1981). To give a specific example, the traumatic reality—the burning house—is described in terms of simulation: "What's burning down is a re-creation of a period revival house patterned after a copy of a copy of a copy of a mock-Tudor big manor house. It's a hundred generations removed from anything original, but the truth is aren't we all?" (14). The narrator takes the disconnection between authentic original and simulation a step further by detaching herself from what she sees as simulations. Shannon sees nothing wrong in burning down this simulated house, after all, "it's not as if this is a real house" (14). The reality the house stood for, a Tudor house somewhere in the past, is long gone; assuming it ever existed. The simulation has taken its place, and Shannon has no interest in simulations; she is "tired of this world of appearances" (291).

Shannon sees Brandy, Evie, and herself as simulations and not real people. Just as the house is a "copy of a copy of a copy" (14), the people are "a product of a product of a product" (217); equally contrived, equally artificial. The stultifying repetition drains the phrase and its referents of vivacity with each recurrence. Rather than living real lives, the characters are performing roles and delivering "dialogue" (16). These three people, in particular, are artificial creations for whom appearances are everything. Brandy Alexander—who is named after a cocktail—is a creation of surgery, artifice, and the designs of the Rhea sisters. Evie—who was Evan— like all fashion models, trades on surface appearances. Shannon, who was beautiful, remade herself an invisible monster: so disfigured that people choose not to see her at all; as radical a transformation in its own way as gender reassignment surgery.

Being artificial creations, to Shannon's reasoning, makes Brandy, Evie, and herself things rather than people. The narrative point of view might seem detached from the events it witnesses, but this outlook is wedded to a world where the death of Bambi's mother can have more impact than a news report about real people dying in real wars, and where an original or authentic event, if it could be accessed, would be difficult to recognize as such.

Invisible Monsters is filled with trauma of all types. However, for most of the narrative the focus is on the overt *appearance* of trauma, a focus which is later undercut. Real trauma tends to conceal itself. It may hide from the affected person who may have no memory of the event, even while he or she relives it in repetitive and harmfully obsessive patterns of behavior or thought. Physically, trauma might refer itself to another part of the body than the part that was initially affected. This chapter will suggest that the conspicuous traumas of *Invisible Monsters* are not the true nuclei of trauma in the novel but instead act to conceal them. It is only when we see how the characters' self-inflicted traumas are themselves repetitions of earlier afflictions that we begin to understand their attempts to treat pain and uncertainty with greater pain.

Trauma theory

Invisible Monsters engages closely with the nature of trauma. At the heart of trauma theory is not a singular disciplinary or methodological approach. Instead there is an event and a response to the event. The event is one that proves exceptionally opaque to understanding, but has a powerful impact on the individual. It overcomes the subject's ability to understand, integrate, and sometimes even speak of it, and as a result can have a devastating effect on the psyche. Caruth defines trauma as "a response, sometimes delayed, to an overwhelming event or set of events, which takes the form of repeated, intrusive hallucinations, dreams, thoughts or behaviors stemming from the event" (*Trauma* 4). The response, delayed or otherwise, is the result of an event that "is not assimilated or experienced fully at the time, but only belatedly, in its repeated *possession* of the one who experiences it" (ibid.). In this way, trauma testifies to the artificiality of our perception that time flows in a sequence, and that we reach an accommodation with the past as we progress through time. In trauma, time repeatedly regroups itself around a profoundly enigmatic event.

Invisible Monsters suggests deeper, or more longstanding, traumas than the ones the characters inflict on themselves by being narratively structured in exactly this kind of discontinuous way. The events to be relayed cannot occur in sequence, and as we discover later, this is because the exact cause of the characters' suffering cannot be definitively known. A wounding of the mind can originate from a traumatic event or a physical trauma to the body, but neither is a necessary precursor. An irony in trauma studies is that the traumatic event is both central and incidental to the sufferer. The event's effect on the subject is of more relevance than the particulars of the event, and knowing the specifics of what happened is not the same as understanding the trauma involved. Laura Brown sensibly observes that "social context, and the individual's personal history within that social context, can lend traumatic meaning to events that might be only sad or troubling in another time and place" (Caruth, *Trauma* 110). Caruth agrees, noting that "the pathology cannot be defined either by the event itself—which may or may not be catastrophic, and may not traumatize everyone equally" (4).

In a similar way, traumatic or apparently causeless suffering is both central and incidental to the characters of *Invisible Monsters*. Brandy and Shannon seek to make trauma central in order to recast and rescript their lives, but this is in part a response to the incidental or ordinary kinds of suffering they have experienced in the past (Brandy's parents' rejection of her after she, as Shane, is molested; Shannon's recognition that she is addicted to adulation). As a result the more genuinely incidental events turn out to be the obvious physical traumas. The central events, it emerges, are the complex uncertainties the characters carry concerning the nature of other people's—including family members'—desires.

In addition, the characters' affectless state speaks of personal trauma and their attraction to chaos hints at unresolved chaos in themselves. They act repetitively, obsessively and self-destructively, and the novel's reverse temporal structure that moves further into the past as it progresses forward suggests a foundational moment or moments that could help explain how the characters stopped being people and became performative roles: "the murderer, the victim and the witness" (16).

Testimony—Rip yourself open. Sew yourself shut.

Trauma, testimony, and witnessing are intricately related. Shannon finds herself thrust into the role of witness, recounting trauma on behalf of Brandy Alexander who, apparently dying, implores her sister Shannon to "Tell me my life. Tell me how we got here" (19). Shannon, backed into a corner, has to take on the role of witness for Brandy and the reader. She offers her testimony of events, but the event is a deliberate perversion of testimony, witnessing, and the unique ethical obligations they are commonly thought to hold.

The ethics of testimony

In trauma studies, testimony is significant and demands special respect. Testimony brings the ethical dimension of writing to the fore. The subject of the trauma bears testimony about an event to a listener who receives the testimony. Each step imparts a moral burden. The suffering subject feels obliged to both the listener and the event itself to give true testimony that does justice to the personal force of the event—a perceived obligation that sometimes results in silence, preventing testimony from happening. In turn, the recipient of the testimony enters into a special relationship with the subject bearing witness, and is not merely a cipher in this process. Dori Laub, himself both a personal witness to the Holocaust and someone who, as an archivist interviewer, received a great deal of testimony regarding it, suggests there is something special in the process that allows the witness to begin personally "repossessing" the event that has previously possessed him or her: "It is the encounter and the coming together between the survivor and the listener, which makes possible something like a repossession of the act of witnessing. This joint responsibility is the source of the reemerging truth" (Laub in Caruth, *Trauma* 69).

Forced to bear witness

Invisible Monsters, however, turns testimony and witnessing on its head. Instead of a traumatized subject offering personal and voluntary testimony to a sympathetic listener as part of a process of healing and repossession of the event, the reader is presented with a reluctant witness compelled to deliver another's testimony. Shannon resents Brandy, and is annoyed at having to "document this Brandy Alexander moment" (19). Immediately, two obstacles present themselves. The first is the question of how Shannon, who has known Brandy for only a year, can possibly bear witness to Brandy's life. If there is trauma at the heart of the story, how can Shannon give witness to the trauma of another person? How can the healing process of testimony operate on the basis of a forced testimony given by another? Shannon is forced to become both the person receiving the testimony and the person giving it.

These are questions we might well ask of the late twentieth-century culture that informs the novel, too, where stories of suffering can be treated as commodities to be consumed by talk show audiences who use these stories in the task of managing their own, perhaps unacknowledgeable, pain. Certainly, Shannon's own view at the beginning is that her forced testimony is a product of this sort, used by Brandy in a cynical and self-aggrandizing way. The second obstacle is practical: how can Shannon, whose facial injury prevents her from talking intelligibly, "tell" Brandy her life? There is also a more philosophical issue in one of the questions raised above: how can Shannon deliver *personal* testimony on behalf of another? Felman argues that the burden of testimony is unique and not transferrable: "[. . .] the testimony cannot be simply relayed, repeated, or reported by another without thereby losing its function as a testimony, the burden of the witness—in spite of his or her alignment with the other witnesses—is a radically unique, noninterchangeable, and solitary burden" (Felman and Laub 15).

However, as with so many things in the novel, initial appearances are deceptive. The paradox of delivering another person's testimony is resolved with the realization that Shannon's witnessing of Brandy's life is closely related to her own history. Shannon is able to be an authentic witness because she *was* a witness; after all, she is Brandy's sister and privy to many of the same childhood events, even though Brandy might or might not be aware of the connection at this point in the novel (282). In being forced to bear witness to Brandy's life, Shannon comes to recognize their commonality beyond the sibling relationship. Shannon recognizes in Brandy her own tendency toward self-destruction. Healing comes through recognizing their bond and reclaiming their past, which provides both with a link to a world outside their present identities.

The practical difficulty of delivering testimony is resolved by Shannon writing the life story in blood, a testimony that is almost immediately eaten up by fire as she writes it. The act makes literal certain qualities of testimony. Shannon is writing about a past she finds traumatic; one from which she has been fleeing. Her testimony, and her ink, come from an open wound, both psychical and physical. The fire that chases her writing hand shows that it is the act itself, and not the physical document, that is important. Perhaps it indicates, at last, a genuine ability to give up the past. Prior to this point she has fled her past, but only by confronting it can she transcend it and begin to heal. Shannon and Brandy need healing. Up until the point where Shannon begins her testimony—although it is really a shared testimony—they have been engaged in a repetitive and self-destructive cycle of self-harm for the purpose of trying to escape the past and reinvent themselves. This has the effect of creating a present characterized by constant running; from their past, from their original identities, from the future, and from the police. They fill their lives with a string of false identities, and try to escape their old identities and the pain of thinking about them brings with stolen prescription drugs.

Shannon's testimony allows both Shannon and Brandy to reclaim their past. By bringing into the open the facts neither have ever mentioned—such as their love for each other and the linked revelations that both Shannon's gunshot wound and Brandy's hairspray explosion were self-inflicted—they reclaim their personal histories and strengthen their bond.

Shannon's is not the only testimony in the novel. Another is provided by Brandy's iconic role model, Rona Barrett, whose autobiography *Miss Rona* offers Brandy a model of testimony and self-recreation. In *Miss Rona*, Barrett recalls her personal rise to celebrity. Rona and Brandy both use surgery, which is also the most persistent motif in *Invisible Monsters*, as a metaphor for testimony. In the preface to *Miss Rona*, as reported by Brandy, Rona describes herself as being "like this animal, cut open with all its vital organs glistening and quivering" (86) who knows no one will come along and sew her up. So, she "has to take a needle and thread and sew herself up" (ibid.). This excerpt, taken in context as the preface to an autobiography, compares autobiography and personal testimony with performing surgery on yourself. This reading is corroborated a moment later when Brandy asks Shannon to tell "a gross personal story" and to "Rip yourself open. Sew yourself shut" (88). It is also related to the wider narrative of the novel later when Shannon repeats Brandy's/Rona's surgery metaphor with a twist that reminds the reader of Brandy's initial request to have her life told to her:

> Rip yourself open.
>
> Tell me my life story before I die.
>
> Sew yourself shut. (240)

Both surgery and personal testimony are, or can be, traumatic and painful. They wound, but they have the potential to heal. Palahniuk is making the point that testimony is, in some ways, not unlike trauma itself. Testimony is itself a way of reexperiencing trauma. However, as Caruth and others frequently note, one of the problems with trauma is that it is an event that overwhelms the mind's ability to understand and incorporate it. In a sense, the event is not fully experienced in its first instance, resulting in its possession of the subject and its frequent and uncontrolled return. Testimony and acting as a witness do not necessarily make for a return to trauma; they can mark the first time the pain is truly experienced at all (Caruth, *Unclaimed Experiences* 17).

There are complications in Palahniuk's use of surgery as a metaphor for testimony. For one, most of the surgery in the novel does not appear to heal a wound. The major surgery is gender reassignment surgery. If surgery is being related to testimony, a gender reassignment operation problematizes the metaphor. Gender reassignment changes surface appearances while testimony demands confrontation with the truth. However, the metaphor does still work, with a remaining caveat. Gender reassignment surgery such as Brandy contemplates can be a way of addressing a trauma of identity. Those who seek such surgery are doing so to directly confront something that is, to them, wounding. Rather than hiding or concealing, reassignment surgery can reveal what was previously hidden. The caveat is that since Brandy does not want such surgery, it is hard to see how her surgery can be healing for her.

By aligning surgery and testimony, Palahniuk brings to the foreground the painful but healing qualities of testimony. By using the horrible image of performing self-surgery, he emphasizes the sense of isolation one can experience when bearing witness to one's own personal trauma. However, he also softens the message. Shannon's testimony is not a lonely act; it ends up being a collaborative effort with benefits for both Brandy and Shannon. Shannon's testimony and the bond she rediscovers by reclaiming her past allow her to reconnect with the world outside herself and discover something genuine and authentic in a world she recently considered devoid of value.

The process is not a quick or easy one. Giving testimony allows Shannon to reclaim her past and with it the bond with her lost brother, but most of the events of the novel are spent running from that same past. Just as Brandy flees from her incipient vaginoplasty, so too do the characters spend most of the novel running from the past. Brandy might have helped Shannon give her testimony and recover her history, but she also helped her run from it.

Identity, gender and performance— The Brandy Alexander Witness Reincarnation Project

Escaping the past

Surgery and testimony threaten to come apart for Shannon when, after her accident, she finds herself the recipient of a great deal of unwanted help. This help, if accepted, would ameliorate the full effects of what we later learn has been an intentional and self-inflicted act. Her nurse wants her to start dating, and tries to set her up with criminals and mutilated men. Her speech therapist is trying to teach her to speak again. Both nurse and speech therapist want Shannon to accept life with her injury. Both want her to adapt her personal reality to her new circumstances, whether by accepting her tongue and jaw will not form the same sounds they used to or accepting most men will be put off by her appearance. Shannon is frustrated by their aid. She does not want to base a new life upon the reality of her traumatic injury, and speaks scornfully of those who do: "People are all over the world telling their one dramatic story and how their life has turned into getting over this one event. Now their lives are more about the past than the future" (117).

Shannon caused her injury because she sought to escape what she describes as her addiction to being beautiful (275). Being beautiful has defined her, and Shannon seeks out "the biggest mistake I could think would save me" (286). Her self-inflicted gunshot wound might have saved her from the physical trap of being beautiful, but if she were to allow her mutilation to define her new life, she would only be replacing one physical trap for another. Shannon turns to Brandy Alexander for a different approach.

Brandy solicits testimony from Shannon, asking her what happened to her face. Shannon writes down the details for Brandy to read. Each time Shannon reveals more—which she does honestly if not completely—Brandy seems dissatisfied, and asks "what else?" Eventually Brandy interrupts Shannon:

> "Your perception is all fucked up," Brandy says. "All you can talk about is trash that's already happened."
> She says, "You can't base your life on the past or the present." (60)

Despite soliciting her testimony, Brandy is not interested in the details of Shannon's past. Instead, she asks because she hopes that in the process of telling, Shannon will gain some distance from her personal history and will become able to throw it "into the trashcan" (61). Without the burden of the past, Shannon will be able to reinvent herself and enter what she glibly calls the "Brandy Alexander Witness Reincarnation Project" (225).

Manus also rejects his past in order to join Shannon and Brandy in reinventing his future. His transformative moment occurs when he receives a gift from his mother: a box filled with mementoes of his childhood. In a cathartic act of renunciation, Manus throws away the physical representations of his past, each a reminder of his identity. Report cards, bronzed baby shoes, and even his birth certificate are chucked "out of existence" (215). Almost immediately afterwards, Brandy takes him under her wing, giving him a new name and the same promise of infinite potential she gave Shannon: "I don't want to know who you are, but if you could be anyone, who would you be?" (215). With his past almost literally thrown away, in Brandy and Shannon's view, Manus can claim a new identity or, even better, a myriad of new identities.

Reclaiming personal identity

As in *Fight Club*, *Invisible Monsters'* characters seek personal transformation through self-inflicted trauma. But the novel also explores the kinds of earlier life events that might be expressed through later, ostensibly self-willed engagements with pain and suffering. Both Shannon and Brandy (and, as it turns out, Evie), use elected trauma to change the way the world relates to them. But as we learn more about their lives, we see that in the past each of them was deeply—in Brandy's case traumatically—uncertain about how to interpret other people's desires for them. Pursuing self-willed traumatic events was a response to this deeper uncertainty.

To Brandy, identity is, or should be, a performance, and changing identities should be no more difficult than switching roles. Towing Manus and Shannon in her charismatic wake she frequently alters their identities, giving them new names, new relationships, and even new backstories. The motivation for change can be nothing more significant than accidentally getting "ripped" by eating "Nebalino suppositories" (237). Brandy chooses names and personalities that are gaudy and artificial; drag queen names, soap opera names, puns on drug names, and the names of cars replace each other in quick succession. Each choice, like Brandy Alexander's own cocktail-inspired name, highlights the artificiality of the personalities invoked. Sometimes she chooses familiar corporate names like "Harper Collins" and "Alfa Romeo" (238), turning the subject into a product and equating the identity of a human being with the arbitrary "personality" cultivated for a brand or corporate identity. Her choices make Shannon's suggestion that killing any of them would mean nothing more than "killing a car" (12) horribly close to reality. It is not entirely clear to what extent this response to late twentieth-century life satirically mobilizes corporately produced desires against themselves and to what extent it is an expression of deep-seated alienation.

Even Brandy, who names and renames her companions, and who, aside from the one massive identity change that is the core of her current identity, is seemingly exempt from the constant identity changes, is as much a product as Manus and Shannon; or as much a "product of a product of a product" (217) as Brandy puts it. She has been renamed (or rebranded) by the Rhea sisters, who did for her what she does for Manus and Shannon. Brandy also deliberately reifies herself. Whenever she introduces herself, she enacts a minor ritual of introduction, one that conspicuously fails to affirm her individuality beyond the sum of her parts:

> "And this . . .," Brandy's big ring-beaded hand curls up to touch Brandy's torpedo breasts.
>
> "This . . .," the enormous hand lifts to touch the billowing piles of auburn hair.
>
> "And this . . .," the hand touches thick moist lips.
>
> "This," Brandy says, "is the Princess Brandy Alexander." (25)

Her ritual of introduction conspicuously avoids using the first person pronoun, making her personal introduction distinctly impersonal. Instead of using the first person, she substitutes a series of demonstrative adjectives and finally a demonstrative pronoun, subtly shifting from referring to things to referring to herself but eliding the two in the process. The demonstratives make the introduction shallow, highlighting proximity in time and space while conspicuously avoiding any reference to personal, internal identity exclusive of external reality. Palahniuk assists Brandy's avoidance of the first person pronoun by avoiding using *any* personal pronouns or possessive adjectives in the dialogue tags of this brief scene. Instead of "her hand" it is "the hand" that touches her lips and even within a single dialogue tag the author repeats Brandy's name instead of writing "her." This introduction suggests that the identity of "Brandy Alexander" does not lie in the person; rather it lies in what might otherwise be seen as factors irrelevant to identity: her breasts, lips, hair, clothes, and affected manner. The repetition of "Brandy" makes the word sound like a brand name and the woman herself sound like a thing.

More than a person, Brandy is a role; a living doll. The Rhea sisters, who played a major part in forming what Brandy suggests is the core of her identity—her appearance and manner—are wealthy because they invented an improbably proportioned doll that makes "catty" remarks at the pull of a little gold chain. The doll's proportions if scaled up to human size—46–16–26 (170)—are identical to the stated proportions of Brandy Alexander. The Rhea sisters have turned their plastic creation into a living product.

Brandy's witness reincarnation project also reduces Shannon and Manus to the level of products, but this is not an incidental or unintentional result: Brandy has complete control over the names she chooses. Names and personalities, she implies, are as interchangeable as the facings of cell phones. The further implication is that the name and identity you are born with has no more meaning than one chosen by another person, and neither have any more reality or permanence than a brand name, which only exists as long as it adds value to a balance sheet.

However, there is an undertone to Brandy, Shannon, and Manus renouncing their old identities. They do so in order to escape the trap of having a static identity and to free their personalities from the past. Despite this ostensible reason, there are factors pushing each of them away from their old lives. Manus is obsessed with being physically attractive and fears aging. Shannon claims she is trying to escape the beauty she thinks has limited her development as a human being. Brandy is leaving behind abuse, rejection, and her own self-inflicted wounding: the exploding hair-spray can. Shannon summarizes the situation from her perspective: "We were all running from something. Vaginoplasty. Aging. The future" (239). This aspect of the Brandy Alexander Witness Reincarnation Project is not mentioned by Brandy, but it certainly exists. Because they are fleeing events and realities from their past or future, the entire project becomes questionable. Rather than escaping or transcending the events that trouble them, the characters are acting as a direct result of them and thus giving the events power over their lives.

Brandy, Manus, and Shannon's quick-step identity changes are smaller echoes of the major identity changes that have occurred earlier. Brandy's surgery and reinvention by the Rhea sisters and Shannon's gunshot wound are intended to help them reinvent themselves as different people. Each new personality is a repetition of the earlier act of recreation; an obsessive return to a familiar theme. Rather than being liberated from the past, the characters are trapped in an obsessive loop of invention and reinvention that seems to be a direct result of the past.

It is difficult to reconcile the extreme actions of the characters with the reasons they give for their conduct. Is Shannon really so sick of being beautiful that she shoots herself in the face? Does Brandy really want to have gender reassignment surgery—the tremendous physical hardship of which is graphically described—just because the Rhea sisters want her to and because she wants to rewrite the story of her life? Is Manus really so afraid of growing old that he is willing to join in Brandy and Shannon's crime spree and endure the subtle and not-so-subtle abuse they give him? Perhaps these are good enough reasons on their own, but the text offers other possible readings that might assist in explaining why the main characters are so compelled to recreate themselves.

Escaping trauma: The opposite of a miracle

The reverse structure of *Invisible Monsters*, which moves the narrative deeper into the past as it goes on, is a flashback structure based on revelation. With each foray into the past, the present is explained with greater clarity. Palahniuk's choice of structure is ironic because it makes the past critically important in understanding what is happening in the present while the characters are engaged in strenuously denying the importance of the past to the present. Each step back reveals more, and comes to supersede revelations that take place earlier in the text of the novel but later in the lives of the characters. By causing more important revelations to occur increasingly further back in the past, this structure privileges the past over the present, and suggests that earlier events have more relevance to the present than recent ones.

The earliest events are the most understated, subtle, and ambiguous of the novel; anomalous in a work that otherwise portrays grotesqueries and personal traumas for their shock value. Among these are the father's minor frauds, the family's looting of train wrecks, the indeterminate nonevent of Brandy's molestation by her father, and the determinate real event of Brandy's molestation by Manus and Brandy's rejection by her family. The five events—which have more claim to being genuine psychologically traumatic events than most of the others in the novel—have fine connections to each other.

How Brandy was not abused, then abused, and what it all has to do with a train wreck

The possibility of Brandy's sexual abuse at her father's hands when she was still the boy named Shane is the most ambiguous of the events. No definitive statement is made, and the most conclusive comment is Brandy's. The police investigation, counseling, and interventions went on and on because "I couldn't tell [the police] anything because there was nothing to tell" (249). When, still as Shane, she says the same to a younger Manus, he replies that "He likes a kid who can keep a secret" and sexually abuses her (251–2). Manus's statement implies that he thinks she is lying to protect her father.

Brandy's denials are subtly ambiguous. Saying there was nothing to tell is not the same as saying nothing happened. One imagines a young Brandy talking to counselors and police, unable to find the words to either deny or confirm their suspicions, resulting in the ongoing investigations, questioning, and counseling she and her family experienced. What does "nothing to tell" mean exactly? It could mean nothing happened. It could mean something happened and she is unable to speak of it. Perhaps the memory is one she does not acknowledge. Perhaps it is an event beyond words and "telling." Whatever the case, Brandy's ambiguous denial leaves open a possible space for genuine trauma, trauma that overspills the possibility for expression and, of necessity, hides itself. Her comment that there was nothing she was too afraid to tell the child abuse people (250) is similarly ambiguous. It may not have been fear preventing her from talking. Regardless, someone keeps making anonymous calls to the police; Shannon claims near the end of the novel it was her, but her motivation is unclear (278).

Earlier Brandy began what appears to be a recounting of abuse by her father. "Some nights, Brandy says, her father used to creep into her room while she was asleep." Shannon recognizes Brandy is sharing a "nasty secret" but does not want to hear it. After creeping in, he would sit on the bed and wake her up (246–7).

Palahniuk causes the narrative to cut away at this point at the edge of what a reasonable reader would think is a confession of personal abuse. When the narrative jumps back, the story changes, or appears to change. Their father wakes her and tells her to wake her sister. They get in the truck. The whole family drives for hours to arrive at a train wreck where they loot from the wreck until the authorities arrive. Again, there is ambiguity. With the jump in narrative, this could be a different night, and the testimony of abuse could have been begun but not finished. It could be a continuation of the story, although why the father would "creep in" and "sit down"—implying slow movement, a lack of haste and a desire not to be heard—only to wake her a moment later and tell her to hurry and get dressed is baffling. The abuse, if it occurred at all, does not happen explicitly in the novel. If it takes place, it does so outside the frame of the novel. Here we see a more subtle and disturbing break in the temporality of Brandy's life than that suggested by the repeated phrase "Jump to . . ." that is used throughout the novel to connect disparate events.

If this event had taken place in the context of the novel, it would simply have been another horror in a circus show of horrors, another scene to which the narrative jumps. By moving it outside the frame and turning it into an ambiguous event, Palahniuk makes Brandy's possible abuse an exceptional event and more like trauma as it is experienced by the suffering subject. True psychological trauma can overcome the subject's ability to incorporate, understand, retell, or remember it properly. Describing trauma and recording events is not enough to portray psychological trauma. The ambiguous nonevent of Brandy's abuse is more true to the nature of trauma, which sometimes cannot be directly viewed. As Caruth puts it in *Unclaimed Experiences*, "the most direct seeing of a violent event may occur as an absolute inability to know it" (92). Certainly, as readers we cannot know what Brandy has experienced.

The real event occurs later, but does not seem to affect Brandy as one might expect it to. Despite being abused by him, Brandy does not seem to bear Manus malice. She dismisses the event, saying it "wasn't horrible" but "wasn't love" (252). The actual event seems an anticlimax after the buildup she gave to her father's nighttime visitation. Palahniuk detaches the event from the emotion and from the traumatized reaction of seeking the opposite of a miracle.

If Brandy's father abused her, it occurred outside the frame of
Invisible Monsters; but what stands in its place inside the novel is
revealing. Instead of the expected account of abuse, we are presented
with a late-night drive and a family picking up mass-produced goods
at the site of a train accident. "That's me growing up, those kinds
of train wrecks," Shannon tells the reader (252). Why is the story of
the train wreck woven in with Brandy's aborted story of abuse and
her recollection of real sexual abuse? It seems anomalous.

Some possibilities emerge if we look at the underlying themes
of the novel, however, which grapple with the alienation and
inauthenticity of modern life. The items the family picks up are
all examples of modern mass production. They take objects in
quantities they cannot possibly use, each exactly alike. They do
so for personal gain and to stave off poverty. The event seems a
synecdochal example of modern culture. The family lives in scarcity,
despite being surrounded by the obscene abundance of modern
production. Even the goods' lack of variation is deplored: Shannon
"loathes" the homogenous butterscotch pudding she ate "from the
time I was six to the time I was nine" (252). The identical goods
remind the reader of Shannon and Brandy's scorn for things that
are copies.

The wreck is one example of the many frauds the family commits,
from grinding ice and cereal into beef to bulk it up, to putting bad
potatoes into the middle of a sack of good potatoes. The frauds
and the events of the train wreck are recalled alongside Brandy's
revelations of abuse, giving what appear to be minor events
a sense of importance, as if they are as intimate a disclosure as
recounting sexual abuse. Each fraud—which Shannon and Brandy
seem to deplore ("You ever hear of anything in your whole life
so underhanded?" (245))—is an example of concealing something
bad behind a pleasing appearance. Perhaps the frauds give Shannon
a reason to dislike the shallowness of modern culture that makes
surface appearances the most important, if not the only, thing.

The father's behavior at the train wrecks and in selling pigs and
potatoes at the market also has things in common with Brandy's
and Shannon's seeking out of life-changing traumas. In tricking his
customers by selling rotten or less valuable vegetables and animals
than he appears to be selling Mr McFarland undermines any chance
of building a loyal client base and ensures the need to perpetually
seek out new, gullible customers. Considered in light of these events,

Brandy's and Shannon's attempts to manipulate how other people see and respond to them are not so much radical changes to their earlier lives as continuations of the inexplicably alienating things their parents did.

The cornucopia of the train wreck also conceals something. Shannon does not mention it, but the family's windfall is a *disaster*. A train wreck does not occur without injury or death. The family do not concern themselves with looking for survivors or the injured. The disaster is off-stage. The family is detached from the trauma of the accident, just as Brandy appears detached from her own abuse and Shannon from the inauthentic things and people around her.

Rejection . . . and acceptance

The most galling piece of inauthenticity in the novel occurs as a result of Manus sexually abusing Brandy, still the 15-year-old boy called Shane then. As a consequence of the abuse, Shane catches an STI. His parents react with horror, mostly because they assume he is a sexually active homosexual. They reject Shane on the spot, asking him to leave the family home and stay elsewhere. Shannon also rejects Shane, ignoring him when he comes to Shannon's bedroom window. This event is concealed by Shane/Brandy and Shannon's parents' later ostentatious show of support for lesbian and gay rights and their willingness to believe their son has died of AIDS without seeking more proof than an anonymous phone call. Their parents' hypocrisy is immense. They hide their intolerance behind a flashy show of support. The disjunction between the appearance they cultivate and the intolerance they hide is extreme, and provides an archetypal focus for Shannon's disgust for mere appearance.

However, although Shannon deplores this rejection, she perpetuates it in her thoughts and actions through most of the novel. She frequently reiterates her disgust for the large show that is Brandy Alexander, while following in her footsteps like a helpless thrall. Only in the denouement is Shannon able to reconcile herself with her lost brother.

It is interesting that in a novel that explores disconnections— between people; between appearances and reality; between sex and gender; between identity and personhood—the final moment is one of connection. As Shannon reconnects with her brother, she is able to reconnect with her past and reclaim the actions that led her to where she is. Just as she is able to reclaim her identity, she offers it to Shane in a selflessly altruistic act. This, it seems, is a healing moment. Shannon acts to heal past wrongs by accepting the brother she earlier rejected. By realizing she loves Brandy, she is able to form a genuine connection with another human being, something that would have been impossible for the detached and brutal Shannon we see at the start of the novel. She even manages to symbolically join appearance and reality, giving Brandy the authentic gift of her own womanhood by offering her own identity papers, and, thus, her own prior modeling career. Palahniuk transforms Shannon from invisible monster to noble heroine with the sudden explosion of feeling for the other that can only be summed up in the impassioned words: "I love Brandy Alexander."

6

From Solid to Liquid: *Invisible Monsters* and the Blank Fiction Road Story

Sonia Baelo-Allué

Invisible Monsters is the story of two siblings' journey to discover their own identity and place in a changing world. The novel can be defined as a blank fiction road story that lacks a point of departure and a point of arrival and whose main characters possess liquid identities that are created, shaped, and changed as they travel up and down the West Coast. This is also a novel of secrets that need to be kept hidden, of pasts that should be erased, of futures that nobody wishes for, and of traumatic presents of both amnesia and possibility. All these complex issues are dealt with in the framework of transgressive or blank fiction. Jesse Kavadlo defines Palahniuk's fiction in these terms: "Imagine what it's like to have your eyes rubbed raw with broken glass. This is what reading Chuck Palahniuk is like" (3). The violence and excess the reader encounters in his transgressive novels is not always easy to interpret, especially in *Invisible Monsters*, a book in which the narrator tries to distance herself from the narration while putting a special effort into hiding her feelings. This distancing makes it difficult to determine whether violence is celebrated or condemned. Kavadlo believes that Palahniuk is actually a closet moralist who writes about communication, love, beauty, hope, and survival (22). Eduardo Mendieta also believes that Palahniuk's fiction deals mainly with survival and human resilience in the face of failure, dysfunction, and pathology (408). In a similar line, Francisco Collado-Rodríguez has underlined the ethical impulse behind Palahniuk's fiction and the explosion of feelings for the other that his characters usually experience (194). By contrast, Jonathan Dee sees no morality or ethical claim in transgressive fiction in general, and in Palahniuk's fiction in particular, which only offers a "ready-made rebellion," since the extreme actions of the characters are based on an "undefined existential boredom" (90). The issue here is whether blank fiction, combined with the road story and a fluid sense of identity can really play an ethical role or, rather, if the ambiguities that narrative distance imposes prevent the belief in the power of generous love and resilience to transform identity.

Blank fiction and *Invisible Monsters*

Blank fiction is a term first used by Elizabeth Young and Graham Caveney to refer to a kind of fiction emerging in the mid-1980s and originally developed by New York "Downtown" writers interested in the darkest corners of urban life: "crime, drugs, sexual excess, media overload, consumer madness, inner-city decay and fashion-crazed nightlife" (vi). What was remarkable about these writers was not just their choice of subjects but their prose, which was flat, affectless, uncommitted, and distant, and their characters, mainly "dazed consumers, urban deviants, middle-class bohemians, sexual outcasts and other disconsolate riff-raff" (vii). James Annesley traced the evolution of these writers through the 1990s and together with Downtown writers like Kathy Acker, Dennis Cooper, and Lynne Tillman, and the more commercial "bratpack" writers Bret Easton Ellis, Jay McInnerney, and Tama Janowitz, new names were added to the canon like Susanna Moore, Douglas Coupland, Mark Leyner, Ray Shell, and Evelyn Lau among others. Annesley insists on using the term "blank fictions" because there are obvious differences among these writers even though they share a number of aesthetic concerns.

Chuck Palahniuk's works in general and *Invisible Monsters* in particular can be better understood within this aesthetic context that explains the ambiguous and contradictory readings his novels produce. The main characters in this novel are the "monsters" that society rejects: the gay, the transsexual, the ugly, who seem to believe in self-destruction as a form of social liberation. It is a novel about violence, sex, prescription drugs, and consumerism. In fact, already in the first chapter nearly all the main characteristics of blank fiction come to mind. The initial situation is an image of violence and excess. It is a flash forward on the wedding day of nearly naked Ms. Evie Cottrell who is holding a rifle and whose house is burning to the ground. Brandy Alexander, who has been shot by Evie and is soaked in blood, asks the unnamed narrator (Shannon) to tell her life story and how they got there. At this point we do not know who these mysterious characters are; their real, unstable identities will be revealed throughout the novel in a series of unexpected plot twists. Brandy is apparently a man-to-woman transsexual waiting for her final operation. She is also constantly defined as a drag queen and queen supreme but she does not like labels: "I'm not straight, and I'm not gay [. . .] I'm not bisexual. I want out of the labels. I don't want my whole life crammed into a single word" (261). Brandy is also Shannon's brother Shane, who disappeared when he was a teenager, after his parents threw him out of the house because he had contracted a sexually transmitted disease. Shannon, who witnessed everything and did nothing, thought her brother was dead but still hates him for garnering most of her parents' attention.

One of blank fiction's characteristic features is the inclusion of consumer culture references, brand names, and products of late twentieth-century life (Annesley 6). Bret Easton Ellis's *American Psycho* (1991) is probably the best-known blank fiction novel to use this aesthetic approach. These references are casually introduced in violent passages with no change of tone in the narrative voice. In the first chapter of *Invisible Monsters* we find sentences like: "Brandy is gushing her insides out through a bullet hole in her amazing suit jacket. The suit, it's this white Bob Mackie knock-off Brandy bought in Seattle with a tight hobble skirt [. . .] The single-breasted cut is symmetrical except for the hole pumping out blood" (12–13). Brandy's life and her Bob Mackie suit jacket are apparently equally valuable or valueless in the narrator's numb mind. Curiously enough, Shannon has started the fire by burning a wedding invitation soaked in Chanel Number Five, just like the fashion models who plant bombs in Louis Vuitton bags in Bret Easton Ellis's *Glamorama* (1998). Violence and style usually go together in blank fiction novels, which usually underline the shallowness of a narrative voice that fails to distinguish the important from the superficial.

In fact, there are many examples in the novel of combinations of glamour and beauty with violence and suffering, of objects of consumption and objects of waste. As Zygmunt Bauman points out, waste is the product of the society of consumers and in such a society one of the major issues is the threat of being considered waste: "In a world filled with consumers and the objects of their consumption, life is hovering uneasily between the joys of consumption and the horrors of the rubbish heap" (*Liquid Life* 9). There are many examples in *Invisible Monsters* of this uneasy equilibrium, like the photos of Shannon taken in the emergency room just after the accident where she is topless in her patch underwear, which seem a replica of the ones in her portfolio as a fashion model (36–7). In a similar vein, there are several examples of fashion shoots at junkyards full of wrecked cars, slaughterhouses, and sewage treatment plants: "The uglier the fashions, the worse places we'd have to pose to make them look good [. . .] you only look good by comparison. One shoot for Industry Jeans Wear, I was sure we'd have to pose kissing dead bodies" (163–4). The line between beauty and waste, between life and death is very thin indeed. While the art director asks Evie and Shannon to push their breasts against the wrecked cars, Shannon thinks about the families that died together in those same cars. Even plastic surgery has two sides: the transformation of Shane into Brandy Alexander gives amazing results and Shannon describes in detail her torpedo breasts, her billowing piles of auburn hair, her hourglass waist, her thick moist lips . . . However, this beauty is the result of painful operations like the bottom ribs extracted to obtain her 16-inch waist, the nipples that had to be shaved and relocated, and "[a]dd to this her lipo, her silicone, her trachea shave, her brow shave, her scalp advance, her forehead realignment, her rhino contouring to smooth her nose, her maxomilliary operations to shape her jaw" (198).

Beautiful dresses are painful when they try to wear them, Shannon's clothes are stretched and torn off by Evie's big-boned body, and even the beautiful make-up that they steal in open houses comes with prescription drugs for old people as invisible as Shannon after her accident. In this sense, the beautiful and the painful go together as much as the deep and shallow complement each other.

In the opening chapter Brandy is also concerned with superficial issues even though she is about to die. One of her main worries is if Bon Marché will take her bloodstained suit back (15) or the fact that dying on the floor will make her hair flat in the back (17). As narrator, Shannon is aware of some of these ironies and knows well that everybody in the scene is as shallow as she seems to be: "Evie, Brandy and me, all this is just a power struggle for the spotlight" (16). Bauman has underlined how in a world of consumers and consumer objects the two are the conceptual poles of a continuum along which people move and in which "the two roles intertwine, blend and merge" (*Liquid Life* 10). As Shannon puts it, "[s]hotgunning anybody in this room would be the moral equivalent of killing a car, a vacuum cleaner, a Barbie doll. Erasing a computer disk. Burning a book. Probably that goes for killing anybody in the world. We're all such products" (12). Sherry R. Truffin points out that "[w]hen humans are reduced to commodities, they may respond by turning themselves into monsters" (75). The reification that takes place in Shannon's mind, evident in her commodified language, turns her into a monster but it also seems a mechanism to hide her true feelings and cope with the fact that the house is burning, Evie has shot Brandy, and Brandy is bleeding to death.

Blank fictions are usually first-person, present-tense narratives in which several mechanisms are established to distance the narrator from the narrated events. The first chapter in *Invisible Monsters* already shows the distance that Shannon establishes and keeps throughout most of her narrative. The events are narrated as if they were part of a film: the big West Hills wedding reception is in fact called "scene setting" (11). Actions are not decided by people but are "cues" to scripted movements; for example, Evie's sobbing is the cue for them to look at her (13), which prevents the narrator from feeling any empathy or understanding for Evie. The place is a "set" and Evie, Brandy, and the narrator herself are described as "[t]he murderer, the victim, the witness, each of us thinks our role is the lead" (16). The fire is just "special effects" as they wait for the firemen and paramedics to "make their entrance" (15). Shannon is trying to hide her feelings through the distance the film scenario produces, a situation that is made obvious when Brandy asks her if she loves her, which Shannon is not yet ready to answer (she will, however, at the end of the novel) but does take Brandy's hand in hers, though "[j]ust for a little stage business" (18). In the novel there are other distancing mechanisms like the sentence "Sorry, Mom, sorry, God" that Shannon uses when she feels that society expects her to apologize for something and she does not truly feel the need to do so. After all, she does not care about what others may think. On the contrary, she apologizes only ironically for the mini thong and almost transparent cotton crepe sundress she was wearing the day of the accident or for the fact that her parents wanted her to go to medical school.

However, the most important distancing mechanism in the novel is not a leitmotif sentence or the opening film trope but the use of photographic flashes to fake feelings. Shannon used to be a model before the accident in which she lost her lower jaw and was used to simulating emotions for the camera. The photographer would tell her how to feel and, when hearing the "flash" sound of the camera, she would perform accordingly: "Him yelling, Give me lust, baby. Flash. Give me malice. Flash. Give me detached existentialist ennui. Flash. Give me rampant intellectualism as a coping mechanism. Flash" (13–14). The only feelings Shannon expresses in the novel, at least until her final declaration of love for her brother, are mediated by this narrative technique. She has to imagine the flash to show any feelings that are artificially performed for an imaginary audience. She is in fact a self-aware narrator who is conscious of the whole narrative process and even announces the narrative shape of the events to follow. For Shannon, reading her story is going to be like glancing through the pages of fashion magazines like *Vogue*, *Glamour*, or *Harper's Bazaar*. On the one hand, there will be many references to brand names and mass culture products, to glamour and stylized images. On the other, the narrative process itself is going to simulate the chaotic experience of reading this type of magazine: the unconnected, nonchronological events resulting from the random passing of the pages of Shannon's life. The metaphor is developed in sentences such as "Jump back to. . . ." or "Jump to the next day. . . ." or even "Jump to the truth," when she finally decides to bridge the gap between her feelings and the straightforward expression of them. The technique also resembles the jump-cuts of cinematic language, even if Palahniuk has denied in an interview that he intended to use any film devices. However, he has always been interested in the introduction of nonfictional forms to his writing (in Kavanagh 183–4).

The writer was apparently dissatisfied with the final effect of this narrative strategy since he had intended something else:

> I wanted to do a linear novel, but to break it up, so that it would say to jump from chapter one to chapter seventeen, to chapter thirteen, and you would physically have to jump back and forth throughout the book. It's been done before. Hopscotch. It was a way of underlining the chaotic aspect of the plot, like a fat fashion magazine that each time you open offers something you had not noticed before. It would make the novel "something that would imply the unknowability of beautiful things." (In Switzer 2001)

In any case, the final design shows the fragmented, traumatized mind of Shannon, her broken and chaotic life, and the unexpected, nonlinear journey the protagonists embark on.

Furthermore, the magazine structure contributes to the detached narration and provides the atmosphere of shallowness that blank fiction needs. As the self-conscious narrator puts it, the narration consists of "[a] million trendy accessories, scarves and belts, shoes and hats and gloves, and no real clothes to wear them with [. . .] This is the world we live in" (21). As narrator, Shannon is well aware of the shallowness that surrounds her but she even embraces the superficiality and lifestyle that Brandy brings with her. In blank fiction commercialized products are not just mere reference points since this is a type of fiction that "does not just depict its own period, it speaks in the commodified language of its own period" (Annesley 7). Of course this is one of the sources of ambiguity in the novel since, paradoxically, the narrator rejects her past as a fashion model for everything it represents but she is willing to participate in the shallow world of Brandy Alexander or "*Vogue* on location" (43). The narrator self-consciously chooses the fashion magazine's fragmented structure to tell her tale of narcissism and emotional detachment that, in turn, is to be surmounted at the end. As in all blank fiction these are ideas difficult to reconcile.

Blank fiction and the road story

As contended above, blank fiction helps us to contextualize the obsession the novel depicts with consumer culture, violence, drugs, and the narrator's apparent emotional detachment. However, even though Shannon claims that "[t]here isn't a real pattern to anything" (20), there is a significant pattern that shapes the whole plot: the road story genre. The choice of this genre is significant because, ever since the early frontier narratives, the road story has played a central role in America's imagination and mythology. Blank or transgressive fiction usually subverts our expectations and stops at nothing, not even sacred or taboo subjects. It tries to cross the line of what is acceptable or even understandable and this is what *Invisible Monsters* does. This is a novel in which rimming, fisting, and felching are discussed at a family Christmas dinner table (92–4) and in which vaginas are described as consumer objects in brochures with a wide variety to choose from (223). In a society in which consumer culture absorbs all signs of the counter-culture and turns them into fashion accessories, it is necessary to go beyond expectations. Katie Mills, using an "intermediary" approach to the road story, has underlined how innovative road narratives such as Kerouac's *On the Road* (1957) have become commodified as they have gone through different media and different cycles of rebellion, ultimately being tamed as seen, for example, in the TV series *Route 66* (4, 64). Since rebellion is becoming very difficult to achieve, road stories that aim at transgressing boundaries have become more and more extreme.

In terms of genre, *Invisible Monsters* plays with the conventions of the road story and avoids straight lines and chronological sequences. This is the way Shannon presents the journey they are about to begin:

> Jump to us driving away with the Fiat Spider just piled with luggage. Imagine desperate refugees from Beverly Hills with seventeen pieces of matched luggage migrating cross-country to start a new life in the Okie Midwest. Everything very elegant and tasteful, one of those epic Joad family vacations, only backwards. Leaving a trail of cast-off accessories, shoes and gloves and chokers and hats to lighten their load so's they can cross the Rocky Mountains, that would be us. (180)

The reference to a great American road novel, John Steinbeck's *The Grapes of Wrath* (1939), is significant. The journey of the Joad family captured the suffering of millions of Americans trying to escape from the Dust Bowl and the Great Depression in the 1930s. They leave Oklahoma as a united family with the hope of reaching California and the promise of a new, better life and they only carry the family's few possessions in an old, used truck. In *Invisible Monsters* we also find a family travelling together or, rather, a redefinition of the traditional nuclear family. Shannon is travelling with her brother Shane/Brandy and her boyfriend Manus. In *The Grapes of Wrath* the Joad family gradually separates under the strain, although they keep their humanity to the very end; in *Invisible Monsters* the family also separates but only after finding their own humanity.

Despite the similarities there are some obvious differences. Shannon, Brandy Alexander, and Manus are, if we use Paes de Barros's terminology, "nomadic subjects" who move without any apparent destination: Portland, Santa Barbara, San Francisco, San Jose, Sacramento, Reno, Las Vegas, Salt Lake City, Butte, Calgary, Edmonton, Vancouver, Seattle, Portland. This circular structure is also seen in the fact that the journey starts when Shannon sets Evie's house on fire believing that she has arranged with Manus to have her killed, and ends in the house of Evie's parents, which Shannon also sets on fire. Nomadic subjects resist fixed territory and "the linear mobility of the conventional road" (Paes de Barros, *Fast Cars* 7) since they lack a planned point of departure and a point of arrival. They travel in zigzag but they also follow Interstate 5 and Interstate 15, which is in theory a linear space. However, the journey is conveyed in a nonlinear, fragmented narrative that focuses on especially intense episodes rather than on a chronological development. The journey is constantly interrupted by flashbacks from the past and by traumatic memories and is fuelled by plans of revenge and self-destruction. The identities of Brandy/Shane, Shannon, and Manus change as often as the cars they drive. The Joads' jalopy in *The Grapes of Wrath* becomes here a red Fiat Spider, a big Seville convertible, a family van, a Ford Probe, a Cadillac, and a Lincoln Town car. In this context of conspicuous consumerism, the few possessions the Joad family carries turn into 17 pieces of matched luggage full of accessories.

Ronald Primeau describes four main tendencies within the genre: the road as space for dissent or contestation (33), as search for national identity (51), as search for the individual self and self-discovery (69), and as metanarrative or parody (89). *Invisible*

Monsters seems to draw from all these versions since it shows dissent from the normative and is concerned with both national/cultural identity and self-discovery in a detached narrative. The road is also a space of freedom where social norms are relaxed or simply disappear. For Paes de Barros "[o]nly between arrival and departure is any utopian vision possible. Outside patriarchy, outside compulsory heterosexuality, the road and the process of the negotiation of borders allow for a new (and finite) world [. . .] a space outside boundaries, a state of mind rather than a destination" (*Fast Cars* 17). On the road Shannon, Manus, and Brandy Alexander do not have to conform to any social norms. As Shannon succinctly puts it, they are all "running from something. Vaginoplasty. Aging. The future" (239). Brandy Alexander is trying to avoid her final sex reassignment surgery, Manus is trying to escape the passing of time and the loss of his sexual allure, and Shannon does not want to take hold of her life and confront her future with a disfigured face. The journey is a break for all of them, an eternal present in which they do not need to cope with their fears.

In a way, they have been impregnated by Brandy Alexander's life philosophy. She firmly believes that they are trapped by culture and that there is no way out; even wanting to get out of the system reinforces the trap since people are trained to want everything they want. Her philosophy is to do what one is trained *not* to want, what scares you the most. When Brandy is bleeding to death after Evie shoots her, she confesses to Shannon that she is actually her brother Shane and that she caused the hairspray accident that badly damaged her face because she did not want to be a normal, average child. However, her greatest mistake is that, even though she is only one operation away from her final sex reassignment surgery, she has never wanted to become a woman in the first place. It was only the biggest mistake she could imagine to break with the social trap and its cultural expectations: "Don't you see? Because we're so trained to do life the right way. *To not make mistakes* [. . .] I figure, the bigger the mistake looks, the better chance I'll have to break out and live a real life" (258).

Shannon seems to share this same philosophy since she also confesses that she shot herself in the face on purpose because she also wanted to break with the superficiality of her life as a fashion model. She had become a product, a consumer object that performed and faked her feelings for an audience. Since she was addicted to beauty and attention, the biggest mistake she could make was to do something she was trained not to want to do: to destroy her beauty, "[t]o be saved by chaos. To see if I could cope, I wanted to force myself to grow again. To explode my comfort zone" (286). Shannon and Brandy's confessions only come at the end after the shooting episode, which had been previously arranged by Evie and Brandy, and that goes wrong. Only in the face of death and once their journey has come to an end are Brandy and Shannon capable of explaining and coming to terms with what they have done with their lives. They put their actions in the perspective of time and under the scrutiny of social norms since their utopian space of freedom has finished.

The call to adventure and the trials on the road

Even though the road is a space of subversion and freedom, it is also full of trials that travellers need to overcome. Ronald Primeau has underlined the similarities between Joseph Campbell's concept of the monomyth (1968) and the literature of the American highway. Both share the pattern of a hero that sets out on a quest, goes through a series of trials and adventures, and returns home wiser and ready to share his new knowledge, since the experience on the road also brings about a rebirth of the protagonist. As Palahniuk's novel is narrated by a cynical and detached narrator, the innocence of the heroic figure of the monomyth disappears. Shannon takes to the road because she has nowhere to go and nothing to lose. She does not want to acquire any new knowledge and she does not want to be reborn and reenter society, as this is precisely what she is escaping from.

However, she goes through a series of trials that are mainly conversations with Brandy in which Shannon has to face her emotional detachment, abandon her narcissism, and disclose her inner feelings. When they start their journey, Shannon is not with Brandy for love: "I'm with Brandy right now because I can't imagine getting away with this without Brandy's help. Because, right now, I need her. Not that I really love her. Him. Shane" (197). Besides, her true admiration for Brandy's beauty does not come from any generosity on her part but from recognizing in Brandy's face the way she looked before the accident: "What I love is myself" (197). As Collado-Rodríguez puts it following Emmanuel Levinas, there is an evolution from a "pessimist Lacanian contemplation of the other" to "a return to the other as a Face that summons the subject to react in an ethical way" (201). The road of trials will help Shannon to overcome her narcissism and find the love that she has been trying to hide.

In the road story Primeau also identifies the "call to adventure on the open road, its initiation rites, threshold crossings, conflict, return, and resurrection" as well as "the pattern of flight, trials, and reentry" (7). The call to adventure for Shannon, Brandy, and Manus emerges from the latter's seeming attempt to kill Shannon in Evie's house. However, their reasons to join the journey are more complex. Shannon's decision to go on the road also arises from her dissatisfaction and need to come to terms with her new disfigured face after her "accident." She needs to redefine herself and find out who she really is and her journey with self-confident Brandy Alexander offers her such a chance. Her ulterior motive is that she wants to kill her brother Brandy/Shane for having robbed her of her parents' attention ever since someone told them that Shane had died of AIDS. Brandy's apparent reason to go on the journey is to find her sister but what she really wants is to recover her love since, as she confesses at the end, she knew Shannon's real identity from the very beginning. Manus is blackmailed into joining them at first since Shannon is still emotionally attached to him but then he is willing to travel with them. Manus used to be an undercover vice detective looking for gay men on the prowl for sexual contact. After years of denial and pretence, the journey also gives him his chance to accept his real sexual orientation as he has sex with a man in Seattle and later on with Allen, Evie's bridegroom, the very day of their wedding.

The initiation rite of the journey takes place in Santa Barbara, where Manus teaches Brandy and Shannon how to steal prescription painkillers and expensive make-up from houses open for sale and how to sell them back in discos and clubs, which turns into a routine for them: "Stealing drugs, selling drugs, buying clothes, renting luxury cars, taking clothes back, ordering blender drinks, this isn't what I'd call Real Life, not by a long shot" (257). They are nomads outside the system and function like terrorists "undermining the familiar course of capital," which results in "despotism, violence and subversion, for culture cannot allow resistance to boundaries and property" (Paes de Barros, *Fast Cars* 8–9). As is usually the case in blank fiction, this is an ambiguous act of subversion since they are against the system but also complicit with it: they rob the rich, those who have full access to consumer culture, so that they can also consume carelessly and continue travelling.

There are several threshold crossings along their journey, some physical and some metaphorical. All these crossings are based on the characters' capacity to change their identities. For example, when they cross the American–Canadian border Brandy first pretends she is the wife of Reverend Scooter Alexander travelling with her mute son-in-law Seth Thomas and her daughter Bubba-Joan. She covers her cleavage with a scarf, wears simple gold earrings and a chain with a golden cross. When this identity proves useless with the border guard she simply changes the strategy: "Don't anybody panic [. . .] I can get us back into the States [. . .] but I'm going to need a condom and a breath mint" (65). It is their capacity to adapt to new situations and change their identities accordingly that permits them to advance in their journey. In a more metaphorical sense, it is also the way they get rid of each layer of secrecy and cynicism that they wore at the beginning of their journey that allows them to see themselves beyond preconceptions and finally reconcile and declare their love. As Shannon puts it in one of the final scenes in Evie's house: "We travelled all over the West and grew up together again" (281).

Each episode of the journey brings them closer together; each event contributes to changing their attitudes. In Seattle they visit the observation deck at the top of the Space Needle, built for the 1962 Seattle World's Fair, which represents the idea of the future that never was. The group members write down their fears on postcards of the future and throw them off the top of the Needle. Shannon's fear is that she will never be loved and when she reads it back she confronts her fear and realizes that all she wants is to be loved: "Oh, love me, love me, love me, love me, love me, love me, love me, love me. I'll be anybody you want me to be" (105). Each conversation contributes to the rethinking of Shannon's original plan to kill Shane/Brandy. There is one significant scene (fragmented in Chapters 18, 22, and 26) that takes place in the bathroom of a house they are robbing in Vancouver. Shannon tries to overdose Brandy by feeding her valium while Brandy tells Shannon how her birth family threw her out when they found out that she had gonorrhoea and how the Rhea sisters, three drag queens, have paid for the operations to turn

Shane into Brandy, operations she never wanted in the first place. Shannon also discovers that Brandy has kept her postcard of the future with her fears. This discovery leads to her determination to find a new story about who she really is.

A conversation between Brandy and Shannon in a secondhand store in Idaho also reveals how they share similar memories of their childhood: how their father used to feed the pigs with expired desserts before selling them, how he would stovepipe potatoes, how they were woken up in the middle of the night to go to a train wreck and take as many products as possible. These memories are important because Shannon starts to see that things did not happen only to her, that she can see her life reflected in her brother's and that she can understand what Brandy has gone through. The same episodes are told from Shannon's and Brandy's perspective, sometimes even complementing each other, especially when Shannon discovers that Brandy was abused by the detective who investigated the hairspray accident and that the detective is actually Manus. The way the events are narrated intensifies the pain of their retelling. As Brandy opens her heart in the secondhand store she tries on an evening dress that looks beautiful on the outside but that has been designed not to last long: "The tension, the push and pull of satin and crepe de Chine trying to control the wire and boning inside, the battle of fabric against metal, this tension will shred them. As the outsides age, the fabric, the part you can see, as it gets weak, the insides start to poke and tear their way out" (246). Brandy's confession is constantly interrupted by descriptions of her dress coming apart: "the silk opening at every seam, the tulle busting out [. . .] In a hundred torn holes, bare skin shows through" (251–2). The dress that looked so beautiful from the outside is breaking in the same way that Brandy, who seems so self-confident, is also torn by her emotions.

A blank female road story of fluid identity

The road has traditionally been occupied by white male travellers but in this novel the journey is taken by the "Queen Supreme" one surgery away from being fully female, a former fashion female model without a lower jaw after a drive-by shooting, and a closeted bisexual who is being fed female hormone pills without his knowledge. Paes de Barros has noticed how women in road stories have traditionally played the role of objects rather than subjects (*Fast Cars* 4). As a fashion model Shannon has always felt like an object and curiously enough undertaking this journey is her attempt to finally become a subject. She also has to overcome a series of obstacles and prejudices since, as Susan L. Roberson has pointed out, women have historically been associated with fixity and home, rather than mobility and the road (217). Shannon is not a very active subject during the journey since, together with Manus, she just follows Brandy Alexander around; however, the journey will give her the opportunity to understand her past and come to terms with her present. She will finally find an identity she can stick to.

As Judith Hamera and Alfred Bendixen point out, the construction of American identity is inextricably linked to the journey and was the basis for the politics of Manifest Destiny and the construction of America as a nation of immigrants (1). Obviously, as society changes the genre has also evolved but the role of the journey in the formation of identity (national or personal) has not changed. As Paes de Barros claims:

> [T]his modern road is nearly always, in some way, about the self, and about the way that the self shifts, changes, and finds autonomy. If such autonomy proves difficult in the contemporary world, the road accommodates the need for self. The road—as defined in travel narratives—continuously allows for the re-emergence of the transcendent self. In that sense, it is indeed the site of miracles. ("Driving that Highway" 242)

In this sense, the notion of identity becomes especially important in the book since Brandy Alexander tells Shannon in the speech therapist's office to write down her past so that it becomes just a story that can be thrown in the trashcan. Shannon finally writes down what has happened to her and cries for the first time. No distancing mechanism is used here and there are no flashes prompting an expected reaction. Brandy asks Shannon to stop writing about her past or present and to focus on her future. Her philosophy is not about acting out Shannon's trauma to work through it, hers is a simple strategy of resilience in which past and present are left behind. The journey provides the perfect space for it.

The fixed signification, static domesticity, and identity of
Shannon's past life are undermined by the motion of the aimless
journey that stands outside time: there is only a trauma-free space
that does not fit conventional notions of linear time. This space has
specially been used by women narrators; Paes de Barros mentions
the work of Kate Braverman, Joan Didion, and Marilynne Robinson
and how "the road emerges as both the space where one mourns
loss and the site simultaneously that marks the absence—the
unreality—of any loss at all" (*Fast Cars* 15). The nomad on the road
"rejects cultural nostalgia, easy sentimentality and the illusions and
clichés offered by mainstream society" (16). On the road Shannon
learns to reject the nostalgia for her past as a fashion model, her
perfect face, her boyfriend, her consumer-culture heaven. The past
disappears as she subverts the status quo by rejecting solid forms of
identity and opening herself to change and chaos.

The attitude of Brandy Alexander and Shannon can be better
understood in the context of "liquid modernity" first introduced by
Zygmunt Bauman in 2000. The concept is based on the metaphors
of "fluidity" and "liquidity" used to describe the present phase of
history. The permanent feature of liquid modernity, as opposed to
the previous phase of "heavy modernity," is the "melting of solids":
durability, social class, fixed positions, long lasting structures, even
sexual orientation are undermined. Liquids cannot keep shape for
long, can change at any time and are not easily stopped. Thus, the art
of liquid life is defined as "acceptance of disorientation, immunity
to vertigo and adaptation to a state of dizziness, tolerance for an
absence of itinerary and direction, and for an indefinite duration
of travel" (*Liquid Life* 4). In this world, it is people like Brandy
Alexander who survive, those who can adapt to new situations,
and who, in the face of trauma, do not halt but offer resilience as
an answer. Brandy brings her concept of liquid life to the road and
provides liquid identities for both Shannon and Manus. Shannon's
first identity is Daisy St. Patience, the rightful heiress to the House of
St. Patience, an international fashion house. On the road Shannon
will also become Miss Kay MacIsaac in Vancouver, Bubba-Joan at
the Canadian border, Miss Arden Scotia in Seattle. At the beginning
of the journey what she really wants is a "solid identity": "What I
wanted looked more and more like what I'd always been trained
to want. What everybody wants. Give me attention. Flash. Give me
beauty. Flash. Give me peace and happiness, a loving relationship,

and a perfect home" (220). She wants a niche in society with clearly defined social rules, conformity, established expectations, a boyfriend, and a family. Brandy and their journey provide exactly the opposite, a changing identity as a form of resilience in a time of liquid life.

The list of identities that Brandy provides Manus with is also never-ending: Seth Thomas, Lance Corporal, Chase Manhattan, Dow Corning, Herald Tribune, Morris Code, Denver Omelet, Eberhard Faber, Hewlett Packard, Harper Collins, Addison Wesley, Nash Rambler, Alfa Romeo, and Ellis Island. The list mostly includes names of multinational corporations, brand names, and popular culture references. Characters in blank fiction usually lack individuality in a homogenized society because, as Elizabeth Young underlines "even the most extreme attempts at individuality are doomed because personality itself has become a commodity [. . .] 'character' comes to us in wraiths, projections, pastiche, mutating entities, archetypes, comic cut-outs and intertextual refugees from history, film, fiction and myth" (20). When Brandy constructs their new identities, she borrows them from popular and consumer culture since there is nothing original anymore. Both Shannon and Seth interiorize this ideology as Seth writes, "*You have to keep recycling yourself*" and Shannon, "*Nothing in me is original. I am the combined effort of everybody I've ever known*" (104). Brandy Alexander is also the result of the combined effort and money of the Rhea Sisters, who have paid for all the operations and whose wealth comes from the creation of a doll named Katty Kathy, which has impossible measurements for a woman and is sold naked just for a dollar. Ironically, her clothes and accessories cost a fortune, in a clear authorial comment on how little people are valued and how much their external appearance is appreciated instead.

For Katie Mills, in road stories of the postwar and postmodern periods there is a different approach to the concept of identity since travellers are concerned with *constructing* a sense of self: "The genre encourages us to imagine new lives, teaching us to rewrite prohibitions into narratives of possibility" (19). She contends that road narratives explore the conflicts of modern identity—race, gender, class, sexual orientation, and conformity—and transform passive characters into active agents. According to Mills, identity politics became central in the 1990s and led to the revitalization of the road genre mainly in film, which is the focus of her analysis, but also in literature. Those rejected by strict social norms take to the road to find the space needed to develop new lives and release themselves from fixed identities. Chuck Palahniuk has also questioned in interviews the obsession with fixed identities: "People are so desperate for a complete identity, an instant identity, they grab one off the shelf. Black. Gay. Feminist. Home-owner. All these labeled lifestyles are easy to embrace. Nice off-the-rack identities. Like IKEA furniture. But by accepting them, don't we limit our own capacity for creating a more personal, powerful identity?" (In Switzer 2001). The journey provides physical movement through space, but also inner psychological travel in terms of identity and self-discovery. The journey leads to Shannon's final acceptance of liquid life since this type of life "feeds on the self's dissatisfaction with *itself*" (*Liquid Life* 11).

Conclusion

As we can read in Palahniuk's *Fight Club,* "Only after disaster can we be resurrected. 'It's only after you've lost everything', Tyler says, 'that you're free to do anything'" (70). The final part of the journey is the return or rebirth of the hero and the reentry into society with some newly acquired knowledge or power. Manus has found his real sexual identity and Brandy her independence from the Rhea sisters, whom she does not call when she is back in Portland because "the only vagina worth having is the kind you buy yourself" (265). Shannon has also gained her independence and is ready to part with Brandy and to write her own story. The half a million dollars that she has blackmailed from Evie gives her the possibility of finally shedding her old identity and putting on a new one. It is her chance to leave solid identity and its traps for a liquid, fluid sense of self. The act of giving her brother Shane/Brandy what is left of herself and her solid past is apparently the ultimate act of love and the end of her narcissism. The detached cynicism of Shannon as narrator disappears and only her straightforward declaration of love remains.

In spite of this seemingly happy ending, *Invisible Monsters* is an ambiguous blank fiction novel until the very end, especially if we focus on Brandy Alexander and her future. The character that has most passionately defended liquid life finally receives a solid identity she can fit into seamlessly. Through plastic surgery, expensive clothes, perfume and make-up she has equated beauty with success, embracing the logic of consumer society and turning his/her own body into an example of such logic. She has been trying to become precisely what her sister was so desperate to escape from, to the point that she shot herself in the face. The identity that Shannon rejected is the identity she gives to Shane, which for Andrew Slade is an act of love that "overcomes alienation and hopelessness" (71), whereas Sherry R. Truffin sees it as "simultaneously a gesture of love and an act of profound cruelty" (83). It is ironic that while Shannon confesses her love for her unconscious brother, the Rhea Sisters apply to Brandy's pale face moisturizer and concealer, eyebrow pencil, eyeliner, base, lid and contour colour, lash curler, mascara, lip liner, and lip gloss until Brandy Alexander finally emerges: a literal resurrection of sorts only achieved by hiding Brandy's real face while Shannon takes off her veil in a literal and metaphorical way.

While Shannon embraces liquid identity and escapes her sense of social entrapment, Shane enters a solid life that does not belong to him. Shannon frees her body and identity so that she can start anew, whereas Shane/Brandy seems destined to make the same mistakes as she turns her new body into the mark of success on which to depend. This novel is both a celebration of artificiality and shallowness as a means to find a place in society, as Shane does, and a condemnation of such a life and the need to overcome the obsession with appearances, the way Shannon does. As the case is with most blank fiction novels, Shane and Shannon represent two faces of the same coin. In *Invisible Monsters* the distance between self-destruction and unconditional love can be easily bridged by tossing the coin.

PART III

Choke

Introduction

Although it did not attract as much critical attention as any of the two books previously discussed in this volume, *Choke* was a best seller, also adapted as a film by Clark Gregg seven years after the novel's publication in 2001, only a few months before the tragic events of 9/11. In a sense, as David Cowart points out in his contribution, *Choke* was also a prophetic anticipation of or sign of a desire for ethical change. This novel features many topics already present in both *Fight Club* and *Invisible Monsters*: a psychologically unstable narrator who shows his apparent expertise in a determinate field of knowledge (medicine in this case); the disturbing results of a fatherless infancy; the notion that the human body is constantly exposed to disease and corruption; life as a constant traumatic experience, or the pervasive awareness of living in a reality that is simulated. All these and other subjects reappear in *Choke* but this time to focus on a permanent source of human restlessness: our addictions.

Religion has traditionally considered addiction to certain things or practices as something evil and sinful, which should be avoided. Dogma has been dictated to control the addictions of the faithful and religious preaching has become a powerful instrument to redirect them. As a guarantor of immortality, religion promises the ultimate recuperation of the lost Lacanian phallus, an omnipotent power for the one who, by having refrained from her or his addictions, has reached salvation. While in Eastern religions the control of passions is understood as the path to a virtuous life, in traditional Christian dogma the luring sins of the world, the devil, and the flesh are the three archenemies that the believer has to fight against and reject permanently in order to reach salvation and, therefore, Lacanian completeness. Assaulted by social dogmas, by his own traumatic experiences, and by his permanent need to satisfy his addictions, Victor Mancini, the narrator and protagonist of *Choke*, is exposed to the addictive sins of the world, recognizes the Oedipal devil in himself, and fights an inauthentic combat against the evils of the flesh. His mental struggle is soothed, as prescribed by Trauma Studies, by fighting against his repetitious symptoms by means of fabricating the "coherent" narrative of his life and addictions, the story in *Choke*. Freudian, post-Freudian, and narrative analyses are developed in this third part of the volume to help readers in making more sense of Victor Mancini's strange story, of his addictions and of the way he sees himself in the mirror of the world. The three chapters that follow frequently center their views on the same or similar passages and themes of the novel, but they offer different and complementary views on the life of a deconstructed American young man at the turn of the millennium.

Jesse Kavadlo's "Chuck Palahniuk's Edible Complex" starts with a reflection on the multiple meanings the term "choke" may evoke, to advance from there to recognition of the links existing in the novel between mores and storytelling, and between storytelling and the definition of the storyteller's identity. Choking, Kavadlo writes, "reveals the liminal state Victor occupies in between life and death when he chokes," but it also helps the narrator and protagonist to construct a new identity. The book, in this interpretation, reveals as one of its main concerns the power that narrative discourse has to shape and determine our lives: the addict is defined by his own story. In the case of Victor—ironically a name that means "winner," as Kavadlo also points out—his narrative is strongly motivated by Palahniuk's alteration of the protagonist's Oedipus complex. Such departure from the Freudian psychological notion has called the attention of the three critics in this part of the volume, but each one of them adds different nuances to the interpretation of the authorial conceit. "In the modern Oedipal story," Palahniuk writes in *Choke*, "it's the mother who kills the father and then takes the son" (15–16). This inversion of the classic myth offers Kavadlo a significant bridge to analyze Victor's reaction to the story that he might be Jesus Christ—and therefore his own Father—and the style in which the book is written, with its combination of narrative deferral and character stasis.

The analysis of other reiterative themes in Victor's story—namely eating and starvation, the use of "you," and the binary constituted by blockage and release—are given complementary meanings in the chapter written by Nieves Pascual. Additionally, Kavadlo's emphasis on the almost metafictional quality of the novel and the importance storytelling has in the construction and transformation of the protagonist's identity are complemented by the intertextual traces and literary analysis offered by David Cowart in the second chapter of this part, "Anger, Anguish, and Art: *Choke*." Cowart starts his contribution by observing the similarities the story and the process of narration in *Choke* share with some influential novels that go back 50 years: Ken Kesey's *One Flew Over the Cuckoo's Nest*, Joseph Heller's *Catch-22*, and especially J. D. Salinger's *The Catcher in the Rye*, among others, offer striking similarities that might be pointing at the necessity of a new social change, perhaps at "a truly 'post' postmodernism." Palahniuk's young readers' expectations of authenticity lead Cowart to point out the narrator's story as a fraud which does to the reader what Victor does to his fellow diners when he pretends to be choking to death. Always attentive to literary echoes, he also revises the notion of "literature of alienation" to interpret the symbolic role of simulated Dunsboro, the narrative use of tense, and the writer's *ars poetica*. The invention of art by the Greeks is mentioned by Victor's mother at the beginning of the story, in this way becoming, in Cowart's understanding, "one of the book's important self-referential motifs," which allows the critic to revise the myth of Philomela and provide readers of the volume with a new interpretive angle about the peculiar Oedipus complex that generates in Victor the belief that he is Jesus Christ. Echoing the importance that Kavadlo gives to the binary blockage/release, Cowart concludes by pointing out that the novel seems to signal a return to the rhetoric of sincerity that anticipates the nation's collective mores after 9/11.

Finally, Nieves Pascual's "Addiction in *Choke*" complements but also departs from the previous analyses of the novel by stressing the importance of a Freudian and post-Freudian reading of Victor Mancini's character. If text and sex are important features in the book, and addiction and blockage are two of its basic defining motifs, Pascual also deals with all of them to read *Choke* as a story that hides male–male sodomy as the arch-addiction. The roles that narcissism, masturbation and food play in Victor's story are analyzed to interpret his obsession with the series of pictures showing a dumpy man dressed as Tarzan, with a monkey "trained to poke what looked like roasted chestnuts up the guy's ass" (*Choke* 36). The peculiar version of the Oedipus complex related in the story, also analyzed by Kavadlo and Cowart, is associated in this third contribution with food pornography and auto-erotic asphyxia to unveil new nuances in relation to Victor as the Second Coming of Jesus Christ. Masculinity and Baudrillard's theories are also linked by Pascual in her interpretation of the simulated reality of Dunsboro to read the novel as "the accomplishments of servile eunuchs elevated to the category of heroes." Fragmentation and the stylistic disposition of the text finally take Pascual to reach her provocative conclusions about a narrative that incisively hides so many meanings about the power of textual representation, sex, identity, literature, and ethics. In sum, an archetypal example of Palahniuk's controversial fiction.

7

Chuck Palahniuk's Edible Complex

Jesse Kavadlo

"Choke": a single word, a simple reflex. Yet immediately, Chuck Palahniuk's semi-onomatopoeic title, a noun and a verb, foregrounds the novel's self-consuming themes: eating, but also the failure to eat. "Choke" means failure itself, but particularly failure at something that should have been easy. And of course, since this is a novel by Chuck Palahniuk, "choke" puns on sex and drugs. "Choke" suggests consumption but also obstruction, and potentially death. It resembles Palahniuk's own first name, sounds like "joke" and is synonymous with "gag," but it also suggests the surge of emotion ("choke up") that results, paradoxically, in silence. "Choke" suggests an oral fixation, in keeping with narrator Victor Mancini's entwined obsessions with food and sex—the culture's "continual links between sexual temptation and gluttony" (Paterson 99)—but also desire's suppression. Even more, "choke" evokes speech and, at the same time, blockage, and speechlessness. "Choke" brings the reader to the mouth, the literal and symbolic locus of eating, breathing, and speaking, but also to the throat, where these actions cease, sometimes before they even begin.

Choke, Chuck Palahniuk's fourth novel, traffics in the same playful contradictions and ambiguities as its title. The deceptively simple novel, like the word, is self-consuming, at once presents an action and its simultaneous negation: in *Choke*'s case, the simultaneous depiction and deconstruction of Palahniuk's recurring concerns, sinning and storytelling. *Choke* is neither an unselfconscious, lurid sex comedy—Jennifer Reese's complaint in *The New York Times* that "Palahniuk revels in the gross"— nor a failed work of social satire, suggested by film critic Andrew O'Hehir and again, Reese, who writes that "This book is dark, but it's not deep" (2001). Rather, I read *Choke* as a self-reflexive mediation on the ontological and narrative connections between our mores and our stories, and our stories and ourselves. Yes, the novel's prurience knows no bounds, with descriptions ranging from rape fantasies to sex toys, but this seeming mosaic of immorality still does not quite choke off its sentimental center: the story of a struggling and ambivalent son attempting to afford care for his deservedly estranged mother, who is suffering from Alzheimer's disease. The Library of Congress's primary designation for the novel is "Alzheimer's disease—Patients—Fiction." But in the end, *Choke* is about more than Alzheimer's, although the illness is a metaphor—it is about the ways in which Alzheimer's, like choking, creates a suspended, static, and stuck state. And the novel suggests that narrative itself has the power to release—in every sense of the word—the narrator's blocked body and psyche.

Story and simulation

Choke is the story of Victor Mancini, a medical school dropout and sex addict who, we discover, supports his mother's expensive nursing home facilities by working as a historical reenactor and, when the job does not pay enough, choking in restaurants and allowing himself to be saved by fellow diners. As Victor explains, "Somebody saves your life, and they'll love you forever . . . It's as if now you're their child. For the rest of their lives, these people will write me. Send me cards on the anniversary. Birthday cards. It's depressing how many people get this same idea. They call you on the phone. To find out if you're feeling okay. To see if you maybe need cheering up. Or cash" (49). Yet the choking is about more than Victor's unconscious quest for symbolic surrogate parents— being somebody's "child" and receiving "birthday cards"—or even more than the crude scam for money. "By choking," Victor continues, "you become a legend about themselves that these people [who save him] will repeat until they die. They'll think they gave you life . . . So be the aggressive victim, the big loser. A professional failure" (50–1). Choking, then, reveals the liminal state Victor occupies in between life and death when he chokes, and his liminality extends as well to his acting as both saved and savior, the oxymoronic "aggressive victim," "big loser," and "professional failure." But it also helps Victor, and his would-be saviors, to create a necessary fiction about their heroism, a new identity, and a better story—and, by extension, the novel performs these same actions for the reader.

Victor's name consumes itself as well: he becomes a kind of victor, the perpetrator of the scam, but also its victim, since he suffers. In that sense, he maintains the duality of *Fight Club*'s narrator, and indeed at first the books have much in common. Yet compared with *Fight Club*, *Choke* has garnered little academic attention. Perhaps an offhand aside, in the pseudonymous "Professor X's" discussion of grading student essays in *In the Basement of the Ivory Tower*, best summarizes the general response: "I'd put a Chuck Palahniuk novel such as *Choke* at about a B, being organized but not sophisticated" (133). More than the novels that preceded it—*Fight Club*, *Survivor*, and *Invisible Monsters*—*Choke* is a farce, the word itself suggestive of both situation comedy and, appropriately, stuffing food. Yet *Choke*'s sense of play, comic form, and seeming lack of sophistication mask its intentions, which match those of the previous works.

Certainly at first *Choke* seems overly indebted to *Fight Club*, exploring postmodern confusion between simulation and reality— *Fight Club*'s "a copy of a copy of a copy" (97) becomes *Choke*'s Colonial Dunsboro, a Colonial Williamsburg-style theme park where, for Victor, "My job is I'm supposed to be some Irish indentured servant. For six dollars an hour, it's incredibly realistic" (30). As Alex Blazer puts it, "Victor is forced into a simulated world, a living history museum, with no exit to the real" (147). The sentiment applies equally to Victor's mother's nursing home—and, until the end, to the novel itself, as we will see. *Choke*'s title and chief metaphor also recall the first two rules of *Fight Club*, "You do not talk about fight club," the self-consuming language taboo where speaking the rule also breaks the rule, then breaks it again. And in order for the narrative to progress, as in *Fight Club*, the rule, like the silence, must be broken, the verbal and oral obstructions cleared.

Yet interestingly, *Choke* does not dwell on what could easily have followed *Fight Club*'s satire of consumerism. Asked whether "the gluttonous aspect of consumer culture" as well as "gagging" suggests an ambivalent "response to consumer culture," Chuck Palahniuk replied that "Very little of my work is about consumer culture. . . . I prefer the idea of 'choking' as failing despite your best efforts" (Kavanagh 189). And Victor does fail, choking his addiction and deferred recovery as much as he elects to choke in restaurants. As Eduardo Mendieta writes, *Choke*, like *Fight Club*, examines:

> [H]ow dependency itself becomes an addiction, or rather how in the midst of a culture that flourishes and thrives by promoting and instigating addiction, the very means by which individuals seek to uncouple themselves from these imposed and acquired dependences becomes a major part of their lives. (401)

Thus *Fight Club*'s narrator becomes addicted to 12-step programs themselves; *Choke*'s Victor trawls sex addiction groups not for healing but for hookups: "For me, it's a terrific how-to seminar. . . . When they tell their stories, these addict people are frigging brilliant. Plus there's the jail girls out for their three hours of sex addict talk therapy. . . . It's a Cinderella story, only at midnight she turns back into a fugitive" (16–17). Even here, the joke gives way to Palahniuk's serious intention: the power of narrative to shape and determine our lives, our perceptions of ourselves, and how we treat others. The addict, like a fictional character, is inextricable from, and defined by, his or her story.

Playing God

As the novel continues, the farce goes further: Victor spends more time visiting his mother, Ida, at her care facility, St Anthony's. There he meets Dr Paige Marshall. Dr Marshall has a theoretical cure for Ida's Alzheimer's disease involving genetically compatible embryonic material; to produce it, however, Paige needs Victor to have sex with her. As if this were not enough, later Paige claims to have translated Ida's journals from Italian and discovered that she, Ida, in a parallel madcap conception scheme decades earlier, used genes from the foreskin of Jesus Christ to conceive Victor, making him the son of Christ, or possibly Christ himself. As Paige explains, "Well, if you believe in the Holy Trinity, you're your own father," and that Ida's belief in her son's divinity is "a fairly common delusion among mothers . . . She truly believes you're the second coming of Christ" (146). More joking, of course—but the humor and even verbal repetition ("you're your") plays upon theological and narrative tautology: Victor is not explained as the son or descendent of God, but rather in self-negating, self-consuming terms, again embodying the paradox and liminality of choking itself.

Somehow, perhaps because Paige frames her pregnancy ploy in religious terms, asking Victor to meet her for sex in the chapel, describing "how if we can't explain something we'll just deny it" (89), and telling Victor, in a typically profane pun, "I need you to put your faith in me" (91), Victor at first attempts to acquiesce. Or perhaps it is Palahniuk's brawny prose, which is so consistently over the top that the plan's outrageous technicalities seem trivial. Despite, then, being a former medical student, Victor accepts these ruses as plausible, yet somehow, if the novel succeeds at all, so may the reader, at least temporarily. These details do not require any more suspension of disbelief than the notion that people who administer the Heimlich maneuver would send the choking victim checks for the rest of his life. And indeed, the dual deceptions, since by the end both Victor and Paige are exposed, are narratively and epistemologically intertwined. On the one hand, Paige tries to conceal her story, changing herself from mental patient, as she turns out to be, to a doctor. On the other hand, Victor wants to choke down his story; in his own mind, he is not a medical student but an incorrigible addict. The novel suggests that the stories we tell have redemptive power, but, as Victor understands at the very end, also warns against "letting the world tell us who we are" (292). The line between our stories and our selves becomes another fragile, liminal, and suspended state, akin to suspension of disbelief itself. As we will see, Victor understands by the end that he is not his own father, and he is not God, but rather that he is his own author.

Victor is unwilling to consummate the relationship with Paige and thereby, he believes, rescue his mother. Instead, as Paige suggests, "You don't want her to die . . . and you don't want her to recover" (119), another choking, suspended state, here literally, since Victor keeps Ida at the very brink of conscious awareness but neither fully lucid nor lifeless. But if Victor is ambivalent about saving his mother, he inadvertently, but not unhappily, has already taken on savior status with Ida's fellow St. Anthony's residents. And like the self-negation of choking, Victor's savior complex threatens to consume itself, somehow both diminishing and growing as the novel progresses. First, one patient, Eva, mistakes Victor for the brother who abused her as a child, and Victor thinks, "The trouble is, anywhere else at St. Anthony's it's the same deal. Another old skeleton thinks I borrowed five hundred dollars from her. Another baggy old woman calls me the devil. . . . It's tough not to come here and soak up the blame for every crime in history. . . . The correct way to handle a case like Eva is to redirect her attention. Distract her by mentioning lunch or the weather or how nice her hair looks . . ." (60–1). But Victor instead accepts the blame ("Screw it," he thinks [61]) and admits the transgression—and Eva forgives him. In relieving the older people's emotional suffering by taking on the sins of others, Victor cuts a clear, if ironic, Christ–figure: "If Jesus could die for my sins," he thinks, "I suppose I can soak up a few for other people. We all get our chance to play scapegoat. Take the blame." And then, he introduces a phrase that will recur throughout the novel: "The martyrdom of Saint Me" (61).

The care facility is named after St. Anthony, the patron saint of lost things, yet it is Victor who continues to find that which its patrons have lost, even as he himself remains lost. And so each character— Victor; Ida; Denny, his friend, fellow sex-addict, and Colonial Dunsboro coworker; Nico and Victor's other sex-addicted partners; and the St. Anthony's patients—whether through historical, sexual, or psychological reenactment, as Victor observes, "is trapped in their past" (59). Not surprisingly, after finishing his absolution with Eva, Victor remembers that "I have to be back at work in the eighteenth century by one o'clock" (62), where, as usual, Denny is more than just symbolically stuck: "Denny bent over in the middle of the town square, getting locked in the stocks again" (26), since "any violation of character"—referring to historical reenactment—"and you will be punished . . . you can spend two hours in the stocks" (30). They are all choking, neither able to move forward nor backward (especially Denny), victims of self-administered blockages like the food Victor can neither swallow nor expel.

Victor remains trapped in his narrative past as well. While the most easily summarized aspects of the book—as well as most of the movie adaptation—occur in the narrative present, *Choke* alternates between these farcical, quasi-romantic episodes and Victor's traumatic memories of life on the run with his fugitive mother. The novel begins in the past, eschewing the first person for self-reflexive *diegesis*. The opening sentence, "If you're going to read this, don't bother" (1), instead directly addresses the implied readership not to become a reader; if you do not talk about fight club, you do not read *Choke* when you read *Choke*. Indeed, the whole first page is a paradoxical entreaty to stop reading, even as the delay ironically and rhetorically builds suspense and interest. At first, the book seems to be in the second person, yet unlike Jay McInerney's *Bright Lights, Big City* (1984), the "you" really does seem to refer to the reader, not the main character himself, and "a stupid story about a stupid boy. A stupid true life story about nobody you'd ever want to meet," along with his mother, "The Mommy" (2). It quickly becomes clear, though, that "the boy" is the illeism of a first-person narrator. The effect, like the opening sentence, is at once inviting and distancing, a way for the reader to get to know the character—his self-consciousness, his conflicts with his mother, the self-deprecation underlying the self-deceptive bravado we soon see, and his own version of the story that he nevertheless says he will not tell—all in the guise of not knowing him. The chapter ends in admonition:

> So if you think this is going to save you. . .
>
> If you think anything is going to save you . . .
>
> Please consider this your final warning. (8, author's ellipses)

It is both the opening gambit to and renunciation of narrative, the self-negating warning as de facto invitation to continue. When the reader begins the novel proper, with a first person "I" now clearly referring to narrator Victor in Chapter 2—"It's dark and starting to rain when I get to the church, and Nico's waiting for somebody to unlock the side door, hugging herself in the cold" (9), which soon leads to the first of many sexual encounters and descriptions—the novel has already juxtaposed the past with the present, the self-loathing beneath the playful, occasionally preposterous story and banter. Victor, not the reader, is the one who does not believe that his story can save him. And at this point, despite Palahniuk's own

notion of "failing despite your best efforts," Victor is not trying to
be saved at all.

Choke on words

When Victor and Nico begin having sex in the church, foreshadowing
the later meeting with Paige, Nico implies that Victor must already
be married. Victor narrates the following thought:

> The truth is, every son raised by a single mom is pretty much
> born married. I don't know, but until your mom dies it seems
> like all the other women in your life can never be more than just
> your mistress.
>
> In the modern Oedipal story, it's the mother who kills the father
> and then takes the son.
>
> And it's not as if you can divorce your mother.
>
> Or kill her. (15–16)

And so Palahniuk rewrites the Oedipal story; with the modern father
preemptively absent, the mother consumes, not consummates, the
relationship with the son. Victor blames his mother for his stasis—
his failure, his choking. But in another sense, he blames a story—the
rewritten Oedipal story—for his being stuck in self-help recovery at
his fourth step, which he explains, tellingly, right after the passage
quoted above, as "My moral inventory notebook. The complete and
relentless history of my addiction" (16). Like Eva, like Ida, and like
the reenactors of Colonial Dunsboro, Victor is trapped in history,
and in his story—a paradoxical problem for a fictional character.
Despite the seeming simplicity and humor, *Choke* borders on the
metafictional, its story increasingly concerned with Victor's attempt
to defer, and then escape from, the Aristotelian constraints of plot
and character.

Stylistically, *Choke* maintains its combination of narrative
deferral and character stasis, in keeping with the thematic and
metaphorical explorations of choking, Alzheimer's disease, historical
reenactment, and Victor's fourth step. Even more than previous
novels, *Choke* employs deliberate repetition—Victor's lament that
he has abandoned his fourth step is reiterated ten times (8, 16, 34,

62, 116, 156, 180, 215, 243, and 273), not including the detail that when Paige first solicits Victor for sex, she is "four steps away" (89)—metaphorically speaking, unachievable. When not repeating directly, the novel substitutes the expression "See also," a device used 41 times. One section uses "See also" to list alternative forms of fatal disease, but Victor uses it primarily to refer to sexual partners (and in one instance to refer to objects that have become lodged inside orifices [11]), to Paige Marshall, and, in Oedipal confusion, to his mother. Victor uses "See also" in Freudian fashion, to conflate lovers and mother, and sex and death. But they also function as an inadvertent, unconscious iteration of his incomplete fourth step; paradoxically, the accumulating "See also" references themselves amount to the very "moral inventory notebook. The complete and relentless history of my addiction" (16) that he ironically professes an inability to compose. The repetition and very language of "See also" combines the book's style and substance, linguistically embodying Victor's stasis in his narrative past, his reductive equivalency, his sense of futility, and *Choke*'s own self-referentiality, since "See also" reminds the reader that she or he is looking at a book, not a life. The cumulative effect is that of a narrator who is trapped by life, language, and literature itself.

Eventually, Victor does change, yet in defiance, he, like the novel itself, deliberately seems to be doing his worst. He began as a calculating con artist, but after his encounter with Eva, he goes further, confessing to all the sins committed against each of the addled patients:

> Two smiling old ladies wander past us, and one points and says to the other, "There's that nice young man I told you about. He's the one who strangled my pet cat."
>
> The other lady, her sweater is buttoned wrong, and she says, "You don't say." She says, "He beat my sister almost to death one time." (115)

While Victor's false admissions seem sadistic, even pathological, Paige understands the women's satisfaction: "'It's sweet,' Dr. Marshall says, 'what you're doing, I mean. You're giving these people completion on the biggest issues in their lives'" (ibid.). Victor's continued denial (to borrow his self-help argot), his fourth-step impasse, forces him to reject the possibility of genuine kindness or redemption; his motive does not come from goodness but from the desire to renounce all goodness. When another old woman recognizes Victor, he assumes that she, like Eva and the others, mistakes him for a man from her past who "[had sex with] her cat," or "drove over her flower beds," or "shot down her husband's fighter plane," or "flushed her hamster down the toilet" (154); Victor has become his own version of "See also." But instead, this woman's son saved Victor from choking. The supposed rescue instilled pride in her son, who, she says, "always felt like a coward until that night" and saved his marriage (154–5). But, Mrs Tsunitsu, the old woman, adds:

> "I knew you were faking. Everybody else saw what they wanted to see."
> She said, "You have an enormous capacity for love in you."
> And as fast as sneezing, I told her:
> "You're a fucking wrinkled old lunatic."
> And Paige winces. (155)

In a sense, Victor is failing despite his best efforts—but he's failing at failing, since he's helping; even after the insult, Mrs Tsunitsu tells Victor that he "can't deny the goodness of your true nature. It's shining for everyone to see" (ibid.). This new version of self-sacrifice develops the book's title and initial premise: just as he continues to endure his near-nightly near-death experiences so that his mother may live, Victor now, despite his adverse motivation, takes on the sins of others so that their victims may live. And unlike the restaurant scam, where at least Victor makes money, there is no profit in being a prophet. He is simply, freely, willing to martyr himself for each nursing home patient. Victor's self-loathing and verbal self-flagellation that "What I am is a dirty, filthy, helpless sexaholic, and I can't change, and I can't stop, and that's all I'll ever be" (156)—choking, stuck at his fourth step—only emphasizes, rather than negates, his self-sacrifice; he rebels against the possibility that he may be God, or even good. Discovering his supposed divinity, Victor turns against what he sees as his new self-knowledge, repeating, in opposition to the popular bracelets, "What would Jesus *not* do?" (182, 216). "What would Jesus *not* do?" functions as another negation, an action that is inaction. But, as the old woman—and reader—understand, he is also doing what Jesus *would* do, offering his very body as sacrifice, with its concomitant food imagery of the Last Supper and Eucharist. Victor allows himself to be consumed so that others may be saved, even when some of those others believe that they are saving him.

Self-consuming narrative

The book then begins working toward its Palahniukesque conclusion, in which the psychological interior of Victor's denial and secrecy must be spectacularly exposed. *Choke* does not have quite the narrative twist of *Fight Club*. Instead, the reader discovers that nearly all that Victor had come to believe during the course of the novel is not true—that Paige Marshall is a doctor when in fact she is a mental patient, or, as Victor says, "a lunatic" (271); that because of his genetic lineage, he says, "I know I'm Jesus Christ" (268) when of course he is not; or even that Ida was his birth mother, when, as she explains: "I stole you out of a stroller in Waterloo, Iowa. . . . I kidnapped you" (269). As his mother confesses, Victor assumes that she is a "poor deluded, demented thing [who] doesn't know what she's saying" (ibid.), even as he continues to feed her compulsively, "spoon[ing] in more pudding," 12 times over 3 pages (267–9), so that she subsequently chokes to death, completing the fatal trajectory of his self-professed reverse-Oedipal complex. The particulars of Ida's death suggest that Victor has ironically feigned near-death choking to prolong Ida's life only to suffocate her with pudding. Yet the details also suggest an odd symmetry between Victor and Ida; as Celia Lury suggests, of addiction in contemporary culture, "one can be addicted not only to too much of a substance such as food . . . but also to its refusal, as anorexics are said to be, or its controlled, intermittent ingestion—as in the case of bulimics" (246). Ida's refusal to eat mirrors Victor's refusal to eat, but it also corresponds with his addictive personality; by the end, even Victor himself thinks that he "is starving but I don't dare eat" (264). Yet these final realizations and disclosures continue Palahniuk's narrative conceit of surprise not for its own sake, not as revelation, but as self-revelation. After Victor absurdly attempts to bring Ida back from the dead ("Just like with Lazarus . . . I've done this before" [270]), he finally realizes, as he says, that "I was the deluded one" (272).

In the end, everything previously concealed is revealed: Victor appears on television, ostensibly to explain the rock structure built from the rocks Denny has amassed "for every day of sobriety. . . . It's what he does at night to stay occupied" (139), but really "to make Denny need me" (262). Victor's fourth step journal is seized by the police, who take him in for questioning based on Eva's imagined allegations:

> In front of all the losers of Colonial Dunsboro, in front of the druggies . . . I'm arrested. It's the same as Denny in the stocks, but for real.
>
> And in another sense, I want to tell them all not to think they're any different.
>
> Around here, everybody's arrested. (275)

Victor, and Palahniuk, presents the pun of "arrested"—another version of stasis, of being stuck at the fourth step, of the Colonial Dunsboro stockade, of choking. And once in police custody, Victor has two other revelations: first, asked by the police, "What's this stuff that looks like maps. All these pages of drawings?" Victor remembers: "It's funny, but I'd forgot all that. Those are maps. Maps I did when I was a little boy [. . .]. You see, my mom told me that I could reinvent the whole word. That I had that kind of power. That I didn't have to accept the world the way it stood, all properly lined and micromanaged. I could make it anything I wanted" (280). But he rejects that vision as one of his mother's illusions—"That's how crazy she was" (ibid.)—and instead attempts to choke himself to death on surrounding objects, the simulated choking made real, the metaphor made flesh. When an officer performs the Heimlich maneuver to rescue the now genuinely choking Victor, the rubber balls lodged in his rectum since the previous week's sexual encounter with Tanya, another fellow sex-addict (216–18), and resultant blockage are released. And somehow, within a mere page, in response to his television appearance, Victor is confronted by a mass of his would-be restaurant rescuers, each bearing a rock for the Denny's televised construction project. But after talking to each other and figuring out Victor's con, "reduced from saviors to fools in an instant" (289), the former Good Samaritans attempt to stone Victor to death, in a final, fatal act of simulated anachronism.

By now, the metaphors are overt, and they are not about choking anymore: Victor needs all his shit, literally and figuratively, to come out:

My entire private life made public.

Nothing left to hide. (287)

And once everything is revealed, the book reaches its conclusion, if not quite resolution, in the tentative moment when "Paige and I just look at each other, at who each other is for the first time" (292), as opposed to their previous meetings, when they were each seeing the fictional character they pretended to be. Paige's name is homophonous with "page," the blank repository of writing. Up until now, Victor suggests, someone else, or the past, has been writing her story, imposing narrative upon her from without; even Victor, earlier conflating Paige's ear with "another hole she can't close, hidden and filled with skin. Framed in soft hair" (89), sees her as a receptacle for sex and speech alike. But at the end, the novel shifts: as a page, she becomes less of a cipher and more of an invitation to open-endedness, possibility, even sublimity. And so does Victor.

For a while, Victor believes he is God: "I *am* the Christ," he impotently iterates when Ida dies (270). He is not, but by the novel's end, he is ready to play God, in the best sense: to make his own world, in the form of his own story. Ida, the mother who is not a mother, the seeming source of all of Victor's neuroses, may have done one thing right—she tried to teach Victor to use language, as Victor comes to understand, repeating again, here in dialogue form, what he remembered after seeing the map held by the policeman:

"I don't want you to just accept the world as it's given," she said.

She said, "I want to you invent it. I want you to have that skill. To create your own reality. Your own set of laws. I want to try and teach you that."

The boy had a pen now, and she said to draw the river in the book. Draw the river, and draw the mountains up ahead. And name them, she said. Not words he already knew, but to make up new words that didn't already mean a bunch of other stuff.

To create his own symbols.

The little boy thought with the pen in his mouth and the book open in his lap, and after a while, he drew it all. (284–5)

Somehow Victor remembered his mouth for choking and his lap for sex addiction, but forgot the pen and the paper. Victor believes that his only possible divine connection comes from the outlandish story of Jesus' foreskin or, somewhat better, his martyrdom of Saint Me, recalled again as he is about to be attacked by his pseudo-saviors (290). But, Victor finally understands, "what's stupid is, the little boy forgot all this. It wasn't until years later that the police detectives found this map. That he remembered he did this. That he could do this. He had this power" (285). Through this repressed memory, unblocked like so much else by this concluding moment, Victor realizes that another way to play God is to create, name, and live his own story.

This conclusion echoes what the novelist John Barth has explicitly stated—that in creating a story, the writer does not comment on or depict the world, but rather creates it:

> My contention . . . is that a novel is not essentially a view of the universe (though it may reflect one), but a universe itself; that the novelist is not finally a spectator, an imitator, or a purger of the public psyche, but a maker of universes: a demiurge. . . . I don't mean this frivolously or sentimentally. I don't even mean it as a figure of speech. . . . I mean it literally and rigorously: The heavy universe we sit in here in Hiram, Ohio, and the two-pound universe of *The Sot-Weed Factor* [Barth's most recent novel at the time], say, are cousins, because the maker of this one and the maker of that one are siblings.
>
> This contention will strike you as immodest. It is. (29)

The novel ends with Victor, Denny, and Paige surrounded by the thrown stones, thinking, "Where we're standing right now, in the ruins in the dark, what we build could be anything" (293). The ending of Palahniuk's story, then, is the beginning of Victor's.

If the final claim that "we could build anything" is, as Barth suggests, an "immodest" contention, it is also an ironic one, placed at the end, rather than the start, of the novel, spoken by a bruised, starved, feces-covered pariah. If the writer is akin to Barth's "demiurge," the novel itself equally seems to be a contemporary example of a "self consuming artifact." As Stanley Fish explains— here, of the *Phaedrus*, but, as Fish suggests, "I will be pleased if others find this study helpful to their consideration of more modern . . . documents" (xiii):

> To read [it], then, is to use it up; for the value of any point in it is that it gets *you* (not any sustained argument) to the next point, which is not so much a point (in logical-demonstrative terms) as a level of insight. It is thus a *self-consuming artifact*, a mimetic enactment in the reader's experience of the Platonic ladder in which each rung, as it is negotiated, is kicked away. The final rung, the level of insight that stands (or, more properly on which the reader stands) because it is the last is, of course, the rejection of written artifacts, a rejection that, far from contradicting what has preceded, corresponds exactly to what the reader, in his repeated abandoning of successive stages of argument, has been doing. (13)

Choke is an exemplary self-consuming artifact: it employs the very direct address of "you" that Fish's seventeenth-century texts often merely imply; puts the reader directly into the position of being trapped with Victor at his fourth step (even using the shared metaphor of Fish's rhetorical ladder with the Twelve Step terminology of addiction and recovery); and it calls for the paradoxical rejection of the very story that we have just read. But it does more: the imagery of choking corresponds directly with the rhetoric of self-consumption and rejection. In offering his body in Eucharistic sacrifice, Victor is, in part, being consumed, but he is also forcing the story to consume itself, as the reader sees, and expels, each of Victor's personas—con artist, sex addict, martyr, Jesus, criminal, outcast—until all that is left at the end is Victor. *Choke* is more than a self-consuming artifact: it becomes a self-consuming *narrative*, for the reader is implored to stop reading the story at the beginning, only to finish the story and understand that the novel eventually renounces everything that has come since the warning. It is not until we have finished the book that we are in any position to understand why we should not have believed it. Like Victor, readers must choke to feel the relief of release. It is catharsis, the word in keeping with choking's expulsion, but it is also consumption, since by the end, the narrative has used itself up.

Victor may have forgotten his mother's lessons about creating a world, but Chuck Palahniuk remembered. Like Victor, Palahniuk rejects the stories others impose; he does not see *Choke* as a critique of consumer culture, just as he refutes John Glassie's contention as well: "The characters in your books do pretty bad stuff. They pretend to choke on dinner rolls for money. They start fight clubs. They stalk sex-addiction support-group meetings. They engage in civil anarchy. Are you an anarchist?" To which Palahniuk replied, "No. I just want to write exciting books" (Glassie, Interview). Writing the novel is the precise opposite of anarchy—it is the imposition of causes and chronologies, of beginnings, middles, and ends, of plots, however inverted or absurd, and characters, however perverted or deluded, onto the chaos and anarchy of real life. It is about, as Victor finally understands, building something. In presenting the contradictions of the word "choke," then, Palahniuk also intimates the paradoxical, liminal nature of the novel itself: like the mouth and the throat, it is another threshold, capable of opening and closing, swallowing or expelling our obstructions, and giving, or even occasionally withholding, our stories.

8

Anger, Anguish, and Art: *Choke*

David Cowart

Butades, a potter of Sicyon, was the first who invented, at Corinth, the art of modelling portraits in the earth which he used in his trade. It was through his daughter that he made the discovery; who, being deeply in love with a young man about to depart on a long journey, traced the profile of his face, as thrown upon the wall by the light of the lamp. Upon seeing this, her father filled in the outline, by compressing clay upon the surface, and so made a face in relief, which he then hardened by fire along with other articles of pottery.

Pliny the Elder, The Natural History, *Book 35, chapter 43*

Certain of his enthusiastic readers see the work of Chuck Palahniuk as *sui generis*, but the more discriminating eye discerns affinities in every postmodern quarter. His novels offer abundant evidence of an energetic and irreverent writer having absorbed lessons in outrage—or outrageousness—from various points on the contemporary literary compass. Indeed, to trace Palahniuk's literary pedigree back only half a century is to observe relationships with, if not apostolic succession from, such looming contemporaries as J. D. Salinger, Joseph Heller, Flannery O'Connor, and fellow Oregonian Ken Kesey. The last of these prompts notice of a temporal intersection or two. Kesey's most famous work, *One Flew Over the Cuckoo's Nest*, came out in 1962, the year of Palahniuk's birth. Kesey died in 2001, the year that saw publication of Palahniuk's *Choke*, which features a medical practitioner as cracked as those she pretends to treat (not that Dr Paige Marshall is the pure monster seen in the loathsome Nurse Ratched). Similarly, the nutty and at times criminal actions of Ida Mancini (who abducts a child in Waterloo, Iowa, and tries to make him an accomplice in various hijackings, pranks, and disruptive adventures) make her another Randall Patrick McMurphy. Both will die while institutionalized. In Palahniuk's grotesque, Jesus-obsessed humor, one encounters traces, too, of Flannery O'Connor, though without the orthodoxy. One imagines that the author of *Fight Club* and *Invisible Monsters* might well concur with O'Connor's defense of comic violence as a strategy to pierce the complacency of an audience bred to spiritual indifference: "to the hard of hearing you shout," she once explained. "And for the almost-blind you draw large and startling figures" (34). Elsewhere on the intertextual spectrum, one senses the presence of O'Connor's great contemporary, Joseph Heller. Palahniuk's penchant for medical gore may owe something to the graphic horror—Snowden's evisceration, the slicing in two of Kid Sampson by an airplane propeller, a defenestrated rape victim, bloody teeth in the street—that gradually squeezes off the laughter in *Catch-22* (1961). The most pronounced of these affinities (one does not call them influences) might be with J. D. Salinger. When Ida Mancini deplores "education" as "[o]ur bite of the apple" (150) and invokes a "cure for knowledge" and all the "living in our heads" (149), she seems to be channeling the boy genius in Salinger's "Teddy" (1953). More obviously, the author of *Choke* shares with Salinger a first-person narrator who, given to profane anger at a world of phonies, dreams of being a savior, a catcher in the rye.

One need not agree with the harsh assessment of Laura Miller, for whom Palahniuk's books "traffic in the half-baked nihilism of a stoned high school student who has just discovered Nietzsche and Nine-Inch Nails," to see that this author is dangerously beholden to a particular demographic. Miller seconds Janet Maslin, who sees in *Choke* little more than "a working definition of the adolescent male state of mind." Although Palahniuk's work offers fresh inflections in the grammar of postmodernism, I suspect that many readers expect from him something more, perhaps a truly "post" postmodernism. Born a generation after John Barth, Grace Paley, Philip Roth, Thomas Pynchon, Toni Morrison, Don DeLillo, and company (not to mention the writers already adduced), Palahniuk inherits a fully developed aesthetic that he shapes to ends that his main audience—Gen-Xers and Millennials—may mistake for the next new thing. These young readers—their keenness a wave that has borne Palahniuk to the top of the charts—find in his pages an irreverence and cynicism and anger that strike them as authentic, not already compromised by accommodation with the smug complacency of the employed and well-adjusted. Certain lines in *Fight Club* strike the generational chord:

> We don't have a great war in our generation, or a great depression, but we do, we have a great war of the spirit. We have a great revolution against the culture. The great depression is our lives. We have a spiritual depression. (149)

> "We are the middle children of history, raised by television to believe that someday we'll be millionaires and movie stars and rock stars, but we won't. And we're just learning this fact," Tyler said. "So don't fuck with us." (166)

Here and elsewhere Palahniuk knows he is recycling the F. Scott Fitzgerald who in *This Side of Paradise* famously declaimed: "Here was a new generation . . . dedicated more than the last to the fear of poverty and the worship of success; grown up to find all gods dead, all wars fought, all faiths in man shaken" (304). But the later generation, restive under a perceived "spiritual depression," enjoys a sometimes disquieting latitude for the expression of its anarchic and, yes, nihilistic humor—as if the "black humorists" of the sixties had spawned unruly grandchildren who delight in every form of advanced adolescent gross-out. Filmmakers and performers such as the Farrelly Brothers, Judd Apatow, Seth Rogen, and Zach Galifianakis have embraced a remarkably coarse comedic standard to enormous success. Called by his publisher "[ou]r funniest nihilist," Palahniuk purveys a comedy, like theirs, so raw as often to throttle the laughter it provokes. Yet here, too, one discerns the outline of an older truculence, for Updike's Rabbit Angstrom announces himself the prophet of such puerility: "If you're telling me I'm not mature, that's one thing I don't cry over since as far as I can make out it's the same thing as being dead" (106).

The sensitive, reasonably erudite reader who seeks the point of any parable may find that of a fiction such as *Choke* elusive, resistant to critical parsing. Because the narration is entirely in the first person, one cannot easily test the picture "Victor Mancini" gives of himself, his foster mothers, his work, his world. Is he really an addict? A sex addict? Has an especially bizarre Christ complex really been foisted on him—or has he embraced it willingly? Did Ida Mancini really kidnap him from a stroller in Waterloo, Iowa? One may, in fact, err to see in Palahniuk's unhappy narrator a study in genuine disaffection and alienation—as opposed to a "bogus little Benedict Arnold" (3), an elaborate fraud who does to the reader what he does to his fellow diners in the restaurants where he stages bouts of choking that become, along with his job at the appalling Colonial Dunsboro, the means whereby he supports himself and, at St Anthony's, the demented woman who has for so many years represented herself as his mother. The anger and anguish, in other words, may seem factitious, two-dimensional, "bogus," and some readers resist taking the spiritual torpor, the sacrilege, and the unvectored anomie at face value. At a certain point, a Palahniuk novel comes to seem like a running parody of such topoi—and for that very reason a peculiarly bleak variation on the unhappiness so often reflected in twentieth- and twenty-first-century literature.

The triumph of Philomela

If not a simple con, Victor Mancini's narrative purports to be the latest bulletin from the frontiers of human misery—a classic study in the alienation that has dogged the human spirit for decades now. As a theme, however, alienation has undergone some interesting transmogrifications since its heyday in the middle of the last century. In his 1956 essay "The Man on the Train," Walker Percy declares that, "strictly speaking . . . a literature of alienation" does not exist: "the only literature of alienation is an alienated literature, that is, a bad art, which is no art at all. An Erle Stanley Gardner novel is a true exercise in alienation. A man who finishes his twentieth Perry Mason is that much nearer total despair than when he started" (83). Looking at more serious claimants to the cachet of alienation, Percy notes that reader and author and character, however individually alienated, escape their condition through a mutual recognition that cancels out the otherness and isolation that true alienation requires: "Neither Kafka nor his reader is alienated in the movement of art, for each achieves a reversal through its re-presenting" (ibid.). If we update his example by substituting Salinger or Palahniuk for Kafka, we discover what may figure in every iconoclast's appeal: an audience that feels itself at odds with the straight, respectable, "phony" world—whether that of Habsburg Prague, the Eisenhower fifties, or the endless eight years of the second Bush administration.

If the "literature of alienation" survived Walker Percy's calling attention to its self-contradictory premises, it stood no chance against post-Freudian psychology, which has complicated the ancient ideal of *gnothi seauton*, know thyself. There is, after all, no single self to know—and the world from which one might be estranged has long since lost its ontological uniqueness. We are all alienated all the time now, and we recognize our truest being amid the proliferating imagoes of a strange, universal psychopathology. Similarly, the ideal of collective self-knowledge that we call history has run onto the rocks of metahistory, where the past splinters to become many pasts, all somehow valid, however mutually contradictory. Univocal history, we have come to see, always falsifies. As Paige Marshall remarks, "[t]hose who remember the past tend to get the story really screwed up" (208).

Choke's narrator and central character, Victor Mancini, works at Colonial Dunsboro, historical reenactment village and "site" of further literary and cultural intersections. Like George Saunders in the title story of *Pastoralia* (published in the same year as *Choke*), Palahniuk seems to be remembering Zwölfkinder, the strange German theme park in Pynchon's *Gravity's Rainbow* (1973), not to mention similar places in the movies of recent decades, notably *Futureworld*, *Jurassic Park*, *Adventureland*. (A similar conceit figures in films— *Fast Times at Ridgemont High*, for example—in which a teen-aged character's job requires that s/he dress up in compliance with some restaurant theme). Locked forever in the year 1734, Dunsboro represents history's calcification, the betrayal of any idea that by remembering the past we can avoid repeating it. Indeed, Palahniuk introduces George Santayana's famous observation only to suggest, in iteration, that knowledge of history offers few assurances about the future. In its superficiality and general cheesiness, Dunsboro gives its visitors little more than history under the postmodern dispensation as sketched by Fredric Jameson—a place without temporal depth or nuance, a simulacrum, the "copy of a copy of a copy" invoked in *Fight Club* (21, 97). According to Victor, such places "always leave the best parts out. Like typhus. And opium. And scarlet letters. Shunning. Witch-burning" (29). He troubles himself to confirm the absence, too, of "a town whore," a "village idiot," a "[p]ickpocket," and a "[h]angman" (ibid.). What Dunsboro replicates accurately, one realizes, is the climate of the Great Awakening (at its height in 1734), in all its puritanical rectitude. "His Lord High Charlie the Colonial Governor" (26, 275) presides over petty officialdom in the form of a "town council" consisting of "six old guys who wear those fake colonial wigs" (29). One smiles at the redundancy of *fake* wigs—the phrase situates authenticity at a double remove. Overrun by teratomorphic poultry (about which more presently), Dunsboro is rife with sex and drugs: perennially giving hand jobs or passing on herpes (28), the staff stay blitzed on glue, weed, ecstasy, acid, hashish, crystal meth, heroin, Vicodin, and "Special K" (Ketamine hydrocholoride). Victor himself suffers, he claims, from sex addiction—but better addiction in any form, he asseverates, than "sadness, anger, fear, worry, despair, and depression" (211). He recognizes what Pynchon calls the "nearly complete parallelism between *analgesia* and *addiction*. The more pain it takes away, the more we desire it" (*Gravity's Rainbow* 348).

The psychological doubling so cleverly developed in *Fight Club* ("There isn't a me and a you, anymore," declares one self to the other [164]) metastasizes in this later novel. In *Choke*, the narration varies between past (in third person) and present (in first person). The narrator is at pains, moreover, to make his childhood self and his ostensible mother figures of conspicuous alterity. Narrating the present, he favors "mom" or, occasionally, "mother"; in flashbacks to the past, he refers nearly always to "the Mommy," a person who veers between arrant lunacy and dubious theoretical patter about Foucault (200) or "people's little identity paradigms" (66). He reviles his own juvenile alter ego as "the little stooge" (159), "this dumb-fuck little boy" (161), "the stupid little shit-heel kid" (196), and 20 or so other such epithets. Why such strenuous and overdetermined contempt? The definite article mocks itself: *the* mother is *any* mother, and *this* mother is eventually revealed as a simulacrum—a foster parent—herself. The "stupid kid" was, similarly, a collective of blind, uninformed, victimized selves. Thus when Victor says, "I don't even pretend to know myself very well" (21) or "it feels like I'm doing a really bad impersonation of myself" (69), the reader must not fall for the invitation to go looking for some authentic, bedrock identity, the key to poor Victor's recovering his psychological and emotional health. Ida begs the psychological question when she muses: "I wonder if Victor has a right to know who he really is" (70). Under the postmodern dispensation, no one has any such right—though everyone, tragically, has the need.

Lacking knowledge of self and world, one must improvise, tell a story about oneself, become an artist, revert to creative child in a sandbox of words: "the only frontier left is the world of intangibles, ideas, stories, music, art" (285). But what is Victor's—or Palahniuk's—understanding of or goal for his own creation? Does the author, in particular, operate according to conscious artistic principle? Does a coherent aesthetic undergird the dark phantasmagoria of his "transgressive" fictions? Rather than issue a manifesto, Palahniuk presents, in *Choke*, a modest parable or two. The author's *ars poetica* appears in disguise—in "outline," as it were—in the story of a primal, sciagraphic depiction of the human form on a wall. One thinks, here, of the brilliant young artist Victor Wind in Nabokov's *Pnin*: at the age of three, invited to draw a picture of his mother (herself as dubious a figure as Ida Mancini), he executes "a lovely undulation, which he said was her shadow on the new refrigerator" (90).

Art began with some such minimalist gesture. "Before the Greeks, nobody had any art" (5), Ida explains. Her fable of "a beautiful girl in ancient Greece, the daughter of a potter" (3), introduces what will become one of the book's important self-referential motifs (277, 289, 292). "[T]he girl traced the outline of her lover's shadow so she would always have a record of how he looked" (4), and "[t]his was how painting pictures was invented" (5). Presently "the girl's father used the outline on the wall to model a clay version of the young man, and that's the way sculpture was invented" (5; cf. 277). Like the myth of Philomela, Ida's story—that of the potter Butades and his daughter Dibutade, as told by first-century scholar Pliny the Elder—credits a woman with the creative gesture in which art has its genesis. But whence the *potter's* art? The answer always leads to the geminate conceits of god as artist and artist as god.

Older than Butades is Keramos, mortal son of Dionysus and Ariadne and patron, in ancient Greece, of those whose work defined a complete artistic spectrum, from humble clay vessels to the most splendid craters (according to Pausanias, their district of ancient Athens, Kerameikos, derived its name from this mythic craftsman [13]). In the mythopoesis of later ages, notably in the poetry of two exact contemporaries, Longfellow and FitzGerald, the primal potter would modulate from craftsman to demiurge to deity. The American versifier, in his long poem "Kéramos," surveys the great artistic variety of pottery and ceramics but cannot bring himself to suggest that the potter's mistakes might mirror those of the deity:

> *Turn, turn, my wheel! This earthen jar*
> *A touch can make, a touch can mar;*
> *And shall it to the Potter say,*
> *What makest thou? Thou hast no hand?*
> *As men who think to understand*
> *A world by their Creator planned,*
> *Who wiser is than they.* (Longfellow 18)

In the bitter questions that figure in the Kuza Nama sequence in *The Rubáiyát of Omar Khayyám*, FitzGerald dispenses with such pious circumspection. The question posed by a deformed pot—"What! did the hand, then, of the Potter shake"?—occurs to every generation that has come to doubt the putative perfection of God's handiwork. Sooner or later, suffering humanity wonders: "Who is the Potter, pray, and who the Pot" (19, 18)? Is God, in other words, thrown on the potter's wheel of the human imagination? Where FitzGerald and his Persian predecessor imagine talking pots, Palahniuk briefly notes Colonial Dunsboro's "potter on methadone" (31) and invites readers to associate the damaged chickens of that benighted institution with the damaged human beings in and outside of St Anthony's. Too many come imperfect from the palsied hand of the divine Potter, a deity as irresponsible, perhaps, as the children who delight in shaking the eggs from which the deformed chickens hatch.

In Pliny's parable, a daughter and a father create painting and sculpture; in Victor Mancini's story of a son and a mother, a third art emerges: storytelling. Though Ida introduces the myth of art's origin in the primal outlining, she swiftly moves beyond ideas of naïve representationalism to become the voice of theory-driven thinking about art and the reality (especially the social reality) it supposedly mirrors. Thus, at any rate, one understands her inchoate teachings about symbols, sign systems, and codes. She characterizes language, by the same token, as "just our way to explain away the wonder and the glory of the world. To deconstruct. To dismiss." She asserts, moreover, that "[w]e don't live in the real world anymore. . . . We live in a world of symbols" (151). Alex Blazer, analyzing the relationship between this novel and Salinger's *The Catcher in the Rye*, emphasizes the tension between phoniness and authenticity in terms derived from Guy Debord and Jean Baudrillard: "Both spectacle and simulation scar the postmodern psyche, leaving the subject feeling inauthentic, fake, phony" (148). Thus it is that Ida argues against passive acceptance of the cultural moment and its simulacra. "I don't want you to just accept the world as it's given," she tells the boy who thinks himself her son, "I want you to invent it" (284). The boy must rediscover, years later, how "[t]o create his own symbols" (285).

But Ida's views are problematic in the end. The reader who considers the ambivalence with which Victor regards his mother and her lessons may come to see in her certain attitudes toward language and symbols that pose a challenge to the literary artist who has imagined both of these characters. With her graduate degree in English (133), Ida becomes at times the nonce representative, in her remarks about the liability of signs, symbols, and language, of the critic or theorist who subjects literary representation and its very medium to "deconstructive" operations. Her offspring, storyteller to a mad civilization, must in some way reinvent that medium and perhaps reality as well. Consanguineous or not (one may doubt the late assertion that she kidnapped Victor), their relationship takes on "symbolic" meaning: an example of what rhetoricians call *hysteron proteron* (reversal of natural order), they are critic and artist in retrograde filiation (an inversion congenial to the postmodern aesthetic). Borges says that "every writer *creates* his own precursors" (201), and here, with something like the uncanniness that Borges saw in Kafka, the critic (Ida) precedes the artist (Victor). Indeed, insofar as his performative choking precludes full ingestion, Victor invites recognition as another "hunger artist."

"Art," declares Ida, "never comes from happiness" (5). Behind this insight lies another myth, a dark parable that distills the paradoxical relationship between suffering and art. Ida's observation has its origin in the story of Philomela, the beautiful Athenian princess raped by her brother-in-law, King Tereus of Thrace, who cuts out her tongue to assure that the crime will go unreported. But Philomela weaves a tapestry to do the office of her severed tongue and so invents art—or at least defines its paradigmatic relation to anguish. From Kyd's Hieronymo to Coetzee's Friday (in *Foe*), the lopped tongue recurs as the wound that, by its nature, precludes direct witness. "Half of my tongue drops to the floor and gets kicked away" (201), observes the nameless narrator of *Fight Club*. Spared this particular violation, Victor Mancini will nonetheless tell a story predicated, like Philomela's, on personal pain.

To what end, however, does Palahniuk equate suffering and art, especially if the suffering is a bit cartoonish? (Who, after all, feels the pain of Wile E. Coyote?) More to the point: does the reader see Palahniuk's tapestry, like Philomela's, as beautiful? One assumes, after all, that what Philomela weaves, like any number of great works about horrific suffering, transcends its subject matter, turns it into the "thing of beauty" (16) that Victor remembers from Keats (who in "Ode to a Nightingale" discovers in supernal birdsong—that of the metamorphosed Philomela—the aesthetic principle that the more terrible the suffering, the more beautiful its artistic transformation can be). Eliot, too, invokes Philomela ("by the barbarous king / So rudely forced") in a work famous at once for showing the twentieth century its true subject—the universal spiritual aridity of the modern wasteland—and pushing the boundaries of the beautiful. The point of the original story, as Eliot understood, lies not in the horror of what happened to Philomela but in the transmutation of her anguish into something rich and strange, whether tapestry or birdsong. The suffering of certain sensitive individuals finds expression as art, in which variously painful events are ordered, universalized, given shape and meaning. However terrible the raw experience—one need only consider the actual subject matter of any Greek tragedy— the artistic representation becomes that rarity, something that legitimately exalts the human spirit, something as tragically beautiful or suggestive as the song of the nightingale. But it may be that art in our time, as a DeLillo character says, has edged up to and away from making "the horror, reality, misery, ruined bodies, bloody faces . . . so fucking pretty" (24). Richard Powers similarly wonders (in his extraordinary novel *Operation Wandering Soul* 1993) about the frequency with which fairytale and fable merely aestheticize ancient enormity.

Tracking the creative impulse to its anguished genesis, the Philomela myth invites even theological amplification. Her terrible victimization notwithstanding, Philomela can be, no less than the potter at his wheel, a figure of the supreme creator. God, too, suffers and, suffering, creates. Turning Milton inside out, one recognizes the Creation as Jehovah's tapestry, woven to articulate and transmute a vast, cosmic violation. In Book VII of *Paradise Lost*, that is, the deity creates humanity and the world to sublimate the anguish, the trauma, of the betrayal narrated in Book VI: rebellion by a third of the angels, collective Tereus to godhead itself.

What would Jesus write?

In the narration of Victor Mancini, who comes to think himself the reincarnate Christ, Palahniuk imagines God the Son as another sufferer who must weave his own tapestry of symbolic witness. Here Palahniuk burlesques the spiritual autobiography, the genre created by St Augustine and refined over the centuries by John Bunyan, Jonathan Edwards, Benjamin Franklin, John Henry Cardinal Newman, Henry Adams, and James Joyce. Thus one discerns in Victor Mancini's narrative a journal of the kind that anchors participants in the 12-step program of Alcoholics Anonymous and similar programs. Like every addict, Victor wrestles with his fourth step, the writing of a "fearless and complete moral inventory" (215) of his addiction and everything that contributes to it (lengthy and complex, this document involves responses to as many as 300 questions). Recurring frequently to this fourth step, he executes it as the novel we read: a serious, crude, nonclinical, self-reproachful, and psychologically revealing document, a postmodern Portrait of the Artist As a Young Addict (Joyce, too, one recalls, moves his narrative toward the journal entries that are at once conclusion and recursive genesis). As narrative, however, the post-Joycean text resists the reader's desire for orientation—not to mention determinacy (whether epistemological, psychological, social, or literary). As document, by the same token, it may be authentic, or it may be little more than a send-up—a case-history pastiche, like something concocted by Vladimir Nabokov's Humbert Humbert (another "sex fiend"), who so loved to toy with the credulity of psychiatrists.

Much energy goes into making the story resemble such a case history, complete with primal scene that the protagonist, arrested, relives over and over again—whether as the crippling neurosis in which the early trauma encysts itself or as the repetition compulsion by which the death instinct gains psychic ground. "Around here," remarks Victor, "everybody's arrested" (275). Thus Victor jokes bitterly about the Oedipus complex from which he himself suffers: "every son raised by a single mom is pretty much born married" (15). When the receptionist at St Anthony's calls Ida "Mrs. Mancini," Victor corrects her: "It's Miss Mancini. . . . My mom's not married, unless you count me in that creepy Oedipal way" (225). Previously, he has noted a significant anomaly in the relationship with Ida: "In the modern Oedipal story, it's the mother who kills the father and takes the son" (16). In the spirit of this modern—or postmodern—Oedipal story, he will reverse the archetype again (not to mention the prescribed sequence of events) when he kills not the father but the mother—as thoughtlessly and as circumstantially as Oedipus slew Laius. Gone, however, is all tragic elevation, for Victor effects the death of the Oedipal parent by spooning chocolate pudding into her mouth. Her death is the ironic consummation of the choking charade by which, on some 300 occasions, Victor has augmented his income: "'Widower' isn't the right word, but it's the first word that comes to mind" (270).

Freud saw in the tragedy of Oedipus a "family romance," the story of a child who, raised in literal or figurative fosterage, discovers the exalted identity of its frequently royal or divine real parents. Moses and Jesus also exemplify the pattern; indeed, the recurrence of this fantasy in myth and literature—its examples include Stephen Dedalus, Jay Gatsby, and more than one hero in Wagner—suggests its cultural and psychological validity. Stories of fabulous parentage feed or mirror a fantasy congenial to childish imagination. Evidently interested in psychoanalysis, Palahniuk seems drawn to Freudian repudiation of supernaturalism. Like the Viennese master, he subjects religious archetype to euhemerization (the grounding of myth in real persons and events). Repeatedly in *Fight Club*, for example, one reads that "your father was your model for God" (140, 141, 186). In *Choke*, the narrator compounds mythic identity: he becomes not only Oedipus but Jesus, central figure in the supreme family romance.

Among its other features, this novel published in 2001 is a comedy of millennial expectations that have come and gone with no sign of the apocalypse, the promised end. Hence the elaborate joke on Victor's paternity, the outrageous idea of his being the son of the son of god, through the agency of DNA allegedly preserved in the "authenticated foreskin" (229, 267) of Jesus. Initially, Victor resists apotheosis. Though he claims "I'm not a monster" (62), he rejects, with increasing desperation, what he takes to be the mounting evidence of his divine identity. Christian youth affected little wristbands with the enigmatic letters WWJD, meaning What Would Jesus Do, and in time the sentiment, which might be traced back to the early fifteenth century in Thomas à Kempis's *De Imitatione Christi*, made its way into other social spheres, including the bumper stickers of green Christians (or simply environmentalists baiting those with the annoying fish symbol adorning their SUVs), which asked rhetorically: What Would Jesus Drive? In defiance of such pietism, Victor tries to live by the principle he repeats like a mantra: "*What would Jesus NOT do?*" (169, 182, 186, 194, 208, 211, 216, 227). Ostensibly a routine piece of flippancy in the vein of *Fight Club*'s "[b]elieve in me and you shall die, forever" (145), this little epithet does something more than declare a disinclination to imitate Christ: it invites ironic recognition that there are in fact things that Jesus would not do. He would not cast the first stone, nor, more importantly, would he sidestep his destiny. He even anticipated the mockery of those who would say to him, on the very cross, *cura te ipsum*, heal thyself. He would not. He did not.

Here one discerns the rationale behind making Victor Mancini, like his mother before him, a failed medical student. His running symptomatologies ("[t]he way to remember the symptoms of melanoma is . . ." [100], "a bruise means cirrhosis of the liver" [104]) coalesce to signal a Kierkegaardian spiritual disease. Unable to heal himself, the quondam medical student begins actually to embrace the absurd identification with Christ. His mother, declares the highly unreliable Dr Paige Marshall (whose mental instability Victor discovers belatedly), "truly believes" that he represents the

long-awaited eschatological consumption, "the second coming
of Christ" (146). As Jesus gravitated to publicans and sinners, so
does Victor prefer the company of slackers and dopers and sex
addicts, the ostensibly preterite in the moral economy of his own
age's Pharisees and Sadducees. In the biblical phrase that Handel
would put into the past tense and set to music, "[h]e is despised
and rejected of men; a man of sorrows, and acquainted with grief"
(Isa. 53.3). As Antonio Casado de Rocha observes, Victor "enacts
his own death and resurrection" every time he chokes (106). He
defends his nasty little game of staging asphyxiation for attention,
sympathy, and dollars as a kind of salvation suited to the times:
"You gain power by pretending to be weak. . . . You save people by
letting them save you" (50). His gloss on the story's primal scene,
when, as a child, he chokes on a corn dog, reframes a familiar
biblical precept and provides the basic meaning for what will
become one of the novel's central conceits: "It seemed that . . . you
had to risk your life to get love. You had to go right to the edge
of death to ever be saved" (3). ("If I don't fall all the way," says
the narrator of *Fight Club*, I can't be saved" [70].) Similarly, by
going along with her cracked notion that he is the individual who
long ago wronged or violated her, he "saves" more than one elderly,
damaged patient who, having misplaced her mind, finds herself in
an institution ironically named for the patron saint of lost things.
Blithely "accepting responsibility for every sin in the world" (274),
Victor pretends contrition for things they have brooded over all
their lives. In feeding their delusions (however therapeutically), he
feeds his own as well, and the reader traces the rise and fall of
his fantasy, the identity he reluctantly embraces: "I'm the savior
who wants you to worship him forever" (33), he says. "I want to
be someone's constant savior" (118). "It sounds," observes Paige
Marshall, "as if you'd like to be God" (119), and Victor, in spite of
his skepticism, arrives at outlandish conviction: "I know that I'm
Jesus Christ" (268). He even tries his hand at literal resurrection,
"just like with Lazarus" (270). In the end, he ruefully yields up his
delusion: "for a while, I really did think I was Jesus Christ" (274).
The punch line to this joke, which Palahniuk tells in a variety of
ways throughout his career, is that Victor may indeed be modeling
the deity's irresponsibility and carelessness.

As G. Christopher Williams has pointed out, Victor Mancini is not
the only Palahniuk protagonist to suffer from messianic delusions

(170). Of course, anyone who has taught English knows that just about any suffering protagonist can be seen as a Christ figure. Small wonder that certain authors—Nathanael West, for example, in *Miss Lonelyhearts*—present parodic versions of this conceit. Characters such as Miss Lonelyhearts and Victor Mancini frustrate the reader's desire for some degree of transparency on the part of a storyteller—transparency regarding the presence of irony, for example. Unable to discern some thematic emphasis or key, readers find themselves in the postmodern limbo of irony that may not be irony, suffering that may be sacramental or hugely specious. Such readers engage in an often painful and frustrating exercise in what—to borrow and modify a term from the Palahniuk novel—might be characterized as tantric hermeneutics. They must read signs that call attention to their own arbitrariness. Yet meaning, thus suspended, becomes spiritually enabling ("tantric") in that possibility resides in every chord unresolved, every closure postponed. Palahniuk characterizes as "Tantric Architecture" (264) the teleologically indeterminate principle behind the rock collecting and wall building to which Victor's friend Denny commits himself. The seismic destruction of the wall Denny, Victor, and their stripper friend Beth have labored over signals the need, periodically, to rebuild—for our mental blueprints are especially susceptible, at the beginning of the third millennium, to being exposed as architectural fantasy, the fanciful work of some deranged Piranesi. Together presently, like good postmodernists, they undertake to fashion a reality, "to build a world" (292). This world-building becomes a paradigm that governs reading as well, not to mention the epistemic striving of philosophy and psychology, which have grappled for centuries with the problem of perception: is it neutral and passive—or does it build a reality that, as Wordsworth says, we half perceive and half create? From Bishop Berkeley in the eighteenth century to F. H. Bradley and his pupil T. S. Eliot, the suspicion that our senses betray us recurs. In *The Crying of Lot 49*, for example, Pynchon's heroine Oedipa Maas contemplates a painting by Remedios Varo and realizes the extent to which reality is not, after all, shared. Everyone makes her own, weaves or embroiders it, a perceptual Philomela, in the cranial tower where the senses, converging, make sense. Whether in the shabby "bordello of the subconscious" or the more expansive "theater of the mind" (131), says Palahniuk, one conjures a reality tinged with prurience and inevitably histrionic.

And decidedly unstable. When Palahniuk reveals, late in the narrative, that Paige Marshall is not the resident psychotherapist at St Anthony's—that, in fact, she is herself one of the patients—he restages and reconceptualizes a classic drama of reality's perspectival liability. Yet another "doctor" unable to heal herself, Paige Marshall burlesques the psychotherapeutic premise and reverses the conceit at the heart of Robert Wiene's celebrated exercise in expressionist horror, *Das Kabinett des Dr. Caligari* (1920). Aimed at destabilizing the viewer's sense of the real and the unreal, the sane and the insane, Wiene's film climaxes with the revelation that its narrative viewpoint is that of an institutionalized mental patient, its sinister title character the director of the asylum. Palahniuk, overturning the *Caligari*-conceit, appropriates and reframes the trope that reflected an earlier generation's sense of disorientation and betrayal (which extended far beyond Weimar, as one sees in the contemporaneous Fitzgerald lines quoted previously—or their even more famous echo in the Gertrude Stein remark on the "Lost Generation" that became one of the epigraphs to Hemingway's *The Sun Also Rises*).

Part of the modernist project that theorists formulate as "representing the unrepresentable," expressionism was an aesthetic aimed at reifying the alienation, the *Verfremdung*, that characterized a lost generation. Making his Dr Paige Marshall a Caligari who is one of the deranged, Palahniuk devises an exercise in what might be called postmodern expressionism, a bringing up to date of the aesthetic crafted by Robert Wiene in film, Edvard Munch on canvas, and Bertolt Brecht on the Weimar stage. Now that alienation has been revealed as part of the very weave of consciousness (not some correctable psychological or social pathology), the artist seeks to represent—the formulation is Lyotard's—"the unpresentable in presentation itself" (81). To put this another way, the expressionists and other moderns could still subscribe to metanarratives and depth models of consciousness and history and art. The postmodernists did not invent self-referential art—they invented an art answerable to what was perceived as a crisis of representation. Grappling with the exhaustion or complete evacuation of the signifier, postmodern art risks making the case for its own inconsequence. Committed to exploring a foundationless world of simulacra, in which every serious thing—history, consciousness, belief, the Good—can be engaged only as text, such art invites dismissal as intellectual self abuse, for its logic is constantly at odds with the practical exigencies of real life. When these exigencies take on sufficient immediacy—when Al Qaeda operatives fly airplanes into tall buildings, for example—an over-subtilized art finds itself unable to represent or transmute the resultant trauma. In *Choke*, however, readers see an understated but stunning anticipation of the challenge to discourse posed by the acts of terrorism that inaugurated the millennium in America.

We can, then, note an unexpected element of timeliness in Palahniuk's novel. In addition to his ludic engagement with Christology, his calculated teasing of the millenarianism so widespread at the beginning of this century, he may in some measure foresee the spirit in which American intellectuals would reflect on the horrors of 9/11 in the days and weeks after the Twin Towers came down. What is remarkable about this fiction, published less than four months before the terrorist attack, is that it anticipates one of the most striking responses to that terrible event, heralded at the time—prematurely, as it turned out—as the moment for a paradigm-shift in intellectual style, a shift away from irony as a culture's discursive and ideational norm. Reflecting on the events of 9/11, Graydon Carter, editor of *Vanity Fair*, observed: "I think it's the end of the age of irony." Roger Rosenblatt, in *Time*, echoed the sentiment:

> One good thing could come from this horror: it could spell the end of the age of irony. For some 30 years—roughly as long as the Twin Towers were upright—the good folks in charge of America's intellectual life have insisted that nothing was to be believed in or taken seriously. Nothing was real. With a giggle and a smirk, our chattering classes—our columnists and pop culture makers—declared that detachment and personal whimsy were the necessary tools for an oh-so-cool life. (2001)

The clumsiness, incoherence, and rhetorical poverty of these remarks offer one gauge of the extent to which events so difficult to process intellectually could rattle thought. Irony was not, of course, invented in 1970—in modern times, it has been a feature of intelligent discourse since World War I exposed the full cost,ten million lives,of rhetorical dishonesty. But yes: on September 12, 2001, and for some months after, lots of otherwise unconnable public intellectuals imagined that sincerity might once again come into its own. Palahniuk, in a novel published scarce weeks before the Manhattan towers fell, registers a prophetic impatience with irony.

In a kind of palinode, Palahniuk disperses, like Prospero, the elements of his romance. He does so with characteristic scatology, and, recapitulating psychogenesis, his narrator brings full circle that moment when, as child, he choked on a corn dog. When he chokes for the last time (evidently wanting to kill himself or cause brain death), a policeman saves him with the usual Heimlich maneuver, but the "[p]eriabdominal pressure" (286) undoes not only the windpipe obstruction but also the intestinal logjam to which Victor has adverted with increasing urgency. The forceful evacuation reminds us—or confirms our suspicions (never really resisted by Mancini)—that the sardonic references to being "full of shit" (239) are, as it were, doubly confessional. But the clearing of the blockage, according to this scatological metaphor, takes on additional meaning of considerable importance to contemporary discourse and postmodern aesthetics. The reader is invited to think about a discourse that is not "full of it" or "bogus"—a discourse, in short, that is *not ironic*. One begins to see the significance of the narrator's plaintive iteration of "for serious" (13 times), "for real" (15 times), and "for sure" (28 times), for Palahniuk's denouement signals the prospect, at least, of a return to the rhetoric of sincerity so long occluded by the default irony of both modernism and postmodernism. "[F]or sure seriously" (227), then, the author of *Choke* grapples resourcefully with the challenge of being late to the postmodern party. His sardonic recycling of Freudian case history and millennial Christology, along with his surprisingly subtle and proleptic problematizing of modern and postmodern irony, reveals more ideational substance, in the end, than his critical disparagers might lead one to expect.

9

Addiction in *Choke*

Nieves Pascual

At the outset of *Choke*, Chuck Palahniuk writes: "This isn't about somebody brave, kind and dedicated. He isn't anybody you're going to fall in love with. Just so you know, what you're reading is the complete and relentless story of an addict" (7–8). In fact, addiction is Palahniuk's great theme. Addiction to violence, suffering, pain, danger, aesthetics, cosmetic surgery, the media, messianism, victimhood, consumption, choking, sex and support groups unabashedly marks his characters' lives. Eduardo Mendieta hits the nail on the head when he says that the moral behind Palahniuk's work is as "simple as this: our culture itself is an amphetamine, an alkaloid that hyper-stimulates our brains and hyper-excites our bodies. Our culture is perpetually turning us into junkies" (402). The paradox is that all those addictions that society creates are "the health of the individual[s]" (395), that is, they constitute "palliatives for a deeper and graver suffering: a void of meaning, a lack of direction" (396). It can be surmised from this: (a) that the boundary between health and pathology is uncertain in Palahniuk's texts; (b) that addicts numb their senses to the suffering of the real world and create their own ideal paradises of gratification; (c) that these paradises are imaginary; and (d) that addiction provides direction to Palahniuk's characters and fills the holes in their identities.

I propose that in *Choke* male–male sodomy is the concealed arch-addiction. Section 1 discusses the protagonist's sodomitic fantasies in the light of Freud's theories of ego defenses. Since addiction interrupts the codes of everyday life and installs addicts in a dream world of their own, the psychoanalytic framework provides a perfect tool for analysis. Section 2 reads sodomy as a displacement from Victor Mancini's compulsion to masturbation. It elaborates on the confusion between the anal and the oral the text plays upon, suggesting that the position of the phallus as the ultimate source of pleasure is in the text usurped by food. Section 3 links digestive and reproductive processes to investigate sodomy and impregnation. In the main, sodomy and masturbation are imbricated in discourses of sterility and waste, but Palahniuk resists this association by transgressing gender norms with women who perform as not women and men who perform as not men, assuming the characteristic of procreation. Section 4 addresses this performative strategy playing out the logic of simulation that undergirds the novel. The last section brings together the sodomitic and the aesthetic. It argues that indications of sodomitic desire are not only present in the metaphors of ingestion and procreation, but are also legible at the level of form: repetition, fragmentation, and orality are prime textual strategies. The final conclusion is that sodomy constitutes the hole in Palahniuk's text—nothing is directly said about it—that subtends the possibility of purpose and meaning.

One caveat: Palahniuk couples sexual and textual play. His text is promiscuous in references ranging from William Shakespeare to Oscar Wilde through Simon and Garfunkel which, unfortunately, have not been researched into. For the purposes at hand, however, I restrict myself to the works of Sigmund Freud, the Bible, and a passing reference to Charles Darwin, the three of which I identify as intertexts for *Choke*.

Narcissism, sodomy, and masturbation

In examining the relevant literature on addiction, one immediately notes the central place narcissism occupies. Psychiatrists Ernst Simmel, Sándor Radó, and Herbert A. Rosenfeld, among others, connected addiction with pathological narcissism, no doubt influenced by Freud who in a letter to Wilhelm Fliess of December 22, 1897, referred to masturbation or self-pleasuring as the "primary addiction" from which all the others derive (272). Versus primary or healthy narcissism which exists in all children and constitutes an essential part of psychic development (love of the other is grounded in love of self), secondary or pathological narcissism is a mental illness characterized by megalomania, that is, an unrealistic sense of self-importance and belief in the omnipotence of thought. The subject takes refuge in megalomania as a defense against an unpleasant reality.

In *Treatment of Addiction*, Neil Springham describes pathological narcissism as "self-interest as an unconscious psychological defense. While its etiology is complex, one relevant strand of the theory suggests that it arises in sustained exposure to unmanageable levels of frustration in the infant's early maternal relationship which results in a distortion of ego development" (143). Let's say that a child cries and the mother does not appear. The child screams in frustration until it eventually falls asleep. Deep down this sleep "is an evasive withdrawal into narcissistic euphoria," and as such bears comparison to the withdrawal of the addict into intoxication (145). In sum, if the mother is not available enough, the child cannot find a mother to love and turns to loving itself. It may also happen that the mother is over-solicitous, giving excessive care to the child, in which case the child's narcissism will also be exacerbated: the child is made to feel that it deserves her whole attention and comes to believe that he is all-important, that all else exists only for his comfort and nourishment.

Paradoxically, Victor Mancini's mother, who earned her living as a masturbation therapist teaching others how to invest their sexual energies in themselves, could not manage her son's masturbation. She was just as incapable of soothing his anxieties or nurturing his needs as she is of nurturing her own. Significantly, at the beginning of the novel she is at a care center because she has lost her appetite: she "needs a feeding tube. She feels hunger, but she's forgotten what the feeling means. Consequently, she does not eat" (23). Addicted to nothingness, she lets herself die. On the one hand, Ida Mancini overfed Victor's narcissism, when he was a child, by making him believe that, like God, he had the power to create reality just by naming it: "Draw the river on our new map," she tells her son when driving on a bridge, "And get ready," she urges him, "there's lot more stuff that needs a name coming up," as if he could redraw the world (285). On the other hand, most of her time was spent in jail or the mental asylum. Because she was found unfit to raise him, Victor was taken up in diverse foster homes, but the safety and security they promised was interrupted unexpectedly, "every time the Mommy came back to claim him" (39), when she was able to escape. Following upon Freud, it is possible to read the recurrent appearance and disappearance of the Mommy as a version of the *fort/da* game that the Austrian therapist theorized in the second chapter of "Beyond the Pleasure Principle" (1920) upon seeing his grandson playing with a reel attached to a string: little Ernst repeatedly threw the object away from him where it could not be seen only to pull it back into view. The toy represents the absent parent while the game expresses the violence that absence implies, which the child tolerates obtaining pleasure. Pleasure, Freud diagnoses, derives from (a) the sense of power that the child experiences: the child conceives of appearance and disappearance as the outcome of his wish; and (b) from the primordial human inclination to destruction. As it is, Freud theorized the existence of mysterious sadist/masochistic trends within the subject that impel him/her to return to sleep, peace, nonexistence, nothingness, the void or the nirvana of the womb. It is from this drive that Freud conceived the "nirvana principle."

The trauma of his mother's absence is not transformed into pleasure by Victor because the game absolutely escapes his control: when he needs her she is never there. Very soon, however, he learns to neutralize the feelings of loneliness, sadness, and fear that her going away generates by looking at a series of photographs posted on a pornographic website picturing a dumpy guy dressed as Tarzan with a monkey "trained to poke what looked like roasted chestnuts up the guy's ass" (36). So, "Every time he was scared, sad or alone, every night he woke up panicked in a new foster home, his heart racing, his bed wet, every day he started school in a different neighborhood, [. . .] the kid would think of those same twelve photos of the fat man bent over" (39). Wherever he is, in his mid-twenties Victor still logs on to the Internet to watch the scene. It is not "the sex part of pornography" that hooks him, he explains, but the nerve of the fat man to bend naked in front of the camera: "It was the confidence. The courage. The complete lack of shame. The comfort and genuine honesty. The up-front-ness of being able to just stand there and tell the world: Yeah, this is how I chose to spend a free afternoon. Posing there with a monkey putting chestnuts up my ass" (37). What *prima facie* seduces Victor, then, what he finds comforting in the image of a monkey stuffing food up a fat man's behind is the man's absolute surrender to debasement, his loss of power, his acceptance of powerlessness which, in his mind, is his very access to power, his form of empowerment. Then, there is also power in Victor's access to the image, which can be retrieved whenever he has the need for peace.

Despite Victor's disclaimer, sexual satisfaction plays a part in his idolatrous worship of the image. The transformation of the short fat man into a god-like ideal invites discussion on two points: identification and the Oedipus complex, both of which Palahniuk parodies. In "Three Essays on the Theory of Sexuality" (1905) Freud states that identification derives from the oral phase of sexual organization and is effected through introjections, in the mouth:

> The first of these [organizations of sexual life] is the oral or, as it might be called, cannibalistic pregenital sexual organization. Here sexual activity has not yet been separated from the ingestion of food; nor are opposite currents within the activity differentiated. The *object* of both activities is the same; the sexual aim consists in the incorporation of the object—the prototype of a process which, in the form of identification, is later to play such an important psychological part. (197)

It will play an important part because through incorporation the ego masters the Oedipus complex. According to the Oedipal scenario, the little boy already experiences great ambivalence with regard to his father with whom he competes for possession of the mother. This ambivalence is manifested in a fear of castration: as punishment for desiring his mother the child becomes anxious that his penis will be cut off by the father figure. Identification diminishes the little boy's castrating anxiety by satisfying this ambivalence. In "Group Psychology and the Analysis of the Ego" (1922), Freud writes: "Identification, in fact, is ambivalent from the very first; it can turn into an expression of tenderness as easily as into a wish for someone's removal. It behaves like a derivative of the first, oral phase of the organization of the libido, in which the object that we long for and prize is assimilated by eating and in that way annihilated as such" (105).

In the photograph of man and monkey introjection is not oral but anal. Phrased differently, the anus or the seat of expulsion is confused with the locus of incorporation. On the other hand, the

absence of paternal agency deflects a more normative Oedipal
trajectory. "In the modern Oedipal story," writes Palahniuk, "it's the
mother who kills the father and takes the son" (16). The son Victor
does not know who his father is and looks for a substitute father;
in fact, the novel is Victor's search for a father. If the mechanism of
identification presupposes, according to Freud, the internalization
of the same-sex parent, the man offering his anus is Victor's imago
of his father. That he identifies himself with the man means that he
wants to be like him and, inevitably, speaks to an unconscious desire
to live the image and entertain an homoerotic fantasy. To Victor:
"that was enlightenment. To be that comfortable and confident in
the world would be Nirvana" (38). The sadist-masochistic inflection
of the nirvana principle is clearly displayed in the "fat man's smile"
(ibid.), resulting from "torture" and "humiliation" (39).

Food porn

Therefore, far from castrating, the fat man bent over saves him:
"'Savior' isn't the right word, but it's the first word that comes to
mind" (ibid.), thinks Victor when looking at the image, reflecting
on its self-soothing potential. "Savior" is not the right word for
Victor either, but it is the first word that comes to the reader's
mind. Victor, who openly claims to be a savior, is not a real
savior, he does not really save (in the real sense of "preserving
from destruction," *Webster's*) anybody, not even himself; rather,
he is a simulacrum of a savior, an imitation. One of his preferred
scenarios to act the role of savior is restaurants. Since he cannot
afford the "three grand each month" (50) for the care that his
mother is receiving, Victor goes to restaurants and causes himself
to choke mid-way through his meal, luring "Good Samaritans"
(ibid.) into saving his life:

> Why I do this is to put adventure back into people's lives.
> Why I do this is to create heroes. Put people to the test.
> Like mother, like son.
> Why I do this is to make money.
> Somebody saves your life, and they'll love you forever. (49)

Victor makes people "feel like God" (51), and they, in return, send him money to help him pay his made-up bills. He keeps a list of everyone who saves him and sends them letters asking for help. Going by the example of the picture of the ersatz sodomites, Victor becomes powerless so as to gain power over others: "You gain power by pretending to be weak. By contrast, you make people feel so strong. You save people by letting them save you" (50). His choking is "the martyrdom of Saint Me" (51). Martyrdom demands a death and implies some form of witnessing or bearing witness, as is testified to by the Greek word *martus*, meaning "witness." However, what readers witness is not Victor's real death, but a series of simulacra or a succession of masturbation-related deaths which require spectators that bear testament and pay: "God only knows how many deaths I'll have to almost die to pay for a stomach tube" he tells himself (78). It is worth noting the close liaison built between ecstasy and death in martyrs' texts (Baldwin Smith 41–62). As to the relationship between food and self-fellatio, it becomes tangible in the following description of the erect penis and ejaculation: "From not breathing, the veins in my neck swell. My face gets red, gets hot. Sweat springs up on my forehead. Sweat blots through the back of my shirt. With my hands, I hold tight around my neck, the universal sign language for someone choking to death" (48). Victor's neck/shaft swells as with an erection, the face/glans becomes tumescent and sweat/semen is emitted. The oral tract is obstructed through food, which usurps the position of the phallus as the ultimate source of pleasure, causing autoerotic asphyxia. The term "autoerotic asphyxia" or "asphyxiophilia" is used to designate the desire for a state of oxygen deficiency to enhance sexual excitement and attain orgasm. Defined as "a subcategory of sexual masochism," asphyxiophilia is not normally "practiced with a partner" but as a "solitary act" (Greenberg 505). As we realize that by watching Victor choking to death we are watching him choking to orgasm, witnessing transforms into voyeurism.

Palahniuk's parody reaches epic proportions when the imitation becomes the original and Victor discovers that he is, in fact, the second coming of Christ. The story goes like this: "According to Paige Marshall, it's in my mom's diary that six women were offered embryos created from this genetic material [the relic remains of the foreskin of Jesus Christ]. Five of them never came to term. The sixth is me" (153). At this moment Victor stops looking for his father: he has become his own father; he is God. Paige says: "if you believe in the Holy Trinity, you're your own father" (145). If this is so, within the catachresis of the terms "oral" and "anal" woven through the text, bearing in mind that what the monkey is stuffing up the fat man's behind is a food item (a roasted chestnut), it can be hypothesized that the photograph of the "tubby savior with his beatific smile" (262) is, in essence, a displacement from Victor's compulsion to autoerotic behavior. This suggestion gains credence with the choice of a monkey as a partner.

The question is: why a monkey? Nothing escapes Palahniuk's parodistic intentions. He parodies Freud just as he parodies the history of Christ and the theory of evolution. Leaving aside the obvious meaning of the word "monkey" as "addiction" (*Webster's*), its presence brings to mind that, according to Charles Darwin, the monkey is the origin of man. When Victor confesses that what he most admires in the monkey is "honesty" (37), he refers to the absence of guile or deceit in its nature, and, by implication, to the monkey's originality. A monkey may well copy the behaviors of others but it necessarily represents the origin: "original" meaning both "existing first or at the beginning" and "not a copy" (*Webster's*). Incidentally, it should be pointed out that the word "primate" derives from *primus*, "first" or original. I will come back to the issues of originality, fakery, and the simulacra that saturate the novel in order to examine how they contribute to understanding the process of addiction. What matters for now is that by bringing together the father and the primate Palahniuk is comically reconciling creationism with evolutionism: Victor, the ultimate Father or prime cause, is also the monkey.

The reproductive imperative

It is no accident that Victor is obsessed with parenthood as it constitutes the major source of his narcissistic supply: "Parenthood is the opiate of the masses," says Paige (112). Addicted to this opiate, he parents the old women institutionalized at St Anthony's Constant Care Center, willfully assuming the role of a sacrificial scapegoat. In the following citation, with an explicit reference to sodomy he takes upon himself the blame for the traumas that brought them

into the sanatorium: "I tell them, heap it on me. Make me play
the big bottom in your guilt gang bang. I'll take everybody's load"
(72). During his visits, Victor mothers his mother by trying to make
her eat, but she keeps her mouth closed, flailing like an infant, just
like him when choking, a likeness that does not escape the son:
"Heaving and flopping, her hands clawing at her throat. This is
how I must look choking in public" (270). At all costs, Victor wants
to save her life but only to keep her crippled so that he can be in
charge. He confesses:

> All my life, I have been less my mother's child than her hostage.
> The subject of her social and political experiments. Her own
> private rat. Now she's mine, and she's not going to escape by
> dying or getting better. I just want one person I can rescue. I want
> one person who needs me. Who can't live without me. I want to
> be a hero, but not just this time. Even if it means keeping her
> crippled. I want to be someone's constant savior. (118)

In his mother's crippling behavior he discovers the underlying cause
of his chauvinism. In his view, "a male chauvinist pig isn't born,
he's made, and more and more of them are being made by women"
(ibid.). Women are clearly inferior and easily replaceable to Victor.
He tells Denny:

> We don't need women. There are plenty other things in the world
> to have sex with, just go to a sexaholics meeting and take note.
> There's microwaved watermelons. There's the vibrating handles
> of lawn mowers right at crotch level. There's vacuum cleaners
> and beanbag chairs. Internet sites. And those old chat room sex
> hounds pretending to be sixteen-year-old-girls. For serious, old
> FBI guys make the sexiest cyberbabes. (205)

Behind Victor's overt depreciation of women, his petulance and
cynicism hide fear. Above I suggested that in Palahniuk's inversion
of the Oedipus myth, the mother takes the son who, in turn,
focuses his libido upon the father. In this rendition, it is not the
father but the mother that causes castration anxiety. Powerful
and domineering, Victor's mother choked him as an infant. Now,
as an adult, he takes revenge by keeping her castrated; the words
"cripple" and "choke" being euphemisms for castration, the power

of which is owned by women. Thus, old Ida represents the castrated mother who by refusing food repudiates her own lack (of penis). In the Freudian imaginary castration defines womanhood, but this requires elaboration.

In her essay "Giving Death," Erin Soros examines the relationship between castration and anorexia, and intimates that through lack of appetite a woman masks her essence and avoids accounting for it. In her words: "The fantasy of anorexia defines the self as phallus, completely self-contained [needing nothing, lacking nothing], absolutely independent of another" (27). Herein lies a fundamental paradox: if through anorexia a woman disavows her castration, through anorexia she also makes the lack present, the absent signified (food) being visible in her emaciation. Regardless, especially interesting is Soros' alliance of digestive and reproductive processes. As she recounts her experience with pregnancy and anorexia, Soros comes to the conclusion that they are two sides of the same coin since the pregnant mother can hardly eat when nauseated by food. Moreover, both processes complete the woman: while anorexia defines the self as phallus, the pregnant mother replaces the lack inherent to her being with a child. If, in Freud's argument, a woman becomes complete by giving birth, it follows that she gains a penis through a baby. In the novel, however, Ida remains incomplete. A crucial moment happens when she tells Victor that he is not her own child: "She says, 'I stole you [Victor] out of a stroller in Waterloo, Iowa'" (269). Soros says: "If a fetus is what allows a woman to complete herself as properly female," then, not carrying a fetus or not bearing a baby "performs one as a not-woman" (23). To clarify: by assuming the physical characteristic typical of men, incapacity for pregnancy, a woman performs herself as incomplete or as not a real woman.

In contrast to Ida, 90-year-old Eva Muehler, also exiled in St Anthony's, represents the castrator who by biting decapitates the phallus and by spitting it out spews its organic significance. "Diddled" or raped as a child by her big brother, she adopted the disgusting habit of spitting out chewed food and putting it in her pockets or her handbag as if these were a mouth (54). The logic of confusing the mouth and the anus that structures the novel does not exclude the biting rhetoric of the vagina as the site of badness and destructive impulses. No long considerations are needed to understand that the image of Eva's biting recalls the toothed vagina myth, largely read as a symbol of male castration for obvious reasons. Elizabeth Grosz writes that the fantasy of the *vagina dentata* results in "the identification of female sexuality as voracious, insatiable, enigmatic, invisible and unknowable, cold, calculating, instrumental, castrator/decapitator of the male, dissimulatress or fake, predatory, engulfing mother, preying on male weakness." She goes on to say that these "are all consequences of the ways in which male orgasm has functioned as the measure and representative of all sexualities and all modes of erotic encounter" (293). From a slightly different angle, again feeding on Soros, it should be noted that another way to make oneself not-a-complete-woman, she explains, is by "having an abortion—cutting off the fetus as penis" (23). In this mode of thinking, if the equation food= penis= baby delivered by Soros is true, Eva's castrating fixation is none other than an aborting fixation. "To abort or castrate it," writes Soros, "If a baby promises to be a maternal phallus, what can an abortion be but a castration?" (ibid.). If the phallus promises to be food, what can a compulsion for castration be but a compulsion for chewing and spitting?

In this logic, the man who performs procreation performs himself as "incomplete," a not-man. In attempting to move from masturbation, whose attribute is that of sterility, to procreation my argument may seem to have landed in a contradiction. Even if this is so, the contradiction is Palahniuk's; still, I would claim, it is less a contradiction than a strategy to bring autoerotic desire to the text while holding it at bay. Masturbation and procreation are engaged as a linked pair via Victor's delusional fantasies of fatherhood and parthenogenesis. In the belief that he is God, he assumes the capacity of self-birth or of creating ex-nihilo, so that every time he chokes in orgasm and aborts the food stuck in his throat, unbitten, he gives himself life, living his masculinity as a continuous rebirth.

Perhaps not surprisingly, fascinated by the thought of procreation as he is, Victor imagines that his best friend Denny creates babies out of stones. Victor first met Denny, compulsive masturbator, at a sexual addiction support group. They worked together at Colonial Dunsboro theme park but when Denny is fired he begins collecting stones from around the city and brings them home:

The oven is full of rocks. The freezer is full. The kitchen cabinets are so full that they're coming down off the wall. Even though the plan was only one rock a day, Denny's got such an addictive personality that he ends up carting home half-dozen rocks a day. (189)

To hide the rocks he has stolen, Denny transports them in a stroller, wrapped in pink baby blankets, as if they were babies. But in his fascination by the idea of procreation, instead of rocks Victor sees "those babies that Denny adopts . . . A whole generation piling up" (ibid.).

Simulated paradises

Playing on the pun of "stoner" and "getting stoned," that is, affected by a drug, Victor patiently explains to Denny that "Just because it's rocks doesn't mean this still isn't substance abuse" (190). The comment should be read within the parallelism of babies and foods drafted above. Enclosed within is the exchange of foods and stones, a syncretism that goes back to the Scriptures, specifically to the passage by Lk. 4.3–4, when in the wilderness the devil said to Jesus: "'If you are the son of God, command this stone to become bread.' But Jesus answered him, saying: 'It's written, Man shall not live by bread alone, but by every word of God'." Yet, deprived of their nutritive function, foods are as sterile as stones in the novel (and as sterile as the treasured organ of the penis, for that matter). It should be added that the text provokes another biblical reverberation: Matt. 16.18, when Peter is announced that on a rock God will build His church. Certainly, Denny is building "no doubt a Satanic church" (262) on the old Menningtown Country Townhouses block (219), which church brings us back to the church where Victor's sex-addiction meetings are held at the beginning of the novel (9).

It is inevitable to see in the symbol of the church/therapy room a fantasized return to the nirvana of the womb. At this point, allow me a brief digression on womb fantasy and male reproduction. Departing from Freud's theory of penis envy as a defining feature of women (women envy the penis and desire to possess it), Catherine B. Silver in her investigation of the maternal body, interprets womb envy as a repressed desire driving men to manipulate the womb through technology. According to her, scientific experimentation manifests their desire to monitor women's bodies, possess the womb, and assume its creative potential. Three moments in *Choke* allude to procreation technology. One happens when Dr Marshall proposes that Victor impregnates her so as to abort the fetus and inject its brain in Ida's head to cure her illness, but Victor cannot produce an erection (123). The second occurs when Denny imagines that the secret of Victor's mother is that his son is a cyborg and not a real person (125). The third refers to the embryo created from Jesus Christ's foreskin cells implanted, or so we are led to believe, in Ida's womb (153). In light of Silver's reflection, they unmistakably signal Victor's narcissistic wish for self-creation.

Primarily, at stake is the symbolism of the novel. "We don't live in the real world anymore," Ida claims, "We live in a world of symbols," (151), where the real is replaced by representations so that nothing is what appears to be. This reality of symbolization or simulation is the reality of the addict who creates an imaginary paradise of gratification where s/he assumes control and eradicates the chaos of everyday life. Jean Baudrillard in *Simulacra and Simulation* (1981) argues that this simulated world makes the real disappear and becomes truth in its own right (1). In *Choke*, "the unreal is [indeed] more powerful than the real" (160); yet, against Baudrillard, Palahniuk opens the gulf between the copy and the model, situating in the knowledge of difference the origin of all addictions: "Every addiction, she [Ida] said, was just a way to treat this same problem [knowledge]. Drugs or overeating or alcohol or sex, it was all just another way to find peace, to escape what we know. Our education. Our bite of the apple" (150). The goal is to escape to the period before the Fall and recuperate the innocence lost, but "a peek at reality" (151), a bite of knowledge or a taste of the apple is needed to know what to escape from. The self-medication strategy that addiction is starts, then, with substituting a roasted chestnut for the apple and the anus for the mouth, as if by altering the symbols of the original sin, the history of moral transgression could be removed too.

As expected, paradises of gratification multiply in the novel: the church, the community center conference room, the strip club, St Anthony's Hospital, Victor's mother's house and his workplace, Colonial Dunsboro, a living history museum that recreates eighteenth-century life where he is employed as an indentured servant. Through simulation Palahniuk dissociates history from truth just as he dissociates symbols from reality. The truth of history is exposed in the metamorphosis of the Pilgrim Fathers who went to America in search of God into modern addicts anxiously looking for salvation. Victor tells the reader:

> The only funny part about Colonial Dunsboro is maybe it's too authentic, but for all the wrong reasons. This whole crowd of losers and nutcases who hide out here because they can't make it in the real world, in real jobs—isn't this why we left England in the first place? To establish our own alternate reality? Weren't the Pilgrims pretty much the crackpots of their time? For sure, instead of just wanting to believe something different about God's love, the losers I work with want to find salvation through compulsive behaviors. (31–2)

The excess of authenticity the museum tends toward emphasizes the value of origins while insisting on artificiality. Even though excess destabilizes the opposition between the model and the copy (Where is the real origin? Is it the copy that engenders the model?), it does not cancel the disagreement. In summary: (a) too much reality in the simulated betrays a lack that is only pacified through consumption; (b) we consume in the hope of finding the real origin; (c) when the origin cannot be found we spend as much time consuming as we can, we become addicts controlled by simulation, servants to it. Another way to put what is at issue here is to say that simulation is the opiate of the masses, who are left with a history reduced to a rapid succession of alternate realities, origins that are not original, sham foods, make-believe saviors, substitute fathers, counterfeit gods, fake babies, spurious consumption, phony sex, mock pornography, simulated masturbation, fraudulent penises, bogus deaths, fictitious procreation, women in drag and men who are not real men.

In the opinion of Kevin Alexander Boon, not real men is precisely what the men's liberation movement is demanding; to wit, that they renounce the traits that have historically defined them as male, read: violence and power. In his study of masculinity in *Fight Club*, Boon argues that the unnamed narrator "attempts to satisfy the first demand by substituting material possessions for conquest."

The second is addressed by going to the gym. That neither succeeds in getting men "in touch with their primal masculinity" indicates that "true manhood lies elsewhere." He goes on to allege that the tragedy of the novel "is that in the cultural milieu of the late 20th century manhood can only be found in death [. . .]. In death [man] gains an individual identity and recaptures the name of the father" (267). As seen, in *Choke* Palahniuk resituates death in the context of sadist-masochistic masturbation, a substitute for death through which Victor recaptures the father and regains his primitive (or primate) nature. On the one hand, then, true manhood lies in masturbation. "Masturbation," which is the original desire of man, "is the only means of escape" from the cultural milieu of the late twentieth century, as Ida Mancini says (199). On the other hand, by giving men entrance into the arena of procreation, the author gives them a power they never had. Compared to *Fight Club*, which "investigates the frustration of heroic men reduced to servile eunuchs" (Boon 272), I would say that *Choke* investigates the accomplishments of servile eunuchs elevated to the category of heroes.

Text/sex

Much in the manner of eighteenth-century mock-heroic or mock-epic compositions, *Choke* manipulates the contrast between appearances and reality, puts a fool in the role of a hero, and raises the trivial matter of masturbation to the level of art. In Victor's words:

> For sure, even the worst blow job is better than, say, sniffing the best rose . . . watching the greatest sunset. Hearing children laugh.
>
> I think I shall never see a poem as lovely as a hot-gushing, butt-cramping, gut-hosing orgasm.
>
> Painting a picture, composing an opera, that's just something you do until you find the next willing piece of ass. (19)

Even writing a novel diverts the expression of the autoerotic impulse from its unspeakable form to one that is considered culturally acceptable. Writing sublimates sodomitic desires where "sublimate" should be understood in the double sense of diversion of sexual drives to artistic aims and elevation or exaltation in dignity: to make sublime (*Webster's*). This is not the place for a discussion of the sublime, suffice it to say that its unspeakability has served Richard Halpern to equate sublimity and sodomy in literary texts spanning several centuries. His theory of a "rhetoric of sodomitical silence" (48) as presented in *Shakespeare's Perfume* (2002) is based on the idea that the textual is sexual; that is, that textual play can limn the unspoken desire of one man for another. My point is that Palahniuk paints masturbation on the surface of the text using three basic strategies favored by epic poets: heavy use of repetition, mutilation of the body, and orality.

Repetition, which abounds in the form of stock sentences and images, acts out the addict's tendency to repeat the same pleasurable experience over and over again. Reiterated are the sequence of Victor's choking, always recited in the same terms, and references to the figure of the chestnut monkey (invoked at least eight times through the novel and surprisingly absent from the movie version, see Elfman 2008) as well as to the drawing of maps that Ida insistently forced her son into. Related to Victor's obsession with drawing maps is his interest in frames. At a certain point in the novel he says: "It's funny how the beauty of art has much more to do with the frame than with the artwork itself" because it is the frame that makes the artwork be understood as such (100). In *The Truth in Painting* (1987) Jacques Derrida equates the framing with the form or signifier and the framed with the content or signifier. Forcefully he argues that form is central to the process of meaning production (73). In like manner, Palahniuk in *Choke* emphasizes the significance of form as the frame for meaning with the purpose of cutting open the opposition of form and content: the unspoken content (male-male/autoerotic desire) becomes form or is intelligible in the form of the text.

In his recovery group Victor is advised to write down a diary inventorying his life, that way the pain that triggered the addiction can be analyzed and overcome, "Because supposedly, those who forget their past are condemned to repeat it" (8). His therapists forget, though, that there is a mysterious link between pain and pleasure, so that far from helping, remembrance moves Victor to repeat and experience indefinitely the pain that activated his compulsive behavior in the first place. Instead of reading as a self-help book, *Choke*, Victor's diary, operates as a how-to manual. The pleasure of repetition is further supplemented by catalogs used by Victor to bring peace and order; in fact, they operate as prayers (Chandrasoma 200–2). It goes without saying that they also assist his memory. He observes a mole on Cherry Daiquiri's skin and proceeds with his usual physical dissection:

> The way to remember every step to a physical examination is CHAMP FASTS. It's what they call *mnemonic* in medical school. The letters stand for:
>
> Chief Complaint.
>
> History of Illness.
>
> Allergies.
>
> Medications.
>
> Past Medical History.
>
> Family History.
>
> Alcohol.
>
> Street Drugs.
>
> Tobacco.
>
> Social History.
>
> The only way to get through medical school is mnemonics. (101–2)

Medical student that he was, Victor retains the ability of fragmenting the body into pieces. The clinical shares this tendency to fragment with the pornographic and/or masturbatory discourse. Both pornography and masturbation deconstruct the body, deriving pleasure from its violent mutilation into detachable parts. "In pornography," Annette Kuhn notes, "photographs are often composed in such a way that a particular body part is emphasized or it may even fill the whole picture, in which case the body is fragmented, cut up, by the frame" (36). Kuhn goes on to write that "porn's attention to bits of bodies is never random. Pornography is preoccupied with what it regards as signifiers of sexual difference and sexuality: genitals, breasts, buttocks" (37). This is the condition of the bodies in *Choke*: throats, "tits," "dicks," "clits," tongues and "assholes" float in the text, "always there, always ready to use" (18). What is more, the body of the novel is itself fragmented through the use of flashbacks, changes of place, richness of subplots, short paragraphs, and simple sentences that make the text look like a list of points.

The body part most privileged by pornographic discourse is the masculine phallus as the fount of pleasure. It was argued above that the place of the phallus is colonized by food on which Victor chokes in a spasm of alimentary orgasm. That food replaces the phallus makes sense within the economies of simulation, castration anxiety, and sodomitical silence that rule the novel. At the level of form, one more strategy underwrites Palahniuk's phallocentric narrative of food ingestion: orality. Besides repetition, listing and condensation (of paragraphs and sentences), which are common oral language techniques, Palahniuk uses idioms, slang, swearwords, contractions, questions, and recalling that invoke phallocentrism (whose connection with the prioritizing of speech over narrative is exhaustively investigated by Derrida in "Plato's Pharmacy") and, moreover, build a conversational ethos that facilitates the bond between author and reader.

Conclusion

Choke never expresses, not overtly, a desire for the male body, and yet sodomy is the text's ultimate signifier. In the light of the narcissistic tendency of the addictive personality and Freud's castration anxiety theory, sodomy has been read as autoerotic desire. Departing from the logic of simulation that organizes the novel, it has been argued that masturbation is enacted in the metaphor of food. Given the role of language in the creation of alternate realities and the oral sensuality of the text, the last part has focused on the rhetorical strategies that speak the unspoken desire of Victor Mancini.

Like epic poetry, which begins with an invocation to the gods, the narrator in *Choke* apostrophizes, using the pronoun "you" to invoke the reader. At the outset of the novel, Chuck Palaniuk writes: "This isn't about somebody brave, kind and dedicated. He isn't anybody you're going to fall in love with. Just so you know, what you're reading is the complete and relentless story of an addict"

(7–8). I do not know what kind of love Palahniuk has in mind. If love is of the sadist-masochistic kind, Victor is certainly lovable. Through his addiction Palahniuk offers a warmed-over chestnut for solving the problem of male selfhood that may bring a beatific smile to the face of some readers.

WORKS CITED

Annesley, James. *Blank Fictions: Consumerism, Culture and the Contemporary American Novel.* London: Pluto, 1998.

Baldwin Smith, Lacey. *Fools, Martyrs, Traitors: The Story of Martyrdom in the Western World.* Evanston, IL: Northwestern University Press, 1999.

Barth, John. "More on the Same Subject." 1960. *The Friday Book.* New York: GP Putnam's Sons, 1984. 26–9.

Bartky, Sandra Lee. *Femininity and Domination: Studies in the Phenomenology of Oppression.* New York: Routledge, 1990.

Bataille, Georges. *Erotism: Death and Sensuality.* Trans. Mary Dalwood. San Francisco: City Lights Books, 1986.

Baudrillard, Jean. *Simulacra and Simulation.* Ann Arbor, MI: University of Michigan Press, 1994.

Bauman, Zygmunt. *Liquid Modernity.* Cambridge: Polity Press, 2000.

—. *Liquid Life.* Cambridge: Polity Press, 2005.

Beauvoir, Simone de. *The Second Sex.* 1949. Trans. H. M. Parshley. New York: Vintage Books, 1989.

Bennett, Robert. "The Death of Sisyphus: Existential Literature and the Cultural Logic of Chuck Palahniuk's *Fight Club*." *Stirrings Still* 2.2 (2005): 65–77.

Blazer, Alex. "The Phony 'Martyrdom of Saint Me' *Choke*, *The Catcher in the Rye*, and the Problem of Postmodern Narcissistic Nihilism." In *Reading Chuck Palahniuk: American Monsters and Literary Mayhem.* Cynthia Kuhn and Lance Rubin, eds. New York: Routledge, 2009. 143–56.

Boon, Kevin Alexander. "Men and Nostalgia for Violence: Culture and Culpability in Chuck Palahniuk's Fight Club." *Journal of Men's Studies*, 11.3 (2003): 267–76.

Borges, Jorge Luis. "Kafka and His Precursors." *Labyrinths.* New York: New Directions, 2007. 199–201.

Bray Haddock, Deborah. *Dissociative Identity Disorder Sourcebook.* Chicago: Contemporary Books, 2001.

Burke, Edmund. *A Philosophical Enquiry into our Ideas of the Sublime and the Beautiful.* Adam Phillips, ed. Oxford: Oxford World Classics, 1990.

Cameron, James. *Avatar*. 20th Century Fox, 2009.

Campbell, Joseph. *The Hero with a Thousand Faces*, 2nd edn. Princeton, NJ: Princeton University Press, 1968.

Carter, Graydon. Remarks quoted in Seth Mnookin, "In Disaster's Aftermath, Once-Cocky Media Culture Disses the Age of Irony." *Inside. com*. September 18, 2001. Web, May 9, 2011.

Caruth, Cathy. *Trauma: Explorations in Memory*. Baltimore: Johns Hopkins University Press, 1995.

—. *Unclaimed Experiences: Trauma, Narrative, and History*. Baltimore: Johns Hopkins University Press, 1996.

Casado de Rocha, Antonio. "Disease and Community in Chuck Palahniuk's Early Novels." *Stirrings Still* 2.2 (2005): 105–15.

Chandrasoma, Shahin. "Physicians, Shamans, and Personal Trainers: An Interview with Chuck Palahniuk." *The Western Journal of Medicine* 176.3 (2002): 200–3.

Coleman, Philip. "Hauntedness: Edgar Allan Poe and Chuck Palahniuk." In *The Ghost Story From The Middle Ages To The Twentieth Century*. Helen Conrad O'Briain and Julie Anne Stevens, eds. Dublin: Four Courts Press, 2010. 166–79.

Collado-Rodríguez, Francisco. "From Theory to Practice: Blank Fiction, Ethics, and Hybridism in Palahniuk's *Stranger Than Fiction* and *Invisible Monsters*." In *Masculinities, Femininities and the Power of the Hybrid in U.S. Narratives: Essays on Gender Borders*. Nieves Pascual, Laura Alonso-Gallo and Francisco Collado-Rodríguez, eds. Heidelberg: Universitätsverlag Winter, 2007. 189–200.

Costa, Jordi. "Hombres salvajes, bestias salvajes: megamostrencos, kamikazes y neobárbaros." *Mondo Brutto* 26 (2002): 9–13.

De Lauretis, Teresa. *Technologies of Gender: Essays on Theory, Film, and Fiction*. Bloomington: Indiana University Press, 1987.

Dee, Jonathan. "Ready-Made Rebellion: The Empty Tropes of Transgressive Fiction." *Harper's Magazine*, April 2005. 87–91.

DeLillo, Don. *Mao II*. New York: Viking, 1991.

Derrida, Jacques. "Plato's Pharmacy." *Dissemination*. Chicago: University of Chicago Press, 1981. 61–172.

—. *The Truth in Painting*. Chicago: University of Chicago Press, 1987.

Dobkin, David. *The Change-Up*. Universal Pictures, 2011.

Elfman, Mali. "Interview: Clark Gregg and Chuck Palahniuk of *Choke*." *screencrave.com*. September 23, 2008. Web, May 10, 2011.

Erikson, Kai. "Notes on Trauma and Community." *American Imago* 48.4 (1991): 455–71.

Favazza, Armando R. *Bodies under Siege: Self-Mutilation and Body Modification in Culture and Psychiatry*. Baltimore: Johns Hopkins University Press, 1996.

Felman, Shoshana and Dori Laub. *Testimony: Crises of Witnessing in Literature, Psychoanalysis, and History*. New York: Routledge, Chapman and Hall, Inc., 1992.

Fink, Bruce. *A Clinical Introduction to Lacanian Psychoanalysis: Theory and Technique*. Cambridge, MA: Harvard University Press, 1997.

Fish, Stanley. *Self-Consuming Artifacts: The Experience of Seventeenth Century Literature*. Berkeley: University of California Press, 1972.

FitzGerald, Edward. *Rubáiyát of Omar Khayyám: A Critical Edition*. Christopher Decker, ed. Charlottesville: University Press of Virginia, 1997.

Fitzgerald, F. Scott. *This Side of Paradise*. New York: Scribners, 1921.

Freud, Sigmund. "Beyond the Pleasure Principle." *The Standard Edition of the Complete Psychological Works of Sigmund Freud*. James Strachey, ed. New York and London: The Hogarth Press, 1953. Vol. XVIII: 1–64.

—. "Extracts from the Fliess Papers." *The Standard Edition of the Complete Psychological Works of Sigmund Freud*. Vol. I: 173–280.

—. "Family Romances." In *The Uncanny*. Adam Phillips, ed. *The New Penguin Freud*. New York: Penguin, 2003.

—. "Group Psychology and the Analysis of the Ego." *The Standard Edition of the Complete Psychological Works of Sigmund Freud*. Vol. VXIII: 65–143.

—. "Three Essays on the Theory of Sexuality." *The Standard Edition of the Complete Psychological Works of Sigmund Freud*. Vol. VII: 123–243.

Friday, Krister. "A Generation of Men Without History." *Postmodern Culture* 13. May 2003. Web, May 13, 2011.

George, Sean M. "The Phoenix Inverted: The Rebirth and Death of Masculinity and the Reemergence of Trauma in Contemporary American Literature." Diss. Texas A&M University, 2010.

Gerrig, Richard J. *Experiencing Narrative Worlds: On the Psychological Activities of Reading*. New Haven and London: Yale University Press, 1993.

Girard, René. *Violence and the Sacred*. Trans. Patrick Gregory. Baltimore: Johns Hopkins University Press, 1977.

Giroux, Henry A. "Private Satisfactions and Public Disorders: *Fight Club*, Patriarchy, and the Politics of Masculine Violence." *Jac* 21.1 (2001): 1–31.

Glassie, John. "The Pugilist Novelist." An Interview with Chuck Palahniuk. *The New York Times Magazine*. September 29, 2002. Web, May 15, 2012.

Gold, Steven N. "*Fight Club*: A Depiction of Contemporary Society as Dissociogenic." *Journal of Trauma and Dissociation* 5.2 (2003): 13–34.

Greenberg, Jerrold S., Clint E. Bruess, and Sarah C. Conklin. *Exploring the Dimensions of Human Sexuality*. Sudbury, MA: Jones and Bartlett, 2007.

Grosz, Elizabeth. "Animal Sex: Libido as Desire and Death." *Sexy Bodies: The Strange Carnalities of Feminism*. Elizabeth Grosz and Elspeth Probyn, eds. New York: Routledge, 1995. 278–99.

Halpern, Richard. *Shakespeare's Perfume: Sodomy and Sublimity in the Sonnets, Wilde, Freud, and Lacan*. Philadelphia: University of Pennsylvania Press, 2002.

Hamera, Judith and Alfred Bendixen. "Introduction: New Worlds and Old Lands—The Travel Book and the Construction of American Identity." *The Cambridge Companion to American Travel Writing*. Cambridge: Cambridge University Press, 2009. 1–9.

Hartman, Geoffrey. "On Traumatic Knowledge and Literary Studies." *New Literary History* 26.3 (1995): 537–63.

Hedegaard, Erik. "A Heartbreaking life of Staggering Weirdness." *Rolling Stone*, June 30, 2005: 124–30.

Herman, Judith. *Trauma and Recovery*. New York: Basic, 1992.

Jameson, Fredric. 1988. "Postmodernism and Consumer Society." In *Studies in Culture: An Introductory Reader*. Ann Gray and Jim McGuigan, eds. London: Arnold, 1997. 192–205.

Janoff-Bulman, Ronnie. *Shattered Assumptions: Toward New Psychology of Trauma*. New York: Free Press, 1992.

Kant, Immanuel. *The Critique of Judgment*. 1790. Trans. Werner S. Pluhar. Indianapolis: Hackett, 1987.

Kavadlo, Jesse. "The Fiction of Self-Destruction: Chuck Palahniuk, Closet Moralist." *Stirrings Still* 2.2 (2005): 3–24.

Kavanagh, Matt. "On Failed Romance, Writer's Malpractice, and Prose for the Nose: A Conversation with Chuck Palahniuk." In *Sacred and Immoral: On the Writings of Chuck Palahniuk*. Jeffrey A. Sartain, ed. Newcastle upon Tyne: Cambridge Scholars Publishing, 2009. 178–92.

Kuhn, Annette. *The Power of the Image: Essays on Representation and Sexuality*. London: Routledge and Kegan Paul, 1985.

Lacan, Jacques. "The Mirror Stage as Formative of the *I* Function as Revealed in Psychoanalytical Experience." *Ecrits*. Bruce Fink, ed. and trans. New York: Norton, 2006.

Laub, Dori and Nanette C. Auerhahn. "Knowing and Not Knowing Massive Psychic Trauma: Forms of Traumatic Memory." *International Journal of Psychoanalysis* 74.2 (1993): 287–302.

Lefebvre, Henri. *The Production of Space*. Trans. Donald Nicholson-Smith. Oxford: Blackwell, 1991.

Lizardo, Omar. "*Fight Club*, or the Cultural Contradictions of Late Capitalism." *Journal for Cultural Research* 11.3 (July 2007): 221–43.

Longfellow, Henry Wadsworth. "Kéramos." *Kéramos and Other Poems.* London: George Routledge, 1878. 11–33.

Lury, Celia. *Consumer Culture.* New Brunswick: Rutgers University Press, 1996.

Lyotard, Jean-François. *The Postmodern Condition: A Report on Knowledge.* 1979. Trans. Geoff Bennington and Brian Massumi. Minneapolis: University of Minnesota Press, 1984.

Maslin, Janet. "An Immature Con Man with a Mom Problem. Review of *Choke,* by Chuck Palahniuk." *The New York Times.* May 24, 2001. Web, May 16, 2012.

Mathews, Peter. "Diagnosing Chuck Palahniuk's *Fight Club.*" *Stirrings Still* 2.2 (2005): 81–104.

McLuhan, Marshall. *Understanding Media: The Extensions of Man.* London: Routledge and Kegan Paul, 1964.

Mendieta, Eduardo. "Surviving American Culture: On Chuck Palahniuk." *Philosophy and Literature* 29.2 (2005): 394–408.

Miller, Laura. "Review of *Diary,* by Chuck Palahniuk." *Salon.com.* August 20, 2003. Web, May 15, 2012.

Mills, Katie. *The Road Story and the Rebel: Moving Through Film, Fiction, and Television.* Carbondale: Southern Illinois University Press, 2006.

Mitchell, Juliet. *Siblings: Sex and Violence.* Cambridge: The Polity Press, 2003.

Mnookin, Seth. "In Disaster's Aftermath, Once-Cocky Media Culture Disses the Age of Irony." *Inside.com.* September 18, 2001. Web, May 15, 2012.

Moyaert, Paul. "Fetishism and the Vicissitudes off the Object in Sublimation According to Freud and Lacan." In *Everyday Extraordinary: Encountering Fetishism with Marx, Freud, and Lacan.* Christopher M. Gemerchak, ed. Leuven: Leuven University Press, 2004. 45–70.

Nabokov, Vladimir. *Pnin.* New York: Vintage, 1984.

Ng, Andrew Hock Soon. "Muscular Existentialism in Chuck Palahniuk's *Fight Club.*" *Stirrings Still* 2.2 (2005): 116–38.

Nietzsche, Friedrich. *Thus Spoke Zarathustra.* Cambridge: Cambridge University Press, 2006.

O'Connor, Flannery. "The Fiction Writer and His Country." *Mystery and Manners,* 1961. 25–50.

O'Hehir, Andrew. "Chokin' on Chuck," *Salon.com.* September 26, 2008. Web, May 14, 2012.

Paes de Barros, Deborah. *Fast Cars and Bad Girls: Nomadic Subjects and Women's Road Stories.* New York and Berlin: Peter Lang, 2004.

—. "Driving that Highway to Consciousness: Late Twentieth-century American Travel Literature." In *The Cambridge Companion to American Travel Writing.* Judith Hamera and Alfred Bendixen, eds. Cambridge: Cambridge University Press, 2009. 228–43.

Palahniuk, Chuck. "Afterword." *Fight Club*. New York: Norton, 1996. 209–18.

—. *Fight Club*. New York: Norton, 1996/London: Vintage, 1996.

—. *Survivor*. New York: Norton, 1999/London: Vintage, 1999.

—. *Invisible Monsters*. New York: Norton, 1999/London: Vintage, 1999.

—. *Choke*. New York, Anchor, 2001/London: Vintage, 2001.

—. *Lullaby*. New York: Doubleday, 2002/London: Vintage, 2002.

—. *Fugitives and Refugees: A Walk in Portland, Oregon*. New York: Crown Journeys, 2003.

—. *Diary*. New York: Doubleday, 2003/London: Jonathan Cape, 2003.

—. *Stranger Than Fiction: True Stories*. New York: Doubleday, 2004.

—. *Haunted*. New York: Doubleday, 2005/Jonathan Cape, 2005.

—. *Rant: An Oral Biography of Buster Casey*. New York: Doubleday, 2007/ London: Jonathan Cape, 2007.

—. *Snuff*. New York: Doubleday, 2008/London: Jonathan Cape, 2008.

—. *Pygmy*. New York: Doubleday, 2009/London: Jonathan Cape, 2009.

—. *Tell-All*. New York: Doubleday, 2010/London: Jonathan Cape, 2010.

—. *Damned*. New York: Doubleday, 2011/London: Jonathan Cape, 2011.

—. *Invisible Monsters Remix*. New York: Norton, 2012.

Palmer, Alan. *Fictional Minds*. Lincoln, NB: University of Nebraska Press, 2004.

Paterson, Mark. *Consumption and Everyday Life*. London: Routledge, 2006.

Pausanias. *The Description of Greece*. Vol. 1. C. 160. Trans. Thomas Taylor. London: Priestley and Weale, 1824.

Percy, Walker. "The Man on the Train." *The Message in the Bottle: How Queer Man Is, How Queer Language Is, and What One Has to Do with the Other*. New York: Farrar, Straus and Giroux, 1975. 83–100.

Pliny the Elder. *The Natural History*. C. 77–79. John Bostock and H. T. Riley, eds. *Perseus Digital Library*. February 1, 1999. Web, May 16, 2012.

Primeau, Ronald. *Romance on the Road: The Literature of the American Highway*. Bowling Green, OH: Bowling Green State University Popular Press, 1996.

Professor X. *In the Basement of the Ivory Tower*. New York: Viking, 2011.

Pynchon, Thomas. *The Crying of Lot 49*. Philadelphia: Lippincott, 1966.

—. *Gravity's Rainbow*. New York: Viking, 1973.

Radó, Sándor. "The Psychoanalysis of Pharmacothymia." *Psychoanalytic Quarterly* 2 (1933): 1–23.

Ratner-Rosenhagen, Jennifer. *American Nietzsche: A History of an Icon and his Ideas*. Chicago: University of Chicago Press, 2012.

Reese, Jennifer. "Review of *Choke*." *The New York Times*. May 27, 2001. Web, May 16, 2012.

Roberson, Susan L. "American Women and Travel Writing." In *The Cambridge Companion to American Travel Writing*. Judith Hamera and Alfred Bendixen, eds. Cambridge: Cambridge University Press, 2009. 214–27.

Rosenblatt, Roger. "The Age Of Irony Comes To An End." *Time*. September 24, 2001. Web, May 17, 2012.

Rosenfeld, Herbert. *Psychotic States: A Psychoanalytic Approach*. London: Hogarth Press, 1965.

Rothe-Kushel, Jethro. "*Fight Club*: A Ritual Cure for the Spiritual Ailment of American Masculinity." *Film Journal* 8 (2004). Thefilmjournal.com, May 13, 2011. Web, May 15, 2012.

Sartain, Jeffrey A. "'Even the Mona Lisa's Falling Apart': The Cultural Assimilation of Scientific Epistemologies in Palahniuk's Fiction." *Stirrings Still* 2.2 (2005): 25–47.

Scheff, Thomas J. and Suzanne M. Retzinger. *Emotions and Violence: Shame and Rage in Destructive Conflicts*. Lexington, MA: Lexington Books, 1991.

Silver, Catherine B. "Womb Envy: Loss and Grief of the Maternal Body." *Psychoanalytic Review* 94.3 (2007): 409–30.

Simmel, Ernst. "Psychoanalysis of the Gambler." *International Journal of Psychoanalysis* 1 (1920): 352–3.

Slade, Andrew. "On Mutilation: The Sublime Body of Chuck Palahniuk's Fiction." In *Reading Chuck Palahniuk: American Monsters and Literary Mayhem*. Cynthia Kuhn and Lance Rubin, eds. New York: Routledge, 2009. 62–72.

Slotkin, Richard. *Regeneration Through Violence: The Mythology of the American Frontier, 1600–1860*. Middletown, CT: Wesleyan University Press, 1973.

—. *The Fatal Environment: The Myth of the Frontier in the Age of Industrialization, 1800–1890*. New York: Atheneum, 1985.

—. *Gunfighter Nation: The Myth of the Frontier in Twentieth-Century America*. New York: Atheneum, 1992.

Soros, Erin. "Giving Death." *Differences: A Journal of Feminist Cultural Studies* 10.1 (1998): 1–29.

Springham, Neil. "'All Things Lovely': Art Therapy in a Drug and Alcohol Treatment Programme." In *Treatment of Addiction: Current Issues for Art Therapies*. Diane Walker and Jacky Mahony, eds. London: Routledge, 1999. 141–66.

Sublette, Cammie. "'If We're Too Lazy To Learn *History* History, Maybe We Can Learn Plots': History in the Fiction of Chuck Palahniuk." In *Sacred and Immoral: On the Writings of Chuck Palahniuk*. Jeffrey A. Sartain, ed. Newcastle upon Tyne: Cambridge Scholars, 2009. 22–39.

Switzer, Chris. "From Destruction to Creation: Chuck Palahniuk Discusses *Choke* and his Writing." *turtleneck.net*. August 12, 2001. Web, May 15, 2012.

Tal, Kali. *Worlds of Hurt: Reading the Literatures of Trauma*. Cambridge: Cambridge University Press, 1996.

Thompson, Mark. "The Other 1%." *Time*, 178.20 (November 21, 2011): 34–9.

Truffin, Sherry R. "'This is what passes for free will': Chuck Palahniuk's Postmodern Gothic." In *Reading Chuck Palahniuk: American Monsters and Literary Mayhem*. Cynthia Kuhn and Lance Rubin, eds. New York: Routledge, 2009. 73–87.

Updike, John. *Rabbit, Run*. New York: Knopf, 1960.

Van der Kolk, Bessel. "Complexity of Adaptation to Trauma." In *Traumatic Stress*. Bessel A. Van der Kolk, Alexander C. McFarlane, and Lars Weisaeth, eds. New York: Guilford Press, 2007. 182–213.

Vickroy, Laurie. *Trauma and Survival in Contemporary Fiction*. Charlottesville, VA: University Press of Virginia, 2002.

Walkowiak, James. "Ugly narrative style mars Palahniuk's *Pygmy*." *Buffalo News* (New York), 17 May 2009. F10.

Wallace, David Foster. "John Updike, Champion Literary Phallocrat, Drops One; Is This Finally the End for Magnificent Narcissists?" *New York Observer*, October 13, 1997. Web, May 12, 2012.

Webster's New Encyclopedic Dictionary, 2nd edn, 1994.

Wiener, Norbert. *The Human Use of Human Beings: Cybernetics and Society*. New York: Da Capo Press, 1954.

Williams, G. Christopher. "Nihilism and Buddhism in a Blender: The Religion of Chuck Palahniuk." In *Reading Chuck Palahniuk: American Monsters and Literary Mayhem*. Cynthia Kuhn and Lance Rubin, eds. New York: Routledge, 2009. 170–82.

Young, Elizabeth. "Children of the Revolution: Fiction Takes to the Streets." In *Shopping in Space: Essays on American "Blank Generation" Fiction*. Elizabeth Young and Graham Caveney, eds. London and New York: Serpent's Tail, 1992. 1–20.

Young, Elizabeth and Graham Caveney. "Introduction." *Shopping in Space: Essays on American "Blank Generation" Fiction*. Elizabeth Young and Graham Caveney, eds. London and New York: Serpent's Tail, 1992. V–viii.

Zunshine, Lisa. *Why We Read Fiction: Theory of Mind and the Novel*. Columbus: Ohio State University Press, 2006.

FURTHER READING

Palahniuk's works

Fiction

Palahniuk, Chuck. *Fight Club*. New York: Norton, 1996/London: Vintage, 1996.

—. *Survivor*. New York: Norton, 1999/London: Vintage, 1999.

—. *Invisible Monsters*. New York: Norton, 1999/London: Vintage, 1999.

—. *Choke*. New York, Anchor, 2001/London: Vintage, 2001.

—. *Lullaby*. New York: Doubleday, 2002/London: Vintage, 2002.

—. *Diary*. New York: Doubleday, 2003/London: Jonathan Cape, 2003.

—. *Haunted*. New York: Doubleday, 2005/London: Jonathan Cape, 2005.

—. *Rant: An Oral Biography of Buster Casey*. New York: Doubleday, 2007/London: Jonathan Cape, 2007.

—. *Snuff*. New York: Doubleday, 2008/London: Jonathan Cape, 2008.

—. *Pygmy*. New York: Doubleday, 2009/London: Jonathan Cape, 2009.

—. *Tell-All*. New York: Doubleday, 2010/London: Jonathan Cape, 2010.

—. *Damned*. New York: Doubleday, 2011/London: Jonathan Cape, 2011.

—. *Invisible Monsters Remix*. New York: Norton, 2012.

Non-fiction

Palahniuk, Chuck. *Fugitives and Refugees: A Walk in Portland, Oregon*. New York: Crown Journeys, 2003.

—. *Stranger Than Fiction: True Stories*. New York: Doubleday, 2004.

Criticism on Palahniuk's fiction

There is a growing volume of criticism on Palahniuk's fiction, especially on *Fight Club*, but the books and edited collections currently available, as well as the articles published in peer-reviewed journals, are very limited in number. The following pages offer a selection of book collections, articles, and book chapters that offer a wide range of critical approaches to the novels studied in this volume and to the writer's fiction in general. A limited number of interviews has been added at the end of this selected list, together with a reference to the author's official website.

Books and special issues

Delfino, Andrew. *Becoming the New Man in Post-Post Modernist Fiction: Portrayals of Masculinities in David Foster Wallace's* Infinite Jest *and Chuck Palahniuk's* Fight Club. Saarbrücken (Germany): VDM Verlag Dr. Mueller e.K., 2008.

Kuhn, Cynthia and Lance Rubin, eds. *Reading Chuck Palahniuk: American Monsters and Literary Mayhem*. New York: Routledge, 2009.

Sartain, Jeffrey A., ed. *Sacred and Immoral: On the Writings of Chuck Palahniuk*. Newcastle: Cambridge Scholars Publishing, 2009.

Schuchardt, Read Mercer, ed. *You Do Not Talk About Fight Club*. Dallas, TX: Benbella Books, 2008.

Stirrings Still: The International Journal of Existential Literature 2.2, Special Issue dedicated to Chuck Palahniuk. Erik M. Grayson, General Editor. Fall/Winter 2005.

Selected journal articles and book chapters

Bennett, Robert. "The Death of Sisyphus: Existential Literature and the Cultural Logic of Chuck Palahniuk's *Fight Club*." *Stirrings Still* 2.2 (2005): 65–77.

Bernaerts, Lars. "*Fight Club* and the Embedding of Delirium in Narrative." *Style* 43.3 (2009): 373–87.

Bishop, Kyle. "Artistic Schizophrenia: How Fight Club's Message is Subverted by Its Own Nature." *Studies in Popular Culture* 26.1 (2006): 41–56.

Blazer, Alex. "The Phony 'Martyrdom of Saint Me.' *Choke, The Catcher in the Rye*, and the Problem of Postmodern Narcissistic Nihilism." In *Reading Chuck Palahniuk: American Monsters and Literary Mayhem*. Cynthia Kuhn and Lance Rubin, eds. New York: Routledge, 2009. 143–56.

Boon, Kevin. "Men and Nostalgia for Violence: Culture and Culpability in Chuck Palahniuk's *Fight Club*." *Journal of Men's Studies* 11.3 (2003): 267–76.

Bronfen, Elizabeth. "Chuck Palahniuk and the Violence of Beauty." In *The Future of Flesh: A Cultural Survey of the Body*. Zoe Dedsi-Diamanti, Katerina Kitsi-Mitakou, and Effie Yiannopoulou, eds. New York: Palgrave Macmillan, 2009.

Casado de Rocha, Antonio. "Disease and Community in Chuck Palahniuk's Early Fiction." *Stirrings Still* 2.2 (2005): 116–38.

Clark, Michael J. "Faludi, *Fight Club*, and Phallic Masculinity: Exploring the Emasculating Economics of Patriarchy." *Journal of Men's Studies* 11.1 (2002): 65–76.

Coleman, Philip. "Hauntedness: Edgar Allan Poe and Chuck Palahniuk." In *The Ghost Story From The Middle Ages To The Twentieth Century.* Helen Conrad O'Briain and Julie Anne Stevens, eds. Dublin: Four Courts Press, 2010. 166–79.

Collado-Rodríguez, Francisco. "From Theory to Practice: Blank Fiction, Ethics, and Hybridism in Palahniuk's *Stranger Than Fiction* and *Invisible Monsters.*" In *Masculinities, Femininities and the Power of the Hybrid in U.S. Narratives: Essays on Gender Borders.* Nieves Pascual, Laura Alonso-Gallo, and Francisco Collado-Rodríguez, eds. Heidelberg: Universitätsverlag Winter, 2007. 189–200.

Friday, Krister. "'A Generation of Men Without History': *Fight Club*, Masculinity, and the Historical Symptom." *Postmodern Culture* 13.3 (2003). Web, May 15, 2012.

Giroux, Henry A. "Private Satisfactions and Public Disorders: *Fight Club*, Patriarchy, and the Politics of Masculine Violence." *Jac* 21.1 (2001): 1–31.

Gold, Steven N. "*Fight Club*: A Depiction of Contemporary Society as Dissociogenic." *Journal of Trauma and Dissociation* 5.2 (2003): 13–34.

Grønstad, Asbjørn. "One Dimensional Man: *Fight Club* and the Poetics of the Body." *Film Criticism* 28.1 (2003): 1–23.

Hume, Kathryn. "'Conjugations of the Grotesque' and 'Attacking the Reader's Ontological Assumptions.'" Chapters 3 and 5 of *Aggressive Fictions: Reading the Contemporary American Novel.* Ithaca and London: Cornell University Press, 2012. 77–114 and 141–63.

Iuliano, Fiorenzo. "Roaming Captivities: Assembling Bodies and Territories in Chuck Palahniuk's *Invisible Monsters.*" In *Queerdom. Gender Displacements in a Transnational Context.* Mario Corona and Donatella Izzo, eds. Bergamo: Bergamo University Press, 2009. 107–26.

Kavadlo, Jesse. "The Fiction of Self-destruction: Chuck Palahniuk, Closet Moralist." *Stirrings Still* 2.2 (2005): 3–24.

Kennett, Paul J. "*Fight Club* and the Dangers of Oedipal Obsession." *Stirrings Still* 2.2 (2005): 48–64.

Lizardo, Omar. "*Fight Club*, or the Cultural Contradictions of Late Capitalism." *Journal for Cultural Research* 11.3 (July 2007): 221–43.

Mathews, Peter. "Diagnosing Chuck Palahniuk's *Fight Club*." *Stirrings Still* 2.2 (2005): 81–104.

Mendieta, Eduardo. "Surviving American Culture: On Chuck Palahniuk." *Philosophy and Literature* 29 (2005): 394–408.

Ng, Andrew Hock Soon. "Muscular Existentialism in Chuck Palahniuk's *Fight Club*." *Stirrings Still* 2.2 (2005): 116–38.

Sartain, Jeffrey A. "'Even the Mona Lisa's Falling Apart': The Cultural Assimilation of Scientific Epistemologies in Palahniuk's Fiction." *Stirrings Still* 2.2 (2005): 25–47.

Slade, Andrew. "On Mutilation: The Sublime Body of Chuck Palahniuk's Fiction (*Fight Club, Invisible Monsters, Lullaby, Diary, Haunted, Rant*)." In *Reading Chuck Palahniuk: American Monsters and Literary Mayhem*. Cynthia Kuhn and Lance Rubin, eds. New York: Routledge, 2009. 62–72.

Sublette, Cammie. "'If We're Too Lazy To Learn *History* History, Maybe We Can Learn Plots': History in the Fiction of Chuck Palahniuk." In *Sacred and Immoral: On the Writings of Chuck Palahniuk*. Jeffrey A. Sartain, ed. Newcastle upon Tyne: Cambridge Scholars, 2009. 22–39.

Ta, Lynn M. "Hurt So Good: *Fight Club*, Masculine Violence and the Crisis of Capitalism." *Journal of American Culture* 29.3 (2006): 265–77.

Tuss, Alex. "Masculine Identity and Success: A Critical Analysis of Patricia Highsmith's *The Talented Mr. Ripley* and Chuck Palahniuk's *Fight Club*." *The Journal of Men's Studies* 12.2 (2004): 93–102.

Williams, G. Christopher. "Nihilism and Buddhism in a Blender: The Religion of Chuck Palahniuk." In *Reading Chuck Palahniuk: American Monsters and Literary Mayhem*. Cynthia Kuhn and Lance Rubin, eds. New York: Routledge, 2009. 170–82.

Zeigler, Robert. "Having the last word: Chuck Palahniuk's *Lullaby*." *Notes on Contemporary Literature* 37.4 (2007): 4. *Academic OneFile*. November 12, 2010. Web, May 13, 2012.

Selected interviews

Chandrasoma, Shahin. "Physicians, Shamans, and Personal Trainers: An Interview with Chuck Palahniuk." *The Western Journal of Medicine* 176.3 (2002): 200–3.

Elfman, Mali. "Interview: Clark Gregg and Chuck Palahniuk of *Choke*." *screencrave.com*. September 23, 2008. Web, May 10, 2011.

Glassie, John. "The Pugilist Novelist." An Interview with Chuck Palahniuk. *The New York Times Magazine*. September 29, 2002. Web, May 15, 2012.

Kavanagh, Matt. "On Failed Romance, Writer's Malpractice, and Prose for the Nose: A Conversation with Chuck Palahniuk." In *Sacred and Immoral: On the Writings of Chuck Palahniuk*. Jeffrey A. Sartain, ed. Newcastle upon Tyne: Cambridge Scholars, 2009. 178–92.

Film adaptations

Fight Club (David Fincher 1999) and *Choke* (Clark Gregg 2008) are the only two film adaptations of Palahniuk's works that have been released so far. Both of them have received ample coverage and different responses from film reviewers. *Haunted*, *Rant*, *Snuff* and *Invisible Monsters* have had their movie rights optioned. However, as announced in the writer's official website, "to date there doesn't seem to be any substantial progress on any of those projects."

Official website

The Cult: The Official Chuck Palahniuk website at ChuckPalahniuk.net.
Created in 1999 by Dennis Widmyer, *The Cult* is the most popular site dedicated to Palahniuk. It provides the author's fans with excerpts, reviews and news about his books and movie adaptations. It also features a writer's workshop, and an online shop where a number of items related to the novelist can be purchased, from T-shirts to the DVD *Postcards From The Future: The Chuck Palahniuk Documentary* (2003).

NOTES ON CONTRIBUTORS

Sonia Baelo-Allué is Associate Professor in the Department of English and German Philology at the University of Zaragoza (Spain), where she teaches US literature. She has published articles on the genre of blank fiction, the concept of intermediality, and the representation of violence in literature. Her current research centres on trauma studies and 9/11 fiction. She has recently published the book *Bret Easton Ellis's Controversial Fiction* (Continuum, 2011) and coedited with Dolores Herrero *The Splintered Glass* (Rodopi, 2011) and *Between the Urge to Know and the Need to Deny* (C. Winter, 2011). The research carried out for the writing of her contribution has been funded by the Spanish Ministry of Economy and Commerce and the European Regional Fund (ERFD) (code FFI2012–32719). The author is also grateful for the support of the Government of Aragón and the European Social Fund (ESF) (code H05).

Francisco Collado-Rodríguez is Professor of American Literature at the University of Zaragoza (Spain). He has written on the influence of fantasy, myth, and scientific discourse on recent American fiction. He has published articles on Thomas Pynchon, Bharati Mukherjee, Kurt Vonnegut, E. L. Doctorow, Bobbie Ann Mason, Cormac McCarthy, Jeffrey Eugenides, and Jonathan Safran Foer among others. He has authored and coedited a number of books, among them *El orden del caos: literatura, política y posthumanidad en la narrativa de Thomas Pynchon* (Valencia: Prensas Universitarias, 2004) and *Masculinities, Femininities and the Power of the Hybrid in U.S. Narratives: Essays on Gender Borders* (with Nieves Pascual and Laura Alonso, C. Winter, 2007) and is also the coeditor, with Celia Wallhead, of a special volume of *Pynchon Notes*: *V. Is for*

Varo Too: Exploring Pynchon's Hispanic (and Other) Global Connections (2009).

David Cowart, Louise Fry Scudder Professor at the University of South Carolina, is completing a book on literary generations in the postmodern period. He is the author of *Thomas Pynchon and the Dark Passages of History* (University of Georgia Press, 2011) and other books on contemporary American fiction, notably *Don DeLillo: The Physics of Language* (University of Georgia Press), which won the SAMLA Literary Studies Award in 2003, and *Trailing Clouds: Immigrant Writing in Contemporary America* (Cornell University Press, 2006). A second, augmented edition of his 1993 book, *Literary Symbiosis: The Reconfigured Text in Twentieth-Century Writing* (University of Georgia Press), came out in 2012. A consulting editor for the journal *Critique*, Professor Cowart has been an NEH fellow and held Fulbright chairs at the University of Helsinki and at the University of Southern Denmark in Odense. In 2005, he toured Japan as a Fulbright Distinguished Lecturer.

James R. Giles, a native of Texas, is Distinguished Professor Emeritus at Northern Illinois University, where he taught in the Department of English from 1970 to 2007. He is the author of nine books and the coeditor of eight others including *The Spaces of Violence* (University of Alabama Press, 2006), *Violence in the Contemporary American Novel* (University of South Carolina Press, 2000), *The Naturalistic Inner-City Novel in America* (University of South Carolina Press, 1995), and six volumes of the *Dictionary of Literary Biography* (all coedited with Wanda H. Giles; Gale/Thompson Gale, 1994–2003). In addition, he has published over 30 articles or short stories in various journals. Most recently, he published essays in *The Oxford Handbook of American Literary Naturalism* (Oxford University Press, 2011) and *A Companion to Twentieth-Century United States Fiction* (Wiley-Blackwell, 2010).

Jesse Kavadlo is Associate Professor of English and Humanities, Writing Center Director, and University Seminar Coordinator at Maryville University of St Louis. He teaches courses in American literature, college writing, and special topics in literature and culture, such as Monsters, Conspiracies, Rock & roll, and Superheroes. He received his PhD in English from Fordham University and is the author of *Don DeLillo: Balance at the Edge of Belief* (Peter Lang, 2004) as well as essays and book chapters about contemporary fiction, popular culture, and pedagogy.

Eduardo Mendieta is Professor of Philosophy at the State University of New York, Stony Brook. He is the author of *The Adventures of Transcendental Philosophy* (Rowman & Littlefield, 2002) and *Global Fragments: Globalizations, Latinamericanisms, and Critical Theory* (SUNY Press, 2007). He is also coeditor with Jonathan VanAntwerpen of *The Power of Religion in the Public Sphere* (Columbia University Press, 2011), and with Craig Calhoun and Jonathan VanAntwerpen of *Habermas and Religion* (Polity, forthcoming), and with Stuart Elden of *Reading Kant's Geography* (SUNY Press, 2011). He is presently at work on another book entitled *Philosophy's War: Logos, Polemos, Topos.*

Nieves Pascual is Associate Professor at the University of Jaén in Spain. She teaches American Literature and her research interests cover Cultural Studies, Feminism, Food, and Popular Culture. She has edited *Witnesses to Pain: Essays on the Translation of Pain into Art* (Peter Lang, 2005), and has coedited *Masculinities, Femininities and the Power of the Hybrid in U.S. Narratives: Essays on Gender Borders* (C. Winter, 2007), *Feeling in Others: Essays on Empathy and Suffering in Modern Culture* (Lit, 2008), and *Stories Through Stories, Theories Through Stories: Native American Storytelling and Critique* (Michigan State University Press, 2009). She has authored two books: *El otro oficio de los profesores. La novela académica anglo-americana* (Universidad Complutense, 1997), and *A Critical Study of Female Culinary Detective Stories: Murder by Cookbook* (Edwin Mellen Press, 2009). Recently she has completed *Hungering as Symbolic Language* (Edwin Mellen Press, 2012). She has also published papers in such journals as *Mosaic, Style,* and *Journal of Intercultural Studies.*

Andrew Slade is Assistant Professor of Literary Theory in the Department of English at the University of Dayton. His research focuses on the philosophy of art and literature, with special attention to the aesthetic of the sublime. He has published scholarly articles on the theory of tragedy and the representation of traumatic histories. He is also the author of *Lyotard, Beckett, Duras, and the Postmodern Sublime* (Peter Lang, 2007).

Eluned Summers-Bremner is Senior Lecturer in English at the University of Auckland, New Zealand. The author of *Insomnia: A Cultural History* (Reaktion, 2008), and the forthcoming books *Ian McEwan: Sex, Death and History* (Cambria), and *A History of Wandering* (Reaktion), she is currently working on a history of the sea and human emotions for Reaktion, and on the literature of the Second World War.

Laurie Vickroy is Professor of English at Bradley University. Her scholarship and teaching have focused on trauma studies, particularly the interrelationship of trauma, culture and women's identity. She is the author of *Trauma and Survival in Contemporary Fiction* (University of Virginia Press, 2002) and coeditor of *Critical Essays on the Works of Dorothy Allison* with Christine Blouch (Edwin Mellen, 2005). She has written on a number of contemporary authors including Margaret Atwood, Toni Morrison, Dorothy Allison, Jeanette Winterson, Pat Barker, Marguerite Duras, Reinaldo Arenas, and Larry Heinemann, among others. Her work has appeared in the following journals: *Mosaic, The Comparatist, MELUS, Modern Language Studies, Women and Language, Obsidian II*, and *CEA Critic*. Recent publications include: "That was Their Deal: Trauma Narratives' Ethical Re-framings" in *Between the Urge to Known and the Need to Deny: Trauma and Ethics in Contemporary British and American Literature* (C. Winter, 2011) and "You're History: Living with Trauma in *The Robber Bride*" in *Margaret Atwood: The Robber Bride, The Blind Assassin, and Oryx and Crake* (Continuum, 2010).

Richard Viskovic is a PhD student at the University of Auckland in New Zealand. He is writing a PhD on metaphysics in Philip K. Dick's works. His research interests are in popular fiction, and the intersection of literature and philosophy.

INDEX